Modern Critical Views

Chinua Achebe
Henry Adams
Aeschylus
S. Y. Agnon
Edward Albee
Raphael Alberti
Louisa May Alcott
A. R. Ammons
Sherwood Anderson
Aristophanes
Matthew Arnold
Antonin Artaud
John Ashbery
Margaret Atwood
W. H. Auden
Jane Austen
Isaac Babel
Sir Francis Bacon
James Baldwin
Honoré de Balzac
John Barth
Donald Barthelme
Charles Baudelaire
Simone de Beauvoir
Samuel Beckett
Saul Bellow
Thomas Berger
John Berryman
The Bible
Elizabeth Bishop
William Blake
Giovanni Boccaccio
Heinrich Böll
Jorge Luis Borges
Elizabeth Bowen
Bertolt Brecht
The Brontës
Charles Brockden Brown
Sterling Brown
Robert Browning
Martin Buber
John Bunyan
Anthony Burgess
Kenneth Burke
Robert Burns
William Burroughs
George Gordon, Lord
    Byron
Pedro Calderón de la Barca
Italo Calvino
Albert Camus
Canadian Poetry: Modern
    and Contemporary
Canadian Poetry through
    E. J. Pratt
Thomas Carlyle
Alejo Carpentier
Lewis Carroll
Willa Cather
Louis-Ferdinand Céline
Miguel de Cervantes

Geoffrey Chaucer
John Cheever
Anton Chekhov
Kate Chopin
Chrétien de Troyes
Agatha Christie
Samuel Taylor Coleridge
Colette
William Congreve & the
    Restoration Dramatists
Joseph Conrad
Contemporary Poets
James Fenimore Cooper
Pierre Corneille
Julio Cortázar
Hart Crane
Stephen Crane
e. e. cummings
Dante
Robertson Davies
Daniel Defoe
Philip K. Dick
Charles Dickens
James Dickey
Emily Dickinson
Denis Diderot
Isak Dinesen
E. L. Doctorow
John Donne & the
    Seventeenth-Century
    Metaphysical Poets
John Dos Passos
Fyodor Dostoevsky
Frederick Douglass
Theodore Dreiser
John Dryden
W. E. B. Du Bois
Lawrence Durrell
George Eliot
T. S. Eliot
Elizabethan Dramatists
Ralph Ellison
Ralph Waldo Emerson
Euripides
William Faulkner
Henry Fielding
F. Scott Fitzgerald
Gustave Flaubert
E. M. Forster
John Fowles
Sigmund Freud
Robert Frost
Northrop Frye
Carlos Fuentes
William Gaddis
Federico García Lorca
Gabriel García Márquez
André Gide
W. S. Gilbert
Allen Ginsberg
J. W. von Goethe

Nikolai Gogol
William Golding
Oliver Goldsmith
Mary Gordon
Günther Grass
Robert Graves
Graham Greene
Thomas Hardy
Nathaniel Hawthorne
William Hazlitt
H. D.
Seamus Heaney
Lillian Hellman
Ernest Hemingway
Hermann Hesse
Geoffrey Hill
Friedrich Hölderlin
Homer
A. D. Hope
Gerard Manley Hopkins
Horace
A. E. Housman
William Dean Howells
Langston Hughes
Ted Hughes
Victor Hugo
Zora Neale Hurston
Aldous Huxley
Henrik Ibsen
Eugène Ionesco
Washington Irving
Henry James
Dr. Samuel Johnson and
    James Boswell
Ben Jonson
James Joyce
Carl Gustav Jung
Franz Kafka
Yasonari Kawabata
John Keats
Søren Kierkegaard
Rudyard Kipling
Melanie Klein
Heinrich von Kleist
Philip Larkin
D. H. Lawrence
John le Carré
Ursula K. Le Guin
Giacomo Leopardi
Doris Lessing
Sinclair Lewis
Jack London
Robert Lowell
Malcolm Lowry
Carson McCullers
Norman Mailer
Bernard Malamud
Stéphane Mallarmé
Sir Thomas Malory
André Malraux
Thomas Mann

Modern Critical Views

Modern Critical Views

SØREN KIERKEGAARD

Edited and with an introduction by
Harold Bloom
Sterling Professor of the Humanities
Yale University

CHELSEA HOUSE PUBLISHERS
New York ◊ Philadelphia

©1989 by Chelsea House Publishers, a division
of Main Line Book Co.

Introduction © 1989 by Harold Bloom

Printed and bound in the United States of America

10   9   8   7   6   5   4   3   2   1

∞ The paper used in this publication meets the minimum
requirements of the American National Standard for
Permanence of Paper for Printed Library Materials, Z39.48-1984.

Library of Congress Cataloging-in-Publication Data
Søren Kierkegaard./
    (Modern critical views)
    Bibliography: p.
    Includes index.
    1. Kierkegaard, Søren, 1813–1855. I. Bloom, Harold. II. Series.
B4377.S58   1987   198'.9   87–16715
ISBN 1–55546–304–5

Contents

Editor's Note

This book gathers together a representative selection of the best criticism available in English on the work of Søren Kierkegaard. The critical essays are arranged here in the chronological order of their original publication, rather than of their appearance in English. I am grateful to Suzanne Roos for her assistance in editing this volume.

My introduction, centering upon "The Case of the Contemporary Disciple" in Kierkegaard's *Philosophical Fragments*, relates Kierkegaard's concepts of irony and of "repetition" to his defensive, strong misreading (or revision) of Hegelian "mediation." The Hungarian Marxist critic Georg Lukács begins the chronological sequence with the appreciative argument that Kierkegaard's heroism was manifested by his drive to create forms from life.

Theodor W. Adorno, the leader of the Frankfurt school of social philosophy, analyzes Kierkegaard's *Works of Love,* and finds both the best and the worst aspect of it to be Kierkegaard's love for the dead. Karl Jaspers, philosopher and psychologist, provides an overview of Kierkegaard's importance and stresses that Kierkegaard, like Nietzsche, represented truth-telling and the full individuation of the self. Evil and its symbolism in Kierkegaard is the subject of the French philosopher Paul Ricoeur, who locates a transfer from negative theology to anthropology as a crucial element in the most characteristic writings.

The American philosopher Stanley Cavell, commenting upon Kierkegaard's *On Authority and Revelation,* notes that the indirectness, irony, and theatricality of Kierkegaard's religious writing are all part of the cost of confirmation of his authenticity. Paradox is emphasized as the salient mark of that authenticity in the tribute of Jean-Paul Sartre.

Bertel Pedersen focuses upon Kierkegaard's many "authorial effacements," ironic strategies and pseudonymity and polynymity, that set particular conditions for producing meaning, in a manner we now think of as Borgesian but which Borges largely derived from Kierkegaard. Kierkegaardian irony is Sylviane Agacinski's subject, while Henning Fenger traces the Danish genius's willing falsification of his personal history, even in his *Journals,* as part of his heroic effort to make his life into a work of art, an effort he shared with Nietzsche.

The distinction between the natural and the ethical in Kierkegaard's life-long quest for the maximum individuality of selfhood is worked through by Mark C. Taylor. A witty disquisition by Louis Mackey returns us to *Repetition* and its life-enhancing paradoxes. Kevin Newmark then fitly concludes this volume with an acute analysis of the difference between Hegel and Kierkegaard, taking us full circle back to the introduction, with its description of Kierkegaard's misprision of Hegel. But Newmark, working in the deconstructive mode of Jacques Derrida and Paul de Man, is necessarily more Hegelian than Kierkegaardian.

I end by affirming again Kierkegaard's permanent originality, which he shares with Nietzsche and Kafka, rather than with Hegel and Heidegger. It is the originality of a mode more literary than philosophical, and perhaps more authentically speculative than German speculative philosophy and its Gallic dependents have ever managed to be.

Introduction

What Kierkegaard called "repetition" is what any of us experiences when we will to take yet again a possibility believed to have transcendental aspects. That is dangerously close to the perpetual self-deception most of us call "falling in love," so that you can reduce Kierkegaard's "repetition" to the Freudian repetition-compulsion of the Death Drive, if that reduction pleases you. Like Freud, Kierkegaard is a great erotic ironist, but that is all these two great consciousnesses share. "Irony is an abnormal growth . . . it ends by killing the individual." That Kierkegaardian realization divides the two repetitions, and allows the Danish thinker to praise the married man who has been faithful as the true hero of his repetition: "He solves the great riddle of living in eternity and yet hearing the hall clock strike, and hearing it in such a way that the stroke of the hour does not shorten but prolongs his eternity."

Such "repetition" is an ironical revision of the Hegelian trope of "mediation." If Hegel's Christ is the great mediator, then Kierkegaard's Christ is the master of repetition, of a scene in which we are instructed in repetition. Kierkegaard, to me, is less a religious writer than he is a poetic speculator, and one of the crucial areas of his speculation is the process of instruction. I do not mean that Kierkegaard was interested primarily in speculative philosophy, which for him meant Hegel's speculative mediation. Rather, the truly speculative enterprise was the immense difficulty of becoming a Christian in a society ostensibly Christian. Becoming a Christian was for Kierkegaard as perpetual an *agon* as becoming a strong poet was for Keats. For teachers, Keats was found by Wordsworth, Milton, and Shakespeare. Kierkegaard, seeking an even more rugged originality, was found mostly by himself, and by Christ, the only absolute founder of a Scene of Instruction.

I turn to Kierkegaard as the great theorist of the Scene of Instruction, particularly in his brilliantly polemical text, the *Philosophical Fragments* (1844). The title page of this short book asks the splendid triple question: "Is an historical point of departure possible for an eternal consciousness; how

1

can such a point of departure have any other than a merely historical interest; is it possible to base an eternal happiness upon historical knowledge." Kierkegaard's intent is to refute Hegel by severely dividing Christianity from Idealist philosophy, but his triple question is perfectly applicable to the secular paradox of poetic incarnation and poetic influence. For the anxiety of influence stems from the ephebe's assertion of an eternal, divinating consciousness that nevertheless took its historical point of departure in an intratextual encounter, and most crucially in the interpretative moment or act of misprision contained in that encounter. How indeed, the ephebe must wonder, can such a point of departure have more than merely historical rather than poetic interest? More anxiously, even, how is the strong poet's claim to poetic immortality (the only eternal happiness that is relevant) to be founded upon an encounter trapped belatedly in time?

Two sections of the *Fragments* are closest to the dilemmas of the poetic Scene of Instruction. These are the essay of the imagination called "The God as Teacher and Savior," and the ingenious chapter called "The Case of the Contemporary Disciple." The first is a concealed polemic against Strauss and Feuerbach as left-wing Hegelians, and the second is an overt polemic against Hegel himself. Against left-wing Hegelianism, Kierkegaard contrasts Socrates as a teacher with the Christ. Socrates and his student have nothing to teach one another, no *davhar* or word to bring forward, yet each provides the other with a means towards self-understanding. But the Christ understands himself without the aid of students, and his students are there only to receive his incommensurable love. Against Hegel, Kierkegaard separates history from Necessity, for Christian truth is not a human possession, as Hegelian Idealism would believe. The contemporary disciple of the God as teacher and savior "was not contemporary with the splendor, neither hearing nor seeing anything of it." There is no immediacy by which one can be a contemporary of a divinity; the paradox of the peculiarly Kierkegaardian variety of "repetition" is at work here, and by an exploration of such repetition we can displace Kierkegaard's polemical wit into a speculation upon the Scene of Instruction, and simultaneously expose again an inadequacy in Freud's account of the compulsion to repeat, and that compulsion's relations to origins.

Repetition, in Kierkegaard, goes back at least to theses XII and XIII of his Master of Arts dissertation, *The Concept of Irony* (1841). Thesis XII smacks at Hegel for defining irony while considering only the modern but not so much .he ancient Socratic form. Thesis XIII, also directed against Hegel, is one of the founding apothegms for any study of poetic misprision:

Irony is not so much apathy, divested of all tender emotions of the

2

soul; instead, it is more like vexation over the fact that others also enjoy what it desires for itself.

True repetition, for Kierkegaard, is eternity, and so only true repetition can save one from the vexation of irony. But this is an eternity in time, "the daily bread which satisfies with benediction." Indeed, this is the center of Kierkegaard's vision, and necessarily also of *his* anxiety of influence in regard to his reviled precursor, Hegel, for Kierkegaard's "repetition" is a substitute trope for Hegel's trope of "mediation," the process of dialectic itself. Kierkegaard's dialectic, by being more internalized, is doomed to even more subjectivity, a limitation that Kierkegaard characteristically sought to represent as a philosophical advance. If repetition is primarily a dialetical re-affirmation of the continued possibility of becoming a Christian, then its aesthetic displacement would reaffirm dialectically the continued possibility of becoming a poet. No contemporary disciple of a great poet then could be truly his precursor's contemporary, for the splendor is necessarily *deferred*. It can be reached through the mediation of repetition, by a return to origins and the incommensurable Election-love that the Primal Scene of Instruction can bestow, there at the point of origin. Poetic repetition repeats a Primal repression, a repression that is itself a fixation upon the precursor as teacher and savior, or on the poetic father as mortal god. The compulsion to repeat the precursor's patterns is not a movement beyond the pleasure principle to an inertia of poetic pre-incarnation, to a Blakean Beulah where no dispute can come, but rather is an attempt to recover the prestige of origins, the oral authority of a prior Instruction. Poetic repetition quests, despite itself, for the mediated vision of the fathers, since such mediation holds open the perpetual possibility of one's own sublimity, one's election to the realm of true Instructors.

But was there a mediated vision of the fathers for Kierkegaard himself? The answer, alas, can only be Hegel, the inventor of mediation. Kierkegaard was not Schopenhauer or Emerson or Nietzsche, who were what they would have been had Hegel never written a sentence or delivered a lecture. Rather, Kierkegaard was post-Hegelian as we are post-Freudian; there is no other option for us. Freud is there, making us belated, writing commentaries upon him, whether we wish it or not. Hegel would have made Kierkegaard belated, but like Emerson and Nietzsche the Danish speculator refused to be a secondary man. The modes of creative misinterpretation are numerous, and most of them reduce to ironies. "Repetition" ironically was Kierkegaard's path out of irony, lest he fall into the irony of irony, and so lose all invention.

Kierkegaard's most inventive moment nevertheless is necessarily an irony, in which "the moment" is destroyed, and the idea of contemporaneity dies forever. That is the authentic literary achievement of "The Case of the Contemporary Disciple," since it demonstrates that true passion is always for the past, that only the past can be a poet's or a Christian's lover. The future belongs to repetition, to a marriage with what one has made, to a constructed joy. The past was a spontaneous joy, and spontaneity is not the taking up again of possibility one has taken up before, and always must take up again. Authentic passion, delirium of the senses, excludes the future, in Kierkegaard and in Kafka, his legitimate son.

Kierkegaard became one of the strongest modern poets at a very high price, again like Kafka, or like Nietzsche. Creative misreading needs to sacrifice the present moment, because the Scene of Instruction depends upon placing all love in the past. Kierkegaard puts this slyly: "Love is presupposing love; to have love is to presuppose love in others; to be loving is to presuppose that others are loving." And yet: "If there were no repetition, what then would life be? Who would wish to be a tablet upon which time writes every instant a new inscription? or be a mere memorial of the past?"

Kierkegaard's Nebuchadnezzar, recollecting when he was a beast and ate grass, mused upon the God of the Hebrews, and understood that only this Mighty One was free of the Scene of Instruction. Speaking for Kierkegaard, Nebuchadnezzar teaches us where creative misreading has touched its limit, and where the difficulty of becoming a Christian at last is resolved: "And no one knoweth anything of Him, who was His father, and how He acquired His power, and who taught Him the secret of His might."

GEORG LUKÁCS

The Foundering of Form against Life: Søren Kierkegaard and Regine Olsen

Fair youth beneath the trees, thou canst not leave
Thy song, nor ever can those tree be bare;
Bold lover, never, never canst thou kiss,
Though winning near the goal—yet do not grieve;
She cannot fade, though thou has not thy bliss,
For ever wilt thou love, and she be fair!
          —JOHN KEATS, "Ode on a Grecian Urn"

What is the life-value of a gesture? Or, to put it another way, what is the value of form in life, the life-creating, life-enhancing value of form? A gesture is nothing more than a movement which clearly expresses something unambiguous. Form is the only way of expressing the absolute in life; a gesture is the only thing which is perfect within itself, the only reality which is more than mere possibility. The gesture alone expresses life: but is it possible to express life? Is not this the tragedy of any living art, that it seeks to build a crystal palace out of air, to forge realities from the insubstantial possibilities of the soul, to construct, through the meetings and partings of souls, a bridge of forms between men? Can the gesture exist at all, and has the concept of form any meaning seen from the perspective of life?

Kierkegaard once said that reality has nothing to do with possibilities; yet he built his whole life upon a gesture. Everything he wrote, every one of his struggles and adventures, is in some way the backdrop to that gesture; perhaps he only wrote and did these things to make his gesture stand out more

From *Soul and Form*. © 1971 by Hermann Luchterhand Verlag. English translation © 1974 by The Merlin Press Ltd. Translated by Anna Bostock. This essay first published 1909.

clearly against the chaotic multiplicity of life. Why did he do it? How could he do it—he of all men, who saw more clearly than any other the thousand aspects, the thousand-fold variability of every motive—he who so clearly saw how everything passes gradually into its opposite, and how, if we look really close, we see an unbridgeable abyss gaping between two barely perceptible nuances? Why did he do this? Perhaps because the gesture is one of the most powerful life-necessities; perhaps because a man who wants to be "honest" (one of Kierkegaard's most frequently used words) must force life to yield up its single meaning, must grasp that ever-changing Proteus, so firmly that, once he has revealed the magic words, he can no longer move. Perhaps the gesture—to use Kierkegaard's dialectic—is the paradox, the point at which reality and possibility intersect, matter and air, the finite and the infinite, life and form. Or, more accurately still and even closer to Kierkegaard's terminology: the gesture is the leap by which the soul passes from one into the other, the leap by which it leaves the always relative facts of reality to reach the eternal certainty of forms. In a word, the gesture is that unique leap by which the absolute is transformed, in life, into the possible. The gesture is the great paradox of life, for only in its rigid permanence is there room for every evanescent moment of life, and only within it does every such moment become true reality.

Whoever does more than merely play with life needs the gesture so that his life may become more real for him than a game that can be played by an infinite choice of moves.

But can there really be a gesture vis-à-vis life? Is it not self-delusion—however splendidly heroic—to believe that the essence of the gesture lies in an action, a turning towards something or a turning away: rigid as stone and yet containing everything immutably within itself?

II

In September 1840 it happened that Søren Aabye Kierkegaard, Master of Arts, became engaged to Regine Olsen, State Councillor Olsen's eighteen-year-old daughter. Barely a year afterwards he broke off the engagement. He left for Berlin, and when he returned to Copenhagen he lived there as a noted eccentric; his peculiar ways made him a constant target for the humorous papers, and although his writings, published under a variety of pen-names, found some admirers because they were so full of wit, they were hated by the majority because of their "immoral" and "frivolous" contents. His later works made still more open enemies for him—namely, all the leaders of the ruling Protestant Church: and during the hard fight he fought against them—

contending that the society of our time is not a Christian one and indeed makes it practically impossible for anyone to remain a Christian—he died.

A few years previously Regine Olsen had married one of her earlier admirers.

III

What had happened? The number of explanations is infinite, and every newly published text, every letter, every diary entry of Kierkegaard's has made it easier to explain the event and at the same time harder to understand or appreciate what it meant in Søren Kierkegaard's and Regine Olsen's life.

Kassner, writing about Kierkegaard in unforgettable and unsurpassable terms, rejects every explanation. "Kierkegaard," he writes, "made a poem of his relationship with Regine Olsen, and when a Kierkegaard makes a poem of his life he does so not in order to conceal the truth but in order to be able to reveal it."

There is no explanation, for what is there is more than an explanation, it is a gesture. Kierkegaard said: I am a melancholic; he said: I was a whole eternity too old for her; he said: my sin was that I tried to sweep her along with myself into the great stream; he said: if my life were not a great penitence, if it were not the *vita ante acta*, then . . .

And he left Regine Olsen and said he did not love her, had never really loved her, he was a man whose fickle spirit demanded new people and new relationships at every moment. A large part of his writings proclaims this loudly, and the way he spoke and the way he lived emphasized this one thing in order to confirm Regine Olsen's belief in it.

. . . And Regine married one of her old admirers and Søren Kierkegaard wrote in his diary: "Today I saw a beautiful girl; she does not interest me. No married man can be more faithful to his wife than I am to Regine."

IV

The gesture: to make unambiguous the inexplicable, which happened for many reasons and whose consequences spread wide. To withdraw in such a way that nothing but sorrow may come of it, nothing but tragedy—once it was clear that their encounter had to be tragic—nothing but total collapse, perhaps, just so long as there was no uncertainty about it, no dissolving of reality into possibilities. If what seemed to mean life itself to Regine Olsen had to be lost to her, then it had to lose *all* meaning in her life; if he who loved Regine Olsen had to leave her, then he who left her had to be a scoundrel and a seducer, so that every path back to life might remain open to her. And since Søren Kierkegaard's penitence was to leave life, that penitence had to be made the greater by the sinner's mask, chivalrously assumed, which disguised his real sin.

Regine's marriage to another man was necessary for Kierkegaard. "She has grasped the point very well," he wrote, "she understands that she must get married." He needed her marriage so that nothing uncertain, nothing vague should remain about the relationship, no further possibility, only this one thing: the seducer and the jilted girl. But the girl consoles herself and finds the way back to life. Under the seducer's mask stands the ascetic who, out of asceticism, voluntarily froze in his gesture.

The transformation of the girl follows in a straight line from her beginning. Behind the fixedly smiling mask of the seducer frowns, as fixedly, the real face of the ascetic. The gesture is pure and expresses everything. "Kierkegaard made a poem of his life."

V

The only essential difference between one life and another is the question whether a life is absolute or merely relative; whether the mutually exclusive opposites within the life are separated from one another sharply and definitively or not. The difference is whether the life-problems of a particular life arise in the form of an either/or, or whether "as well as" is the proper formula when the split appears. Kierkegaard was always saying: I want to be honest, and this honesty could not mean anything less than the duty—in the purest sense of the word—to live out his life in accordance with poetic principles; the duty to decide, the duty to go to the very end of every chosen road at every crossroads.

But when a man looks about him, he does not see roads and crossroads, nor any sharply distinct choices anywhere; everything flows, everything is transmuted into something else. Only when we turn away our gaze and look again much later do we find that one thing has become another—and perhaps not even then. But the deep meaning of Kierkegaard's philosophy is that he places fixed points beneath the incessantly changing nuances of life, and draws absolute quality distinctions within the melting chaos of nuances. And, having found certain things to be different, he presents them as being so unambiguously and profoundly different that what separates them can never again be blurred by any possible nuance or transition. Thus Kierkegaard's honesty entails the paradox that whatever has not already grown into a new unity which cancels out all former differences, must remain divided forever.

Among the things you have found to be different you must choose one, you must not seek "middle ways" or "higher unities" which might resolve the "merely apparent" contradictions. And so there is no system anywhere, for it is not possible to *live* a system; the system is always a vast palace, while its creator can only withdraw into a modest corner. There is never any room for life in a logical system of thought; seen in this way, the starting point for such a system is always arbitrary and, from the perspective of life, only relative— a mere possibility. There is no system in life. In life there is only the separate and individual, the concrete. To exist is to be different. And only the concrete, the individual phenomenon is the unambiguous, the absolute which is without nuance. Truth is only subjective—perhaps; but subjectivity is quite certainly truth; the individual thing is the only thing that *is;* the individual is the real man.

And so there are some major, typical cycles of possibilities in life, or stages to use Kierkegaard's language: the aesthetic, the ethical, the religious stage. Each is distinct from the other with a sharpness that allows of no nuances, and the connection between each is the miracle, the leap, the sudden metamorphosis of the entire being of a man.

VI

This, then, was Kierkegaard's honesty: to see everything as being sharply distinct from everything else, system from life, human being from human being, stage from stage: to see the absolute in life, without any petty compromises.

But is it not a compromise to see life as being without compromises? Is not such nailing down of absoluteness, rather, an evasion of the duty to look at *everything?* Is not a stage a "higher unity", too? Is not the denial of a life-system itself a system—and very much so? Is not the leap merely a sudden transition? Is there not, after all, a rigorous distinction hidden behind every compromise, hidden behind its most vehement denial? Can one be honest in face of life, and yet stylize life's events in literary form?

VII

The inner honesty of Kierkegaard's gesture of separation could only be assured if everything he did was done for Regine Olsen's sake. The letters and diary entries are full of it: had they remained together, not even Regine's bubbling laughter would have broken the sombre silence of his terrible melancholy; the laughter would have been silenced, the lightness would have fallen wearily to the stony ground below. No one would have benefited from such a sacrifice. And so it was his duty (whatever it may have cost him from the point of view of human happiness, of human existence) to save Regine Olsen's life.

But the question is whether Regine's life was the only thing he saved. Was not the very thing which, as he believed, made it necessary for them to part, essential to his own life? Did he not give up the struggle against his melancholy (a struggle which might have been successful) because he loved it more dearly, perhaps, than anything else, and could not conceive of life without it? "My sorrow is my castle," he once wrote, and elsewhere he said (I quote only a few examples to stand for many more): "In my great melancholy I still loved life, for I loved my melancholy." And writing about Regine and himself: "She would have been ruined and presumably she would have wrecked me, too, for I should constantly have had to strain myself trying to raise her up. I was too heavy for her, she too light for me, but either way there is most certainly a risk of overstrain."

There are beings to whom—in order that they may become great—anything even faintly resembling happiness and sunshine must always be forbidden. Karoline [Schelling] once wrote of Friedrich Schlegel: "Some thrive under oppression, and Friedrich is one of them—if he were to enjoy the full glory of success even once, it would destroy what is finest in him." Robert Browning rewrote Friedrich Schlegel's tragedy in the sad history of Chiappino, who was strong and noble, delicate and capable of deep feeling so long as he remained in the shadows and his life meant only wretchedness and fruitless longing; when misfortune raised him higher than he had ever hoped in his wildest dreams or most foolish rantings, he became empty, and his cynical words could barely disguise the pain he felt at becoming conscious of that emptiness—the emptiness which came with "good fortune." (Browning called this disaster "a soul's tragedy.")

Perhaps Kierkegaard knew this, or perhaps he sensed it. Perhaps his violently active creative instinct, released by the pain he felt immediately after the break with Regine, had already claimed in advance this only possible release. Perhaps something inside him knew that happiness—if it was attainable—would have made him lame and sterile for the rest of his life. Perhaps he was afraid that happiness might not be unattainable, that Regine's lightness might after all have redeemed his great melancholy and that both might have been happy. But what would have become of him without his melancholy? Kierkegaard is the sentimental Socrates. "Loving is the only thing I'm an expert in," he said. But Socrates wanted only to recognize, to understand human beings who loved, and therefore the central problem in Kierkegaard's life was no problem for Socrates. "Loving is the only thing I'm an expert in," said Kierkegaard, "just give me an object for my love, only an object. But here I stand like an archer whose bow is stretched to the uttermost limit and who is asked to shoot at a target five paces ahead of him. This I cannot do, says the archer, but put the target two or three hundred paces further away and you will see!"

Remember Keats' prayer to nature:

> A theme! a theme! great nature! give a theme;
> Let me begin my dream.

To love! Whom can I love in such a way that the object of my love will not stand in the way of my love? Who is strong enough, who can contain everything within himself so that his love will become absolute and stronger than anything else? Who stands so high above all others that whoever loves him will never address a demand to him, never be proved right against him— so that the love with which he is loved will be an absolute one?

To love: to try never to be proved right. That is how Kierkegaard described love. For the cause of the eternal relativity of all human relationships, of their fluctuations and, therefore, of their pettiness, is that it is now the one who is right, and now the other; now the one who is better, nobler, more beautiful, and now the other. There can be constancy and clarity only if the lovers are qualitatively different from one another, if one is so much higher than the other that the question of right and wrong (in the broadest sense) can never be posed, even as a question.

Such was the ideal of love of the ascetic mediaeval knights, but it was never to be as romantic again. Kierkegaard's psychological insight robbed him of the naive belief (naive for a Kierkegaard) that the beloved woman whom the troubadours renounced in order to be able to love her in their own fashion—or even the dream image of such a woman, who can never and nowhere be real—might be different enough from reality for their love to become absolute. This, I believe, was the root of Kierkegaard's religiosity. God can be loved thus, and no one else but God. He once wrote that God is a demand of man, and man clings to this demand to escape from the wretchedness of his condition, to be able to bear his life. Yes, but Kierkegaard's God is enthroned so high above everything human, is separated from everything human by such absolute depths—how could he help a man to bear his human life? I think he could, and for that very reason. Kierkegaard needed life to be absolute, to be so firm that it tolerated no challenge; his love needed the possibility of embracing the whole, without any reservation whatsoever. He needed a love without problems, a love in which it was not now the one, now the other that was better, not now the one, now the other that was right. My love is sure and unquestionable only if I am never in the right: and God alone can give me this assurance."You love a man," he wrote, "and you want always to be proved wrong against him, but, alas, he has been unfaithful to you, and however much this may pain you, you are still in the right against him and wrong to love him so deeply." The soul turns to God because it cannot subsist without love, and God gives the lover everything his heart desires."Never shall tormenting doubts pull me away from him, never shall the thought appal me that I might prove right against him: before God I am always in the wrong."

VIII

Kierkegaard was a troubadour and a Platonist, and he was both these things romantically and sentimentally. In the deepest recesses of his soul burned sacrificial flames for the ideal of a woman, but the self-same flames fed the stake upon which the self-same woman was burned. When man stood face to face with the world for the first time, everything that surrounded him belonged to him, and yet each separate thing always vanished before his eyes and every step led him past each separate thing. He would have starved to death, tragically, absurdly, in the midst of all the world's riches, had woman not been there from the start—woman who knew from the start how to grasp things, who knew the uses and the immediate significance of things. Thus it was that woman—within the meaning of Kierkegaard's parable—saved man for life, but only in order to hold him down, to chain him to the finiteness of life. The real woman, the mother, is the most absolute opposite of any yearning for infinity. Socrates married Xanthippe and was happy with her only because he regarded marriage as an obstacle on the way to the Ideal and was glad to be able to overcome the difficulties of marriage: much in the way that Suso's God says: "You have always found recalcitrance in all things; and that is the sign of my chosen ones, whom I want to have for myself."

Kierkegaard did not take up this struggle; perhaps he evaded it, perhaps he no longer needed it. Who knows? The world of human communion, the ethical world whose typical form is marriage, stands between the two worlds of Kierkegaard's soul: the world of pure poetry and world of pure faith. And if the foundation of the ethical life, "duty," appears firm and secure compared with the "possibilities" of the poet's life, its eternal evaluations are yet, at the same time, eternal fluctuations compared with the absolute certainties of the religious. But the substance of those certainties is air, and the substance of the poet's possibilities is likewise air. Where is the dividing line between the two?

But perhaps this is not the question to ask here. Regine Olsen was for Kierkegaard no more than a step on the way that leads to the icy temple of nothing-but-the-love-of-God. Committing a sin against her merely deepened his relationship to God; loving her with suffering, causing her to suffer, helped to intensify his ecstasies and to fix the single goal of his path. Everything that would have stood between them if they had really belonged to each other only gave wing to his flight. "I thank you for never having understood me," he wrote in a letter to her which he never sent, "for it taught me everything. I thank you for being so passionately unjust towards me, for that determined my life."

Even abandoned by him, Regine could only be a step towards his goal. In his dreams he transformed her into an unattainable ideal: but the step that she represented was his surest way to the heights. In the woman-glorifying poetry of the Provençal troubadours, great faithlessness was the basis for great faithfulness; a woman had to belong to another in order to become the ideal, in order to be loved with real love. But Kierkegaard's faithfulness was even greater than the troubadours', and for that very reason even more faithless: even the deeply beloved woman was only a means, only a way towards the great, the only absolute love, the love of God.

IX

Whatever Kierkegaard did, and for whatever reason, it was done only to save Regine Olsen for life. However many inner meanings the gesture of rejection may have had, outwardly—in Regine Olsen's eyes—it had to be univocal. Kierkegaard sensed that for Regine there was only one danger, that of uncertainty. And because, for her, no life could grow out of her love of him, he wanted with all his strength—sacrificing his good name—that she should feel nothing but hate for him. He wanted Regine to consider him a scoundrel, he wanted her whole family to hate him as a common seducer; for if Regine hated him, she was saved.

Yet the break came too suddenly, even though long and violent scenes had helped to prepare the way. Regine suddenly had to see Kierkegaard as different from the man she had previously known; she had to re-evaluate every word and every silence of every minute they had spent together if she was to feel that the new was indeed connected with the old—if she was to see Kierkegaard as a whole man; and from that moment onwards she had to see whatever he might do in that new light. Kierkegaard did everything to make this easier for her, to channel the current of her newly formed images in a single direction—the direction he wanted, the only one he saw as leading to the right goal for Regine: the direction of hate against himself.

This is the background to Kierkegaard's erotic writings—especially the *Diary of a Seducer*—and it is this that gives them their radiance, received from life itself. An incorporeal sensuality and a plodding, programmatic ruthlessness are the predominant features of these writings. The erotic life, the beautiful life, life culminating in pleasure, occurs in them as a world-view—and as no more than that; a way of living which Kierkegaard sensed as a possibility within himself, but which not even his subtle reasoning and analysis could render corporeal. He is, as it were, the seducer *in abstracto,* needing only the possibility of seduction, only a situation which he creates and then enjoys to the full; the seducer who does not really need women even as objects of pleasure. He is the platonic idea of the seducer, who is so deeply a seducer and nothing else that really he is not even that; a man so remote, so far above all other humans that his appeal can scarcely reach them any longer, or if it does, then only as an incomprehensible, elemental irruption into their lives: the absolute seducer who appears to every woman as the eternal stranger, yet who (Kierkegaard was incapable of noticing this aspect), just because he is so infinitely remote, barely avoids appearing comic to any woman who, for whatever reason, is not destroyed when he looms up on the horizon of her life.

We have already said that the role of the seducer was Kierkegaard's gesture for Regine Olsen's sake. But the possibility of being a seducer was already latent in him, and a gesture always reacts back upon the soul that makes it. In life there is no purely empty comedy: that is perhaps the saddest ambiguity of human relationships. One can play only at what is there: one cannot play at anything without it somehow becoming part and parcel of one's life; and although it may be kept carefully separate from the game, life trembles at such play.

Regine, of course, could only see the gesture, and the effect of the gesture forced her to re-evaluate everything in her life so that it became the exact opposite of what it had been before. At least, that was what Kierkegaard wanted, and on this he staked everything. But something that has been lived in corporeal reality can, at most, only be poisoned by the realization that it was a mere game; a reality can never be completely and unchallengeably re-evaluated; only one's view of that reality and the values one attaches to that view can change. What had passed between Regine and Kierkegaard was life, was living reality, and it could only be shaken and irretrievably confounded in retrospect, as the result of a forced re-evaluation of motives. For if the present forced Regine to see Kierkegaard differently, then this way of seeing him was sensual reality only for the present; the reality of the past spoke in a different voice, and could not be silenced by the feebler voice of her new knowledge.

Soon after the actual break Kierkegaard wrote to Bösen, his only dependable friend, that if Regine knew with what anxious care he had arranged everything and carried it through once he had decided that the break had to come, she would by that very fact recognize his love for her. When, after Kierkegaard's death, Regine read his posthumous writings, she wrote to Dr. Lund, his relative: "These pages put our relationship in a new light, a light in which I too saw it sometimes, but my modesty forbade me to think that it was the true light; and yet my unshakable faith in him made me see it like that again and again."

Kierkegaard himself felt something of this uncertainty. He felt that his gesture remained a mere possibility in Regine's eyes, just as Regine's gesture had in his own eyes. The gesture was in no way sufficient to create solid reality between them. If there was a way in which he could find true reality, it was the way to Regine: but to travel that way, however cautiously, would have been to destroy everything that he had accomplished so far. He had to remain frozen in his outwardly rigid, inwardly uncertain posture because, for all he knew, everything in her life might really be settled and certain, after all. Perhaps, if he had made a move towards her, he would have encountered living reality? But only perhaps. Ten years after the breaking off of the engagement he still did not dare to meet her. Perhaps her marriage was only a mask. Perhaps she loved him as before, and a meeting would have cancelled out all that had happened.

X

But it is impossible even to maintain the rigid certainty of one's gesture— if indeed it ever is a real certainty at all. One cannot, however much one may want to, continually disguise so deep a melancholy as a game, nor can one ever definitively conceal such passionate love under an appearance of faithlessness. Yes, the gesture reacts back upon the soul, but the soul in turn reacts upon the gesture which seeks to hide it, it shines forth from that gesture and neither of the two, neither gesture nor soul, is capable of remaining hard and pure and separate from the other throughout a lifetime. The only way of somehow achieving the outwardly preserved purity of the gesture is to make sure that, whenever the other person momentarily abandons his stance, this is always misunderstood. In this way accidental movements, meaningless words carelessly spoken, acquire life-determining significance; and the reflex produced by the gesture is in turn strong enough to force the impulse back into the same self-chosen stance. When they parted, Regine asked Kierkegaard almost childishly, in the midst of tearful pleas and questions, whether he would still think of her from time to time, and this question became the *leitmotif* of Kierkegaard's whole life. And when she became engaged, she sent him greetings expecting a sign of approval, but by doing so she set off quite another train of thought in his uncomprehending mind. When he could no longer bear the weight of the mask and thought that the time had come for mutual explanations, Regine, by agreement with her husband, returned his letter unopened, making a gesture of certainty to make sure that everything should remain uncertain for ever more—since in any case, for her it had always been so—and to make sure that, once Kierkegaard was dead, she herself should grieve over the uncertainty she had created by refusing to hear his explanation. Whether they met or did not meet, the pattern was always the same: a hasty impulse leading out of the gesture, then a hasty return to the gesture—and the other's failure to understand both.

XI

Where psychology begins, monumentality ends: perfect clarity is only a modest expression of a striving for monumentality. Where psychology begins, there are no more deeds but only motives for deeds; and whatever requires explanation, whatever can bear explanation, has already ceased to be solid and clear. Even if something still remains under the pile of debris, the flood of explanations will inexorably wash it away. For there is nothing less solid in the world than explanations and all that rests upon them. Whatever exists for a reason may have been its opposite for another reason—or, under slightly changed circumstances, for the same reason. Even when the reasons remain the same—but they never do—they cannot be constant; something that seemed to sweep the whole world away at a moment of great passion becomes minutely small when the storm is over, and something that was once negligible becomes gigantic in the light of later knowledge.

Life dominated by motives is a continual alternation of the kingdoms of Lilliput and Brobdingnag; and the most insubstantial, the most abysmal of all kingdoms is that of the soul's reason, the kingdom of psychology. Once psychology has entered into a life, then it is all up with unambiguous honesty and monumentality. When psychology rules, then there are no gestures any more that can comprise life and all its situations within them. The gesture is unambiguous only for as long as the psychology remains conventional.

Here poetry and life part company and become tragically, definitively distinct. The psychology of poetry is always unambiguous, for it is always an *ad hoc* psychology; even if it appears to ramify in several directions, its multiplicity is always unambiguous; it merely gives more intricate form to the balance of the final unity. In life, nothing is unambiguous; in life, there is no *ad hoc* psychology. In life, not only those motives play a role which have been accepted for the sake of the final unity, and not every note that has once been struck must necessarily be silenced in the end. In life, psychology cannot be conventional, in poetry it always is—however subtle and complex the convention. In life, only a hopelessly limited mind can believe in the unambiguous; in poetry, only a completely failed work can be ambiguous in this sense.

That is why, of all possible lives, the poet's life is the most profoundly unpoetic, the most profoundly lacking in profile and gesture. (Keats was the first to recognize this.) That which gives life to life becomes conscious in the poet; a real poet cannot have a limited mind about life, nor can he entertain any illusions about his own life. For a poet, therefore, all life is merely raw material; only his hands, doing spontaneous violence to living matter, can knead the unambiguous from the chaos of reality, create symbols from incorporeal phenomena, give form (i.e. limitation and significance) to the thousandfold ramifications, the deliquescent mass of reality. That is why a poet's own life can never serve as the raw material to which he will give form.

Kierkegaard's heroism was that he wanted to create forms from life. His honesty was that he saw a crossroads and walked to the end of the road he had chosen. His tragedy was that he wanted to live what cannot be lived. "I am struggling in vain," he wrote, "I am losing the ground under my feet. My life will, after all, have been a poet's life and no more." A poet's life is null and worthless because it is never absolute, never a thing in itself and for itself, because it is always there only *in relation to something,* and this relation is meaningless and yet it completely absorbs the life—for a moment at least; but then life is made up of nothing but such moments.

Against this necessity, the life of Kierkegaard—whose mind was never limited—waged its royally limited struggle. It might be said that life cunningly gave him all that it could give and all that he could ask for. Yet life's every gift was mere deception; it could never, after all, give him reality, but only lure him deeper and deeper, with every appearance of victory and success—like Napoleon in Russia—into the all-devouring desert.

This much his heroism did achieve, in life as in death. He lived in such a way that every moment of his life became rounded into the grand gesture, appearing statuesquely sure, carried through to the end; and he died in such a way that death came at the right time, just when he wanted it and as he wanted it. Yet we have seen how unsure his surest gesture was when seen from close by; and even if death overtook him at the climax of his most real, most profound struggle, even if it came as he wanted it to come, so that, dying, he could be the blood-witness of his own struggle, yet he could not be its real blood-witness. For, despite everything, his death pointed at several possibilities. In life, everything points at more than one possibility, and only *post facto* realities can exclude a few possibilities (never all of them, so that only one central reality is left). But even those open the way to a million new ones.

He was fighting the Christianity of his time when death overtook him. He stood in the midst of violent struggle; he had nothing more to seek in life outside that struggle, and he could scarcely have been fighting any harder. (Some incidental factors, too, made his death fateful. Kierkegaard had lived off his capital all his life, regarding interest as usury in the way religious men did in the Middle Ages; when he died, his fortune was just running out.) When he collapsed in the street and they took him to the hospital, he said he wanted to die because the cause he stood for needed his death.

And so he died. But his death left every question open: Where would the path which broke off suddenly at his grave have led to if he had gone on living? Where was he going when he met his death? The inner necessity of death is only in an infinite series of possible explanations; and if his death did not come in answer to an inner call, like an actor taking his cue, then we cannot regard the end of his path as an end and we must try to imagine the further meanderings of that path. Then even Kierkegaard's death acquires a thousand meanings, becomes accidental and not really the work of destiny. And then his purest and most unambiguous gesture of his life—vain effort!— was not a gesture after all.

THEODOR W. ADORNO

On Kierkegaard's Doctrine of Love

The observations presented in this study are intended to be philosophical rather than historical. They attempt to throw some light on a text of Søren Kierkegaard, concerning the position of basic concepts of religious ethics in the present situation. At the same time I should like to go beyond a mere critical analysis of the text. There may also be some historical interest involved in the analysis, since the work to be discussed is one of Kierkegaard's lesser known writings. . . . It is the book *Leben und Walten der Liebe* (Works of Love), published in 1847, a collection of so-called edifying discourses linked to each other by the concept of Christian love.

Kierkegaard's literary production falls into two distinctly separate parts, the philosophical writings and the religious sermons. This rough and schematic division is justified in Kierkegaard's case: justified by himself. Whereas all his philosophical writings were published anonymously—even those with the open theological tendencies of his later period, such as the *Krankheit zum Tode* (Sickness unto Death) and the *Einübung im Christentum* (Training in Christianity)—he published the religious sermons under his own name. This distinction was made most methodically. He alternated between these two methods of publication from the very beginning of his literary career, since *Entweder/Oder* (Either/Or). He was guided in this procedure by the basic idea that one ought to lure man into Truth. That is to say, truth, according to Kierkegaard, is no "result," no objectivity independent of the process of its subjective appropriation, but really consists in the process of subjective appropriation itself. In his philosophical writings, Kierkegaard goes so far as

From *Studies in Philosophy and Social Science* 8, no. 3 (1939). © 1940 by the Social Studies Association, Inc.

to say that subjectivity is the truth. This sentence is not, of course, to be understood in the sense of philosophical subjectivism, such as Fichte's, of whose language it reminds one. Its intrinsic meaning is that Truth exists in the living process of Faith, theologically speaking, in the imitation of Christ. Kierkegaard's philosophical writings attempt to express this process of existential appropriation through its different stages—which he calls aesthetic, ethical and religious—and to guide the reader by the dialectics of these stages to the theological truth. But he deemed it necessary to contrast as the "corrective" to this process the positive Christianity which one should achieve, though Kierkegaard never pretended to have achieved it himself. This contrast is provided by religious sermons. One may safely assume that Kierkegaard, who did not share philosophy's optimism of being able to produce the Absolute from itself, rebuffed this optimism even where his own philosophy was involved. In other words, he did not believe that a pure movement of thought could possibly lead up to Christianity, but only, in Kierkegaard's language, to the border of Christianity. He regards that Christian standpoint as being based on revelation. Hence, it maintains a transcendence of the movement of thought which does not permit philosophy to reach Christianity by a procedure of gradual transitions. According to this conviction, the Christian, from the very beginning, must face philosophy independently and distinctly. With Kierkegaard philosophy assumes the paradoxical task of regaining the lost position of an *Ancilla theologiae* and, in the last analysis, must abdicate. One may just as easily formulate the relation in the reverse way. The idea of a reason which attains the Absolute not by maintaining itself in complete consistency of thinking, but by sacrificing itself, indicates not so much the expropriation of philosophy by theology as the transplantation of theology into the philosophical realm. Indeed, the Christian, as a stage, fits perfectly into the hierarchy of Kierkegaard's philosophy, and all the categories which Kierkegaard regards as specifically Christian appear within the context of his philosophical deductions. They are, as it were, invested only post festum with the insignia of Christian revelation. This is particularly true of the doctrine of the radically different, of the qualitative jump, and of the paradox. These questions, however, can be settled only in connection with an actual text of Kierkegaard's.

The text to be discussed here has a particular bearing upon these questions. What is introduced here as an exegesis of Christian Love is revealed, through a more intimate knowledge of Kierkegaard's philosophy, as supplementing his negative theology with a positive one, his criticism with something edifying in the literal sense, his dialectics with simplicity. It is this very aim which makes Kierkegaard's sermons such tiresome and unpleasant reading. At every point, they bear the hallmarks of his trend of thought. Yet at the same time, they deny this strain and affect a sort of preaching naiveté. This naiveté, being produced dialectically and by no means primarily, threatens to slip into loquacious boredom at any moment. Verbosity is the danger of all Kierkegaard's writings. It is the verbosity of an interminable monologue which, so to speak, does not tolerate any protest and continually repeats itself, without any real articulation. This loquaciousness is intensified in his religious writings to the point of being painful. A Hegelian philosopher deliberately talks circumstantially, imagining himself a Socrates conducting his conversations in the streets of Athens. There is reason to suspect that even the pain and the boredom are planned by the cunning theologian, as Kierkegaard repeatedly styled himself. If the philosophical writings wish to "cheat" the reader into truth, the theological ones, in turn, wish to make it as difficult, as uninteresting, as insipid to him as possible. In one passage of the *Works of Love*, Kierkegaard says that he actually intends to warn us against Christianity. It is one of the basic aims of all his writings to rejuvenate Christianity into what it was supposed to have been during St. Paul's times: a scandal to the Jews and a folly to the Greeks. The scandal is Kierkegaard's Christian paradox. The folly to the Greeks, however, is the laborious simplicity which Kierkegaard stubbornly upholds throughout the religious sermons.

A brief summary of the book on Love is pertinent at this point. Kierkegaard speaks of Christian Love for man, but in pointed contrast to natural love. He defines love as Christian, if it is not "immediate" or "natural," or as Kierkegaard puts it, if one loves each man for God's sake and in a "God-relationship." Kierkegaard never concretely states what this love means. He comments upon it only by means of analogy. Negatively, however, his concept of love is distinct enough. He regards love as a matter of pure inwardness. He starts from the Christian command "Thou shalt love." He interprets this command by emphasizing its abstract generality. Speaking exaggeratedly, in Kierkegaard's doctrine of Love the object of love, is, in a way, irrelevant. According to Kierkegaard, the differences between individual men and one's attitude towards men are, in the Christian sense, of no importance whatever. The only element of "this man" which is of interest to the Christian is "the human," as revealed in this person. In love, the other person becomes a mere "stumbling block" to subjective inwardness. This has no object in the proper sense, and the substantial quality of love is "objectless." In Kierkegaard's doctrine the "Christian" content of love, its justification in eternity, is determined only by the subjective qualities of the loving one, such as disinterestedness, unlimited confidence, unobtrusiveness, mercifulness, even if one is helpless oneself, self-denial and fidelity. In

Kierkegaard's doctrine of love, the individual is important only with respect to the universal human. But the universal consists in the very fact of individualization. Hence love can grasp the universal only in love for the individual, but without yielding to the differences between individuals. In other words, the loving one is supposed to love the individual particularities of each man, but regardless of the differences between men. Any "preference" is excluded with a rigor comparable only to the Kantian Ethics of Duty. Love, for Kierkegaard, is Christian only as a "breaking down" of nature. It is, first of all, a breaking down of one's own immediate inclination which is supposed to be replaced by the God-relationship. Hence the Kierkegaardian love applies to the farthest as well as to the nearest. The concept of the neighbor which Kierkegaard makes the measure of love is, in a certain sense, that of the farthest: whomever one happens to meet is contrasted, in the very abstractness of such a possibility, with the "preference" for the friend or for the beloved one. Kierkegaard's love is a breaking down of nature, moreover, as a breaking down of any individual interest of the lover, however sublimated it may be. The idea of happiness is kept aloof from this love as its worst disfigurement. Kierkegaard even speaks of the happiness of eternity in such gloomy tones that it appears to consist of nothing but the giving away of any real claim to happiness. Finally, this doctrine of love is a breaking down of nature by demanding from the simple lover the same characteristics Kierkegaard's doctrine of Faith demands from the summit of consciousness. The *credo quia absurdum* is translated into the *amo quia absurdum*. Thus Kierkegaard admonishes the loving person to maintain faith in a once beloved person, even if this faith has lost any rational justification. He ought to believe in the person in spite of any psychological experience which is taboo, according to Kierkegaard, as being "secular." Here, the transformation of love into mere inwardness is striking. This Christian love cannot be disappointed, because it is practiced for the sake of God's command to Love. The rigorousness of the love advocated by Kierkegaard partially devaluates the beloved person. There is a line of Goethe: *Wenn ich dich liebe, was geht's dich an*—if I love you, what concern is it of yours? Kierkegaard would certainly have rejected this dictum as "aesthetic": one may say that it is the implicit theme of the *Tagebuch des Verführers* (Diary of the Seducer). This "erotic immediacy," however, reproduces itself, as it were, in Kierkegaard's religious doctrine of love. It is of no concern, to the Christian beloved one, whether or not he is loved. He has no power over this love. Incidentally, the reproduction of Kierkegaard's "aesthetic" standpoint in his religious stage, for which this example has been given, recurs throughout his work. It is unnecessary to point out how close this love comes to callousness. Perhaps one may most accurately summarize Kierkegaard's doctrine of love by saying that he demands that love behave towards all men as if they were dead. Indeed, the book culminates in the speech *Wie wir in Liebe Verstorbener gedenken* (How to think with love of those who passed away). There is good reason to regard this speech as one of the most important pieces he ever wrote. I should like to emphasize, even at this point, that the death-like aspect of Kierkegaard's love comprises the best and the worst of his philosophy. The attempt to explain this will be made later.

Theologians will not overlook the close connection of this doctrine of love with the wording of the Gospel and also with certain Christian traditions such as the distinction between Eros and Agape. But nor will they overlook the transformation of these motives, which it is difficult to call anything but demonic. The overstraining of the transcendence of love threatens, at any given moment, to become transformed into the darkest hatred of man. Similarly, the humiliation of the human spirit before God comes close to the naked hybris of the same spirit. By means of its radical inwardness, it is prone to conceive itself as the sole ground of the world. In spite of all the talk of the neighbor, the latter is nothing but the stumbling-block to prove one's own creative omnipotence as one of love. The forces of annihilation are scarcely tamed by this doctrine of love. The relapse into mythology and the lordly demonology of asceticism is enhanced by Kierkegaard's reckless spiritualization of love. He sets out to expel nature with a pitchfork, only to become Nature's prey himself. Let us take Kierkegaard's interpretation of the command "Thou shalt love." In its proper place, this command means the suspension of universal "justice." It "sublates" the concept of moral life as a closed interrelation of guilt and punishment insofar as they are regarded as equivalents which can be exchanged for one another. Christian love takes a stand against the mythological notion of destiny as one of an infinite relationship of guilt. It protests against the justice—an eye for an eye, a tooth for a tooth—in the name of Grace. The Christian "Thou shalt love" puts a stop to the mythical law of atonement. Kierkegaard, too, attacks the principle of "an eye for an eye, a tooth for a tooth." But he hardly ever mentions the idea of grace. He "mythifies" the "Thou Shalt love" itself. I have previously stated that it means, in its Christian sense, the barrier against the universal relationship of atonement. Kierkegaard does not understand it as such a barrier. He makes it dialectical in itself. The Hegelian in Kierkegaard dwells on the contradiction of the "Thou shalt" of the command and its content: love cannot be commanded. This very impossibility becomes to him the core of the command. "Thou shalt love" just because the "Shalt" cannot be applied to love. This is absurd, the wreckage of the finite by the infinite which Kierkegaard hypostatizes. The command to love is commanded because of its impossibility. This, however, amounts to nothing less than the annihilation of love and the installment of sinister domination. The command to love degenerates into a mythical taboo against preference and natural love. The protest of love against law is dropped. Love itself becomes a matter of mere law, even if it may be cloaked as the law of God. Kierkegaard's super-Christianity tilts over into paganism.

By so doing, Kierkegaard's doctrine of love offers itself to the smuggest sort of criticism. It is one single provocation, folly in reality and scandal. As far as my knowledge of the literature goes, only Christoph Schrempf has dealt with the doctrine of love in detail. As a matter of fact, he honorably stumbles at every stone Kierkegaard throws in his way. He objects to Kierkegaard on the ground that he neglects the preceding internal relationship between two persons, which he regards the necessary condition of love. He further objects in that love cannot be commanded, whereas this very impossibility makes the paradoxical center or perhaps the blind spot in Kierkegaard's doctrine. Opposing Kierkegaard, he defends preference as something beautiful; he attacks the theory of self-denial, maintaining that no lover ever denies himself but just "realizes" himself in love. At this point, I do not wish to judge the truth or falsity of this criticism. The points made by Schrempf are necessary consequences of that demonic "mythification" of Christianity which I have tried to make clear. It is senseless to discuss the theses on the basis of common sense since, according to Kierkegaard, they presuppose the suspension of common sense. But I would go beyond that. In a way, Schrempf's objections are too cursory. Closer examination shows that Kierkegaard's rigorousness which Schrempf naively takes for granted is not quite rigorous. One might almost say: that it is not rigorous enough. Kierkegaard's doctrine of love remains totally abstract. Of course he repeatedly gives examples such as that of the obedient child. But he always remains on the level of the metaphorical, of illustrations from the treasure of his autobiographical experience, such as the motive of the "poet," or his relation to Regine Olsen. And he never goes into any real, non-symbolical, non-metaphorical case of human love in order to apply his doctrine to it. On the other hand, he always insists on the "practice of real life." His failure to reach this practice by his concepts, and the unyielding abstractness of his doctrine, are symptoms that it is not quite as substantial as it pretends to be. Hence Schrempf's objections bear so little fruit, and it is therefore important critically to analyze the actual presuppositions of Kierkegaard's doctrine. Then I shall try to show the critical elements of Kierkegaard's rigorousness which goes far beyond the limits of that narrowness which it deliberately exhibits.

The main presupposition is the category of the neighbor and the historical changes it has undergone. Let us discuss this more closely. Kierkegaard asks: who is man's neighbor? He answers, according to his idea of absolute inwardness: "The neighbor, strictly speaking, is the reduplication of one's own ego. It is what philosophers would call 'the otherness,' that is, where the selfish element in one's love for oneself is to be revealed. As far as the abstract idea is concerned, the neighbor must not even be here." The abstractness of the neighbor, which has been mentioned earlier, is explicitly acknowledged by Kierkegaard. He even makes it a postulate, as an expression of the equality of men in the eyes of God: "The neighbor is everybody. . . . He is your neighbor by being your equal before God, but this equality is due unconditionally to every man, and everybody has it unconditionally." Thus the neighbor is reduced to the general principle of the otherness or of the universal human. Therewith, the individual neighbor, despite Kierkegaard's incessant talk of "that particular individual" (hiin Enkelte, dieser Einzelne) definitely assumes the character of contingency. "When you open the door behind which you have prayed to God and walk out, the first man whom you see is the neighbor whom thou shalt love." The particular reality which I encounter in my neighbor is thus rendered totally accidental. This implies one thing from the very beginning: that I must accept the neighbor whom I happened to meet as something *given* which ought not to be questioned: "To love thy neighbor means to be essentially and unconditionally present to each person according to the particular position in time given to him"—given to him externally, independent of oneself. In other words, Kierkegaard's doctrine of the neighbor presupposes a providence or, as Kierkegaard states, a "governance" which regulates human relationships and gives one a certain person and no other as a neighbor. In one passage, he frankly demands that one should "put oneself in the place where one may be used by governance." This necessarily gives rise to the objection of how one can maintain the concept of the practice of real life as a measuring rod of the love for the neighbor, if one excludes from this practice the specific being of the world? How is practice possible without the acting person's initiative in the very sphere that Kierkegaard takes for granted as a matter of Providence? It is of particular interest to observe how Kierkegaard surreptitiously raises this objection against himself and how he compromises with it. This happens in the discourse on mercifulness. Here he puts the question to himself of how the love to the neighbor is possible, if the loving person is powerless; that is to say, if this love cannot alter reality given by "Providence." The method he makes use of is exceedingly characteristic. For he is struck by the fact that this possibility of powerless love of the neighbor is actually not thought of in the Gospels. Hence he employs a device hardly compatible with his orthodox dogmatism. He modifies, as it were, biblical parables, in order to make them fit present reality. He tells the story of the Samaritan with the alteration that the Samaritan is incapable of saving the unfortunate man. Or he assumes that the sacrifice of the poor widow, which is supposed to be worth more than that of the rich, has been stolen without her being aware of it. Of course he maintains that her behavior is still that of true love. I should like to emphasize the configuration of the motives at hand. Pure inwardness is made the only criterion of action at the very moment at which the world no longer permits an immediate realization of love. Kierkegaard is unaware of the demonic consequence that his insistence on inwardness actually leaves the world to the devil. For what can loving one's neighbor mean, if one can neither help him nor interfere with a setting of the world which makes such help impossible? Kierkegaard's doctrine of impotent mercifulness brings to the fore the deadlock which the concept of the neighbor necessarily meets today. The neighbor no longer exists. In modern society, the relations of men have been "reified" to such an extent that the neighbor cannot behave spontaneously to the neighbor for longer than an instant. Nor does the mere disposition of love suffice to help the neighbor. Nothing is left to "that particular individual" but to cope with the very presuppositions which Kierkegaard excludes from practice as a product of providence. Kierkegaard denies reification. As a matter of fact the whole personalism of his philosophy aims at this denial, for a thing, "an object is always something dangerous, if one has to move forward. An object, being a fixed point in a finite world, is a barrier and break and therewith a dangerous thing for infinity. For love can become an 'object' to itself only by becoming something finite." In other words, it becomes impossible, if, on the basis of the material presuppositions of their relations, men have become objects, as is the case in our epoch. One could even go further. The form in which the concept of the neighbor is used by Kierkegaard is a reification itself compared with the Gospels. The neighbor of the Gospels implies fishermen and peasants, herdsmen and publicans, people whom one knows and who have their established locus in a life of simple production which can be realized adequately by immediate experience. One cannot imagine the Gospels taking the step from this concrete, unproblematic neighbor to the abstract, universal idea of neighborhood. Kierkegaard has the abstract concept of man of his own period and substitutes it for the Christian neighbor who belongs to a different society. Hence, he deprives both of their sense. The Christian neighbor loses the concreteness which alone made it possible to behave concretely towards him. Modern man is deprived of the last chance of love by moulding love after the pattern of frugal conditions which are not valid any longer. This contradiction is mastered only by Kierkegaard's stubborn maintenance of the "givenness" of social order. The maintenance is socially conformist and ready to lend its arm to oppression and misanthropy. Kierkegaard demands that one should "find the given or chosen object worthy of one's love." Such a demand is not only impossible to fulfill; by its acceptance of the given, it acknowledges the very same reification of man against which Kierkegaard's doctrine of love is directed. It is evident that Kierkegaard here follows the Lutheran doctrine of absolute obedience to the authority of the State. In the face of Kierkegaard's radical theological subjectivism, however, this spiteful orthodoxy leads to absurd inconsistencies and even to insincerity. The presuppositions of this doctrine of the neighbor and, at the same time, of love itself, are untenable.

A doctrine of love which calls itself practical cannot be severed from social insight. Such an insight is denied to Kierkegaard. Instead of any real criticism of inequality in society, he has a fictitious, merely inward doctrine of equality: "Christianity . . . has deeply and eternally impressed the kinship between man and man. Christianity establishes it by teaching that in Christ each particular individual is equally akin to God and stands in the same relation to God. For Christianity teaches each individual without any difference that he is created by God and redeemed by Christ." Sometimes Kierkegaard's way of speaking of the equality of men before God assumes the character of involuntary irony: "The times are gone when only the powerful and noble ones were men and the other people slaves and serfs." The irony cannot escape Kierkegaard's attention. He uses it as a medium of his religious paradox. With some haughtiness, he says: "Christianity simply does not enter into such things. It applies eternity and is at once at its goal. It leaves all differences in existence, yet teaches eternal equality." The more liberty and equality are interiorized, the more they are denounced in the external world: "Externally everything, so to speak, remains as it was before. The man is to be the wife's lord and she is to be subservient to him. Within the inwardness, however, everything is changed, changed by this little question to the wife, if she consulted her conscience whether she wants this man as her lord. . . . What Christ said of this realm, that it is not of this world, applies to everything Christian. Foolish people have tried foolishly, in the name of Christianity, to make it secularly manifest that the wife is empowered with the same rights as the man. Christian religion never demanded or wished anything of that sort. It has done everything for the woman, if she is ready to content herself in a Christian way with the Christian. If she does not want that, the mean external position she might obtain in the world is nothing but a poor substitute for what she loses." Such theorems bring to the fore what was hinted at earlier, namely, that in a certain sense Kierkegaard's religious rigorousness is not seriously meant and that it is better to analyze its presuppositions than sentimentally to criticize it. Kierkegaard raises the objection against himself which is due in a state of universal injustice: "Is it not a fundamental demand that there should be every possible help for the needy and that, if possible, want itself should be abolished?" Kierkegaard dismisses this question all too easily: "Eternity says however: there is only one danger: the danger that mercifulness is not practiced. Even if every want had disappeared, it must not have necessarily disappeared through mercifulness. In such a case, the misery that no mercifulness has been practiced would be a greater misery than any other secular one." The following is symptomatic of the flippancy of a rigorousness which is ready to leave everything in its status quo. Kierkegaard is insatiable in condemning the world, worldliness, and its limited worldly aims. He does not hesitate, however, to qualify his own rigorousness as soon as he speaks, as it were, as a social pedagogue. "Indeed, we do not intend to make an adolescent conceited, and to excite him to condemn the world in a quick, busy way." Kierkegaard's ascetic rigorousness is carried through only abstractly. It is soft-pedaled as soon as it could lead to serious conflicts with the "existing" condemned by Kierkegaard in abstracto. At such a moment, worldliness must not be condemned under any circumstances.

Kierkegaard's doctrine of love keeps itself within the existent. Its content is oppression: the oppression of the drive which is not to be fulfilled and the oppression of the mind which is not allowed to question. Kierkegaard's love is a love that takes away instead of giving. Such he formulates himself: "Then the woman was taken from the man's flank and given to him as company; for love and community first take something away from man before giving anything." But, at the same time, this oppression of the individual implies a criticism of what could be called, in Hegelian language, bad individuality. The individual, in his self-assertion and isolation, is visualized as something contingent and even as a mere veneer. The thesis underlying the present study, the thesis which I should like to put forward for discussion, may be expressed as follows: Kierkegaard's misanthropy, the paradoxical callousness of his doctrine of love enables him, like few other writers, to perceive decisive character features of the typical individual of modern society. Even if one goes so far as to admit that Kierkegaard's love is actually demonic hatred, one may well imagine certain situations where hatred contains more of love than the latter's immediate manifestations. All Kierkegaard's gloomy motives have good critical sense as soon as they are interpreted in terms of social critique. Many of his positive assertions gain the concrete significance they otherwise lack as soon as one translates them into concepts of a right society.

Before going into further detail, I should like to comment on an objection which might be raised at this point. One might consider that the critical insight for which I give Kierkegaard credit is as abstract from the reality as his doctrine of the neighbor. It is possible, perhaps, to attribute this critical insight to his general idea of worldliness, instead of to a specific coinage of it for the present situation. This however, would oversimplify matters. The abstract generality of his doctrine of the neighbor is not altogether voluntary. It is due to a position of constraint: to the incompatibility of the Christian command to love in its pure form with present society. Kierkegaard's philosophy, however, aims in all its stages—even in the aesthetic one—at the "instant," which is supposed to be the paradoxical unity of the historical and the eternal. It is probably uncertain whether Kierkegaard was even capable of "filling out" this paradox or whether it merely remained a program. This much, however, is certain: as a critic, he actually grasped the instant, that is to say, his own historical situation. It is highly significant that his polemic chef d'oeuvre bears the title *Der Augenblick* (The Instant). Kierkegaard was Hegelian enough to have a clean-cut idea of history. He is not satisfied by simply contrasting the eternal with an abstract contemporariness which, at any given moment, is supposedly equally far and near to the eternal. He conceives history to be related to Christianity. His concept of this relation, however, turns the Hegelian idea of the self-realization of the world-spirit upside down. To him the history of Christianity is, roughly speaking, the history of an apostasy from Christianity. He contrasts the conviction of the loss of all human substance to the current conviction of progress, or rather, he conceives progress itself as the history of advancing decay. It is at this point that critics of modern culture such as Karl Kraus followed Kierkegaard most closely. Kierkegaard regards the criticism of progress and civilization: as the criticism of the reification of man. He belongs to the very few thinkers of his epoch (apart from him I know only Edgar Allan Poe and Baudelaire) who were aware of the truly chthonian changes undergone by men, as it were, anthropologically, at the beginning of the modern industrial age: by human behaviour and the total setting of human experience. It is this awareness which invests Kierkegaard's critical motives with their genuine earnestness and dignity. His *Works of Love* contains an extraordinary testimony to that awareness. For here Kierkegaard gives an account of a tendency in today's mass society which, during his time, must have been very latent: the substitution of spontaneous thinking by "reflectory" adaptation taking place in connection with modern forms of mass information. Kierkegaard's hatred of the mass, however conservatively it styles itself, contains something of an inkling of the mutilation of men by the very mechanisms of domination which

actually change men into a mass. "It is as if the time of thinkers had gone."
The following quotation most clearly shows Kierkegaard's realization of the
abolition of thinking by information and "conditioned reflexes": "All communication is supposed to assume the comfortable tone of the easy pamphlet
or to be supported by falsehood after falsehood. Indeed, it is as if, in the last
instance, every communication ought to be manipulated in such a way as to
make it possible to promulgate it in an hour's time at a public meeting. Half
an hour is spent in noisy expressions of applause and opposition, and during
the other half hour one is so dizzy that one is incapable of collecting one's
own thoughts." Kierkegaard, in speaking of the mass meetings of the 1848
period, seems to have heard those loudspeakers which filled the Berlin Sports-
palast one hundred years later.

To return to the social aspect of Kierkegaard's doctrine of love, let me
give the following examples. Kierkegaard, to be certain, does not touch on
secular injustice and inequality. But the misanthrope Kierkegaard has a very
sharp eye for discovering them—the eye of love, one should say. He suspects,
for example, that the doctrine of civic equality has an ideological element. He
is familiar with the fact that members of different classes who behave towards
each other in the name of Christianity as if they were nothing but men, do so,
generally, only in order to maintain the fiction of civic equality and thus better
to preserve civic inequality. Kierkegaard is full of mockery for what he calls
"welfare"—a mockery which easily can be understood as plainly reaction-
ary. But by denouncing the worldly happiness which is aimed at through welfare as something poor compared with eternity, he does not merely mean a
postponement ad Kalendas Graecas. He knows something of the wretchedness of that very happiness welfare provides to men. This becomes particularly evident in a demand that Kierkegaard raises again and again: "In order
to get into a relation with the Christian, one must first become sober." Of
course, the demand of soberness first takes something away: the happiness
gained through drunken ecstasy. But does not this happiness only cheat us of
another happiness which is absolutely denied to us in the world as it is?
Kierkegaard's demand for sobriety is not that of the Philistine. It attacks the
shams of mere individuality, the making absolute of accidental "differences,"
and all the false happiness connected with them. Behind this sobriety lies the
profound knowledge that in the last analysis the differences between men are
not decisive. For all the features of individualization and specification owe
their very existence to the universal injustice which makes this man thus and
not otherwise—whereas he could be different.

The significance of "could be different" is the measure of the "taking
away" of Kierkegaard's love. The counter-concept that he contrasts to the

worldly which he intends taking away is that of possibility. The possibility, according to Kierkegaard, is to be maintained against mere existence. He means by that the paradox Eternal, the Christian *absurdum*. But it is directed at the same time against the typical character I mentioned previously: the character which is no longer capable of the experience of possibility. The theory of possibility is, first of all, directed against knowledge, particularly against empirical knowledge. This, however, is not to be taken as "anti-intellectual." The knowledge against which Kierkegaard struggles is the knowledge of the man who is positive as regards what has taken place since the beginning of the world and what will take place for all the future. It is the knowledge of mere after-construction, the principle of which excludes anything radically new. This is the point attacked by Kierkegaard's criticism of psychology and, as one would call it today, of positivism. To him, psychology is distrust of the possibility. He formulates his attitude towards it as follows: "What is the enticing secret of distrust? It is an abuse of knowledge: by a resolute ergo, that one transforms knowledge into faith. As if this ergo were nothing! As if it ought not to be noticed at all, for everyone has the same knowledge and necessarily draws the same conclusion from it, as if it were eternally certain and settled that preexisting knowledge necessarily determines the act of inference." Against this knowledge there is possibility which he interprets as hope. Hope is, according to Kierkegaard, the "sense for the possibility." "But the hope that remained did so only with the loving one." "The man who knows mankind, who knows its past and future, has a secret affinity to Evil. To believe nothing at all is the very border where the belief in evil begins. For the good is the object of the belief and therefore whoever believes nothing is ready to believe the bad." Kierkegaard goes even beyond that. Fundamentally (and this reveals an Utopian tendency aided even by his conservatism which denies it) he cannot even imagine that one could breathe for one moment without the consciousness of possibility, that is to say, without hope of the transfiguration of the world. "Truly, anyone who does not wish to understand that man's entire life-time is the time of hope, is in despair." The worldliness that Kierkegaard wants to "remove" is actually the stage of despair. Kierkegaard has introduced the concept of the existential seriousness into philosophy. In the name of hope, he becomes the foe of seriousness itself, of the absorption by practical aims which is not suspended by the thought of what is possible. The following passage could very well be used against Kierkegaard's present successors, the German existential philosophers, particularly against Heidegger. Nothing serves to better differentiate between Kierkegaard and his heirs than his turning against "seriousness." Alas, how often reconciliation has failed, because one handled the matter too seriously and also because one did not learn from God the art (which one must learn from God) of achieving something with deep inner seriousness and yet as easily and playfully as truth permits. Never believe that seriousness is peevishness; never believe that the distorted face which makes you sick is seriousness. No one can know seriousness unless he has learnt from seriousness that one can be too serious." The seriousness rejected by Kierkegaard is the bourgeois seriousness of business and competition: "They judge that such a man"—that is, one who hopes—"is not serious. Making money, however, is serious. To make a great deal of money, even through the slave-trade, is serious. To promulgate some truth, if one makes ample money by doing so, (since this and not the truth matters): is serious." Kierkegaard's doctrine of hope protests against the seriousness of a mere reproduction of life which mutilates man. It protests against a world which is determined by barter and gives nothing without an equivalent.

Kierkegaard's view of our love for the dead derives from this protest. I have already mentioned that it is both the worst and the best part of his doctrine of love. Perhaps an explanation can now be attempted. The bad side is obvious: love for the dead is the one which most rigidly excludes the reciprocity of love that necessarily takes the beloved one as living himself. Thus it appears to be the reified and fetish love kat'exochen. But, at the same time, it is love absolutely void of any barter, of any "requital," and, therefore, the only unmutilated love permitted by our society. The paradox that the only true love is love for the dead is the perfect expression of our situation. Let me try to interpret the real experience behind Kierkegaard's theology of love for the dead in the words of a secular philosopher of our own time: "On the death bed, when death is certainty, the rich and the poor are alike in many regards. For with death a man loses his 'relationships': he becomes nothing. The proudest kings of France had to have this experience. The enlightened and humane physician who tries to help the lonely dying man in the hour of his last ordeal, not for the sake of economic or technical interest but out of pity— this physician represents the citizen of a future society. His situation is the present image of a true humanity." What Kierkegaard says of God as the last one who remains with the dying man is in deepest accordance with the "present image" of a true humanity, however little Kierkegaard might have interpreted his idea of the Eternal as such an image.

I should like to conclude with a selection of passages from that sermon *Wie wir in Liebe Verstorbener gedenken* (How to think in love of those who passed away). After the above remarks, they hardly need any interpretation. Kierkegaard calls death the "powerful thinker who does not only think through any sense illusion down to the bottom, but actually thinks to the bottom." This reminds one of that poem of Baudelaire's which invokes Death as *vieux capitaine*. The relation to the dead is characterized as one free of aims: "Truly, if you thoroughly wish to ascertain, how much love is in you or in another person: watch only the behavior to a dead one. . . . For the dead man is cunning. He has really drawn himself totally out of any entanglements. He has not the slightest influence which could aid or hinder his opposite neighbor, the loving one. . . . That we think lovingly of those who passed away is a deed of truly unselfish love." Kierkegaard describes mourning as follows: "We must not disturb the dead by wailing and crying. We must treat a dead person as a sleeper whom we do not dare to awaken, because we hope he will awake voluntarily. . . . No, we ought to think of him who passed away, we ought to weep softly but weep for a long, long time." Kierkegaard realizes the enigmatic interweaving of death and childhood: "It is true that he does not cause any troubles, as the child sometimes does. He is not the cause of any sleepless nights, as least not by the troubles he causes. For, oddly enough, the good child causes no sleepless nights; the better the dead man was, however, the more sleepless nights he causes." To Kierkegaard's contemplation, even death assumes the expression of paradox. The thesis is: Yes, the loving memory must . . . defend itself against reality, lest reality should become too powerful by ever new impressions and blot out the memory. It also has to struggle against time. In brief, it must not allow itself to be induced to forget and must fight for the liberty of maintaining memory in love. . . . Certainly, no one is as helpless as the dead man." Now the opposite: "For a dead man is very strong though he does not seem so. It is his strength that does not change. And the dead man is very proud. Did you not notice that the proud man tries to show nothing to him whom he holds in most profound contempt; that he does everything to appear absolutely unchanged as if nothing had happened, just in order the more deeply to let down the one held in contempt?" And, finally, the lofty bridge between Kierkegaard's criticism of seriousness and the love for those who have died: "If it would not sound so merry (as it can sound only to him who does not know what seriousness is) I should say one could put this inscription over the door of the cemetery: 'Here no one is urged' or: 'We do not urge anybody.' And yet I shall say so and shall firmly stick to what I have said. For I have thought so much about death that I know well: no one can talk seriously about death who is incapable of utilizing the cunning lying in death, the whole deep-thinking roguishness of death—the roguishness to resurrection. The seriousness of death is not the seriousness of the eternal. To the seriousness of death belongs this particular awakening, this deep-thinking jesting overtone. Of course, apart from the thought of eternity, it is often an empty, often cheeky jest, but in connection with the thought of eternity, it is what it ought to be; and then, indeed, something radically different from that insipid seriousness. The latter is least of all capable of conceiving and maintaining something of the tension and bearing of the thought of death." The hope that Kierkegaard puts against the "seriousness of the eternal" is nothing but the hope of the reality of redemption.

KARL JASPERS

The Importance of Kierkegaard

Kierkegaard died in 1855. As late as 1900 he was still little known outside the Scandinavian countries. True, there had been some selected German translations; in 1896 there had appeared a stout volume entitled *Angriff auf die Christenheit* which contained all the documents of the Kierkegaardian struggle against the Church. A wider circle first became aware of him through other sensational publications. In 1904 Inselverlag published letters and notes on his relationship to his fiancée, in 1905 the *Tagebuch des Verführers,* and in the same year the *Buch des Richters.* This last, translated by Gottsched at Basel, is still an excellent selection from Kierkegaard's diaries which provide us with a remarkable impression of his character. In 1909 began the definitive twelve-volume edition of his works edited by Gottsched and Schrempf, through which one can become thoroughly acquainted with his work. Kierkegaard became a figure of the first rank in the German intellectual world. He was like a discovery.

Still his name scarcely appeared in the area of academic philosophy before 1914. It was still absent from our histories of philosophy. Shortly before the first World War he became an event for certain young men who were studying theology or philosophy. Today his work has been translated into French and English. His significance is growing throughout the West and even in Japan. Dialectical theology and all shades of existentialism have relied heavily on Kierkegaard. The source of their fundamental principles is obvious.

From *Cross Currents* 2 (Spring 1952). © 1952 by *Cross Currents.* Translated by Erwin W. Geissman.

Among young students today the interest in Kierkegaard is as great as it is in Nietzsche. Lectures and seminars on the one are as likely to be filled as those on the other. Still the questions of what the real Kierkegaard was, what he signified historically, and what his present influence is, cannot be answered unequivocally. In the short space of this article I will attempt a few demonstrations.

Kierkegaard is a Christian philosopher, but of a remarkable kind. He does not profess himself a Christian and yet he says that the truth of Christianity is everything to him. Furthermore, his works are of very great interest for the unbeliever. He is a writer, a thinker, and a master of language. No reader of *Either/Or,* his first great work and a sensational success in Copenhagen in 1843, is forced to take note that a Christian has written it.

In the pseudonyms under which Kierkegaard published most of his work, he invented "thinkers" whom he permitted to expound his position: the aesthetic man with his sovereign freedom in taking hold of every possibility of life and of spirit; the ethical man with his well-established moral realization in the husband and the citizen; the religious man who out of his own inner cataclysm hearkens to that call of God at which the aesthetic order will be set aside. Through such development in the figures which represent thinking existence Kierkegaard was able as he said "to read once more, where possible in an interior way, the original text of individuals, of the human existence-relationship, known of old and handed down to our fathers."

The event appears to be simple, fair and gratifying: progress through human possibilities leads by ascent over the stages of the aesthetic, the ethical, the humanly religious to the truth, and this truth is Christianity.

But Kierkegaard's position is in no way so direct. He gives no systematic teaching and asks that the opinions of the pseudonyms not to be taken for his own. He shows only the possibilities, so as to leave the decisions to the reader. If the reader wishes to have the decisions made for him by Kierkegaard it is rendered very difficult for him. The reader does not find in the work of Kierkegaard the objective, clearly-defined grounds by which he could hold himself convinced. He may find himself in treacherous quicksand in which he has lost his footing.

Indeed Kierkegaard in retrospect has said of his works that they were all written by him in order as it were to deceive men into Christianity. While he took his stand on the ground of this world (on that which interests the men of this world), he wished to lead mankind there where this ground leaves off and the truth of Christianity shines in its splendor, or perhaps there where the capacity for belief is granted by the grace of God.

Kierkegaard refuses to say that he is a Christian and believes as a Christian, but at the same time he states that Christianity is something so high that he dare not aspire to it as long as his own life is not adequate to it.

We ask: of what sort of Christianity was Kierkegaard thinking?

The belief that God has appeared to the world in the person of Jesus Christ is called Christianity. This belief, moreover, is beyond our understanding. A human being is not God, and God is not a particular human being.

Kierkegaard lived in our own age—an age in which the conception of the God-Man in all its seriousness, literalness, and reality is no longer believed with firm or unquestioned certitude. One seeks to make the conception somehow bearable and comprehensible to his understanding, tries to confirm it by historical research in Scripture, wishes to convince himself through speculative dogmatics.

According to Kierkegaard all of this already involves an abandoning of Christian faith. For the truth of this faith cannot be perceived, cannot be discovered historically, cannot be thought speculatively. It does not like human truth slumber within us as a hidden bud which need only be awakened. It is not like human truth communicated from teacher to scholar, where the scholar learns only incidentally from the teacher what he might well have been able to discover for himself. On the contrary Christian faith develops outside of and in opposition to human truth. It comes to us from elsewhere. God alone gives us the capacity for belief. One statement of Jesus was enough for His contemporary generation: We have believed that in these years God revealed Himself as a humble servant, lived among us and then died. This statement was enough to make them mindful. In later ages man believes because of this account of the contemporary, as the contemporary believed because of the capacity which he himself received from God. All study, all demonstration, all attempts to make it plausible or practical would be to no purpose.

For the understanding the concept of the God-Man is a paradox. Faith is unreason and therefore is to be attained only through the subjugation of the understanding. Kierkegaard understands that this must be so: if God wants to reveal Himself to man He cannot show Himself directly. For in that case there would be no bond between God and man; man would be as it were crushed and undone. Therefore God must show Himself while at the same time He conceals Himself. He dare not be knowable as God. Therefore He appears in the form of a humble servant in all the humiliation of a crucified criminal.

This God-manifestation is an indirect communication. Even when Christ says that He is the Son of God, it is not a direct assertion because since it stands in contradiction to His humanity it is patently absurd. To understand this assertion, an act of faith is necessary.

Indeed Kierkegaard forbids us to hold as Christian faith what is only human religiosity. Faith in God, the One, the Unchangeable, the Eternal Lover; the totality of human consciousness of guilt; life for an absolute end; the intensification of the soul; all of this is merely human but not yet Christian. No—to believe in the unique, the fearful, all the reality exceeding human understanding, all the appearance of God Himself bursting on human thought—this is possible only in a leap thanks to the bestowal of grace, and not through human skill.

But once one believes, then the believer, gaining eternal salvation, stands in a radically different position toward the world and the world toward him. The world must deny him; in the world he must suffer and be denied in order to take up his cross. The distinguishing mark of a Christian is not only the surrender of the understanding ("to believe against reason is a martyrdom"), but is martyrdom itself, whether in boundless pain or in suffering death for following the faith. This is the indispensable sign of being a Christian. It is the consequence of its radical dissimilarity from the world. Christianity implies an irreparable break with the world.

The further consequence of this belief is the breach through mankind: the breach between those who are Christian believers and those who are not. No one can understand the Christian belief (which is humanly unintelligible) except one who is himself a believer. Therefore his faith operates in a detaching, separating, polemic fashion. Its truth is exclusive. The believer experiences "the grief that he cannot sympathize with all humankind as humankind, but essentially only with Christians."

For the believer things can come to the point that he "must hate father and mother." For his feelings will be akin to hatred if he has attached his salvation to conditions which he knows will not be acceptable to them.

It is in this way that that Christianity which he calls the Christianity of the New Testament appears to Kierkegaard. But what, according to Kierkegaard is the situation of Christianity in our time?

Kierkegaard says: New Testament Christianity has disappeared. Today we are all Christians; that is, no one is a Christian.

This is the task Kierkegaard sets himself: to show the real Christianity without deception in order to make becoming a Christian difficult. With this in mind he had written his works for a decade. But then in the last year of his life he proceeds to public and direct attack on the Church, on the Christendom of our times, in order to make genuine Christianity possible again.

Today, says Kierkegaard, we are all born baptized, confirmed as Christians, and everything is in order. But faith cannot come by innate nature. Mankind remains, as it is born, in untruth. It has no way to reach truth of itself. Only when God grants the capacity for belief does man become entirely different; then for the first time does he walk in truth; a sudden leap brings him there. One becomes a Christian through a complete reversal, the second birth. His preceding state was not properly one of existing at all. At the decisive moment he becomes conscious that he was born as himself. He reaches this consciousness not through baptism, since the child knows nothing of the baptism; nor through confirmation since at fourteen he is not yet mature. The consciousness comes to him only through the real second birth.

The open assault on the Church in Copenhagen (1884–5) was the most unrestrained attack on the Christian Church and the one grounded on the deepest seriousness which the nineteenth century had seen. Pointing to the true Christianity of the New Testament, Kierkegaard wished to unmask the Christendom of his own time. He reached a climax in these most drastic statements:

> By ceasing to take part in the public worship of God as it now is, thereby have you constantly one grave sin the less: thereby you take no part in making a fool of God in what is now given out for New Testament Christianity, but which certainly it is not.

He goes further: the proclaimers of Christianity have a pecuniary interest in people calling themselves Christians and in their not getting to know the truth of Christianity. The state is obliged to reduce all preaching of Christianity to a private matter. "Christ demands that one preach the doctrine for nothing; that one preach in poverty, in lowliness, in complete renunciation, in the most absolute dissimilarity from the world."

What motive brought Kierkegaard to this attack? He did not aim at it from the beginning. For years he seemed prepared to become a clergyman. The attack was an ultimate result. In order to find the answer we must draw some hypotheses from his life.

In his early youth the ground was laid. At twenty-two he writes in his diary that he has felt the almost irresistible force of one pleasure after another. He has tasted the fruit of the tree of knowledge and has known a moment of joy in learning, but the knowledge has left behind no deeper mark on himself.

It was necessary for him "to find the truth which is truth for me, and for which I am willing to live and die." He forms the resolution, "Now will I begin to act inwardly." The young man is conscious of having "crossed the Rubicon" because seriousness has been established.

But the realization grows in the course of years to a succession of negative resolutions. The burden of the No! lays itself on Kierkegaard's life. He broke his engagement, marriage was denied him—a fact which, despite numerous interpretations, was largely incomprehensible to Kierkegaard himself—but he remained true to the separated one in a unique way. He entered on no vocation. Whenever he, who had passed the examinations long before, wished to become a clergyman, something was against it which denied it to him.

Nevertheless his thought and poetry grew directly out of the negative. Each *no* produced an almost drunken ferment of creativity.

Kierkegaard was aware of this. Unhappy in love, he was able like no one else to praise the happiness of love. He who did not dare to risk marriage has perhaps written more deeply about marriage than anyone else in world literature.

It was the same with faith. He who could not undertake to be a true believer was able to write about belief. As his description of love has a greater charm than the descriptions of a married man, so his writings on religion have a greater appeal than those of a professional clergyman. What he says moreover is not untrue; what he describes is simply his happier, his better self. In his relations to the world of religion, he is an unhappy lover, not a believer. He has only that which precedes faith—despair—and in it a burning desire for religion.

But this showed the Thinker Kierkegaard that his world might indeed not be true. As a Christian any purely poetic existence is sin to him: to write instead of *being,* to occupy his imagination with good and evil instead of *being,* to think the faith instead of living the faith.

It is the mark of Kierkegaard's seriousness that he cannot be satisfied with the mere display of writing and thinking, no matter how extraordinary his spiritual production might be. What he wrote originated in an earnestness which nothing he wrote could satisfy. This is why his writings are so touching. They are never shallow or arbitrary.

One thing always remained clear to him: it is important to turn from reflection to action. It was Kierkegaard's destiny and his mystery, that this step could not take place in his own life.

In the *Journal* we see the vacillation between willing and not willing, the experimentation in thinking, the preparation, the hesitation. In only two directions was firmness attained:

1. in negative resolutions, in conscious self-appraisal, in fidelity to that which was denied.

2. in the pursuit of literary production, the very variety of his work, the aim of making man the individual mindful.

Only the open attack on the Church, an action full of risk and responsibility, seemed to solve the problem of existence, but this was an action which again as action was only a negation.

How could Kierkegaard endure such living and such thinking?

Kierkegaard's personal piety in the background of his dialectical interpretation of Christianity, of his distinction between human and Christian religiosity, is simple and straightforward, as if there all those refined, tormented thoughts might be forgotten.

So he writes: "The best proof for immortality of the soul, for the existence of God . . . , is, properly speaking, the mark which a man obtains in childhood: this is absolutely certain, because my father has told it to me."

And again: "From earliest childhood on: that is the main point."

Entirely without reflection—he repeatedly admitted it—he lived in secret with God as a child with its father. He saw, though not altogether unequivocally, the direction in his life.

He always spoke simply of the love of God, the eternal love which is without end: "While I sleep, you wake; and when waking I go astray, you shape it that the error has been better than the right."

On his deathbed he answered the question whether he could pray in peace: "Yes, I can. I pray first of all that all may be forgiven me. Then I pray that I may be free from despair in death. . . . Then I pray that I may know beforehand when the last hour has arrived."

He arranged that his tombstone would carry the verses of the Danish poet Brorson:

> But a short time
> And it is won;
> Then will the whole struggle
> Be melted into nothingness.
>
> Then may I refresh myself
> In the stream of life,
> And forever, everlastingly
> Speak with Jesus.

But this piety was not the motive of his thought and his action. In his work it is scarcely visible, except in many passages of edifying discourse.

What Kierkegaard really intended by his attack on Christendom depends also on the foundation of seriousness which he layed in his youth, and which, as he swept to such annihilating negation, remained possible for him throughout the retreat from life because of an unaffected childlike piety. But decisive for the attack itself was a quite definite motive.

He wished no revolution; he did not seek at any time to found a new church. He wanted to have nothing to do with either the Socialists or Liberals, or with any of the politicians or agitators, in the planning of programs for the change of social conditions. He avoided all communication with them although they regarded him as one of themselves. In all these movements he saw only the road to the disastrous destruction of our world.

Did he perhaps wish to fight as a Christian for Christianity? to become a new martyr? He expressly said no: "Although I should by my death become a martyr, it would not be for Christianity." Christianity stands too high for him. He does not dare to confess himself a witness to the truth of Christianity. He does not wish to be mistaken. What then did he wish? Only honesty.

He declares therefore at the height of his open attack:

> I want honesty. . . . Will our generation honorably, honestly, openly, frankly, directly rebel against Christianity and say to God: We can but we will not subject ourselves to this power.— Very well, then, I am with them.
>
> If they will admit to God how it really stands with us men, that the human race in the course of time has taken the liberty of softening and softening Christianity until at last we have contrived to make it exactly the opposite of what it is in the New Testament—and that now, if the thing is possible, we should be so much pleased if this might be Christianity. If that is what they want, then I am with them.
>
> But one thing I will not do. . . . I will not take part in what is known as official Christianity, which by suppression and by artifice gives the impression of being the Christianity of the New Testament.
>
> For this honesty I am ready to take the risk. On the other hand I do not say that it is for Christianity I take the risk. . . .
>
> Suppose that I were to become a martyr: I would not even in that case be a martyr for Christianity, but because I wanted honesty.

As an honest man Kierkegaard felt himself needed by Providence. He is—this one time in his life—completely convinced that God wills what he is doing with his attack.

Is honesty now for him the ultimate end? Not at all, but it is the indispensable condition. Therefore he begins his own activity as discreetly as possible: not a witness to truth, not a martyr, not a warrior for Christianity; he shall do nothing else but unmask falsehood.

Why? Kierkegaard sees his age plunging into the nothingness of groundless reflection, of total leveling, of representation in which nothing is represented, of appearance with no sense of value for a foundation, of the universal godless "as if." Let the new seriousness not be looked for in disease, famine and war; first let the eternal punishments of hell be present and mankind will become serious again.

In these hopeless circumstances Kierkegaard sets forth the challenge. The Church should only acknowledge honestly that her action and her weakened teaching is not New Testament Christianity. Let this honesty become a reality, this least minimum, and then man must see. It lies in no man's power to direct the progress of the world. The realization of this honesty he understands as a question to the deity. These changes have taken place. Let it appear whether they have the approbation of providence. If not, all must break asunder, in order that in this dread individuals may again emerge who can endure the Christianity of the New Testament.

This attack on the Church (just as Kierkegaard's interpretation of Christianity) appears to us to be plainly ruinous. Christianity, which must have duration, in time, permanency in the world, is bound to the Church. That with it is bound up accommodation, limitation, perversion, the Christian of the first centuries understood. The Church is never brought to perfection. The Christian element in it is the constant question, the measure, the claim, the task—and it is always corrupted in the secular world. It is enjoined to destroy itself because one wishes to destroy the bearer of its worldly surrender—the Church.

Furthermore, if the Christian faith through so cunning a dialectic shall be delivered into absurdity, so Christianity, rightly understood in this way, would be impossible for rational man as long as he is neither insane nor dishonest.

In short, if Kierkegaard's interpretation of Christianity was the true one, then this Christianity had no future. Kierkegaard's work for its defence was in reality a work for its destruction, in still another direction than the deceptions and accommodations destroy it.

Is not the life and thought of Kierkegaard also proven to be absurd? Is the self-exclusion from the world and the community, from every realization in the world, not like a form of suicide rather than a faith, which is only discernible in negations:

what he believes is for the human reason not only beyond
reason but is clearly impossible

the act of believing in principle shows itself only as suffering
and martyrdom

every realization—marriage, his vocation,—he meets with
negative resolution and turns away.

These signs Kierkegaard himself has expressed: he is no model; he is no authority; he does not show the way; he does not preach.

So one must ask in astonishment: what actually was Kierkegaard? what kind of a man, with what mission, with what accomplishment? We see him above all in his personal reality. What an unfortunate man, to whom everything was denied, except that he was a genius in thinking and in writing, and that he knew the deep satisfaction of creating!

At the age of twenty five he writes of himself, "Like a solitary fir, egoistic, secluded and elevated, I stand, cast no shadow, and only the wood dove builds its nest in my branches." And then, "It surely must be frightful on the day of judgment, when all souls again walk into life, there to stand altogether alone, solitary and unknown of all, of all."

And on his deathbed as Boesen reminds him of how many wonderful things had befallen him in life, "Yes, I am very happy about that, and very sad, because I can share the joy with no one."

He speaks of himself as a kind of trial-man, a guinea pig so to speak for existence, and even in his youth he thinks that perhaps in each generation two or three are sacrificed in order to discover through horrible suffering what will be good for others.

Kierkegaard was conscious of his own fate, of this radical and total deprivation of all humanity and of worldly activity. An entry in his diary, one among countless comparable entries, states:

Now I completely understand myself to be a solitary man
without reference to anyone. . .

with only one comfort: God who is Love,

with longing after only one joy, that I might altogether
belong to the Lord Jesus Christ,

with longing after a dead father,

worse than isolated through the death of the only living
man whom I have loved in any final sense.

In the course of his negative resolution Kierkegaard has outlined possibilities in his work. There is no radical plan of the manifold forms of the lost aesthetic life. There is no grandiose design for marriage and for human (and according to him not yet Christian) religiousness. His work reveals the basic human situation and lack of proportion with unheard of richness. It would not be possible in this brief space to describe the ideal world which Kierkegaard has unfolded.

However everything remains for him in the form of possibility. It is "thought" by the pseudonym, represented in poetic form. The truth appears to be nowhere. The wealth of form of the aesthetic life is everywhere a lost existence. Moreover, the apparent perfection, the ethically bound, metaphysically grounded marriage, human religion, each has its limits. He dares not be sure of himself.

Therefore we are driven from one to another, we have gained no ground. Christianity demonstrating itself in negative resolutions may be understood as absurd—as untrodden a path as the fruitless ground of Nietzsche, of the eternal return, the dionysiac life and the will to power.

But Kierkegaard does not wish to work for this Christianity, but only for honesty. He constantly repeats that he is not an authority, only a corrective. He calls himself a policeman, a spy in the service of the Almighty.

In point of fact Kierkegaard and Nietzsche will remain ambiguous figures. They are illuminators and at the same time tempters. They are purifying agents for seriousness and admit of being called as witnesses for every fraud. They are masters of honesty and yet they make available methods of thought which allow every truth to slip away. They unsettle in order that each may come to himself, and they destroy in the abyss of nihilism.

Therefore it is not possible to follow them as teachers. But all modern philosophizing would be insufficient if it did not come to know the purgatory of their inward search, even in every corner where one may hide himself or strengthen himself.

I am convinced that neither theology nor philosophy can base itself on Kierkegaard. That foundation of forty years ago was not the establishment of a new basis; it was the awakening from a sleep.

When we assimilate his work—and it will not be destroyed in the process—we must not forget his own words: "I will leave behind a not inconsiderable intellectual capital; and alas I know who will probably be my heir, that figure which is so offensively dreadful to me, the lecturer, the professor. And when the professor comes to read even this, the real consciousness will still not touch him. Even this will be lectured about."

In reality, when we speak of Kierkegaard, we must almost certainly succumb to this danger to which we are exposed. In order to escape its power it is necessary that we do not confine ourselves to the intellectual capital but that we allow ourselves to capture the seriousness as well.

We today, on the universal voyage in the storm, look into the darkness. Some of us are permitted to remain for yet a while as if on a happy island, deliberating on a glimpse of the sun. By reflecting under such conditions, the importance of Kierkegaard and Nietzsche grows. Their names have risen to stars of the first magnitude, before which the many post-Hegelian philosophers of the nineteenth and twentieth centuries fade away.

To discuss the question in the world-historical style which Kierkegaard himself so detested, with Hegel something came to an end, something which remained a unity among all differences for a thousand years, and was a matter of course in his own shattering fundamentals. For more than a hundred years, fixed in matter we have been losing our way, and perhaps constantly accumulate more knowledge. Amid the progress in this new world we see Kierkegaard and Nietzsche as storm birds before a hurricane. They show the unrest, the precipitation, and then the strength and clarity of an instantaneously high flight, and again something like circlings and whirls and rapid falls.

They know themselves as sea beacons; by them orientation is possible, but only while one holds himself at a distance from them. To follow them is forbidden by themselves.

They work in such a way that they bring others to themselves to look for decisions from them, but they do not give the decisions.

For the more an age, losing its historical connections, falls into the slavery of the mass, the stronger becomes the claim made by the individual as individual: to be himself; every man is an individual; here is the last basis on which reality can appear.

At such a time, when living on a stage or within a fiction becomes increasingly dubious, one thing remains worthwhile: honesty.

Kierkegaard's claim, closely corresponding to that of Nietzsche, is to be an individual and to be honest. But this claim is recognized by them first in their entire self-testing. What is the Self? What is honesty? Both have experienced it and thought it out to the utmost.

The claim itself is uncommonly small. It has not yet produced what can perhaps be awakened by it. In the case of Kierkegaard and Nietzsche it stands square in the midst of the spiritual riches of the European tradition. Their claim alone remains indivisible and inexorable, while in them the riches of the European tradition focus to a great drama of introspection and interior development.

Or with Kierkegaard is it more than this? When we let pass all the absurdity of a Christian belief so violently understood by him, and all the seductive variety of possibility, does he not still offer us the eternal truth of human religion with a wonderful purity? This truth sets forth

the immutability of God, the presence of this awesomeness and this rest, so that for Kierkegaard all is determined and does not change

that before God we are always in the wrong; that all our rebellion miscarries in the eternity of His unfathomable depth

that God is unending Love, so that even at the most frightful time trust can remain in that Providence which we, despite firm obedience to it, do not understand in its enduring ambiguity

These eternal truths, moreover, in the absence of dogmas point only to the possibility of endless fulfillment. They do not endure; their meaning disappears. So much the more wonderful when, in spite of this they always appear again.

The other truths in Kierkegaard's thought are present on biblical grounds:

the world is wrong and it is not to be set right as such, but rather it must go through time in constant change, constantly failing and trying again,—

therefore the unrest of our soul which in this world finds no final resting place. We are the question capable of eternal happiness, and therefore of absolute seriousness, but we remain without an objective answer guaranteed.

Today when we philosophize in consciousness of the cosmic moment, when we know that something irrevocable has happened, through which all human history experiences a revolution,—

when we see that no man and no people can make satisfaction for this event by any ethical religious reality, through which disaster might be averted and the elevation of man made possible.—

when we think in this ever poor, growing world to discern something as the end of western philosophy in that form which was a single great continuity from Parmenides to Hegel,—

then will we perceive in this era of considerable transition the primitiveness of thinkers such as Kierkegaard and Nietzsche who, in the possession of the medium of thought burst forth as it were, orient us, but yet do not show the way,—

then will we not look to the professional philosophy of the past century

PAUL   RICOEUR

Kierkegaard and Evil

The task of celebrating Kierkegaard, who had no pity for ministers and professors, may call forth derision. Can we talk about Kierkegaard without excluding either him or ourselves? We are here to face this ridicule as honestly and modestly as possible. After all, we must also confront Kierkegaard's sarcasm. It is still the best way of honoring him. In any case, it is better to run this risk than to prove him correct out of good manners or through convention.

. . . We shall attempt to listen and to understand by simply putting before ourselves a few texts upon which we shall concentrate as narrow and intense attention as possible. These texts are taken from two writings, *The Concept of Dread,* which dates from 1844, and *The Sickness unto Death,* published five years later, in 1849. I want to extract from these two essays Kierkegaard's thought concerning evil by means of as rigorous an exegesis as possible. It is through this *explication de texte* that we run the biggest risk of excluding ourselves . . .

We are we stopping with these two texts and why the question of evil?

Let us consider the question of evil first. There is scarcely any need to emphasize that evil is the critical point for all philosophical thought. If it comprehends evil, this is its greatest success. Yet evil understood is no longer evil. It has stopped being absurd, scandalous, beyond right and reason. Yet if philosophy does not comprehend evil, then it is no longer philosophy—at least if philosophy ought to comprehend everything and set itself up as a system

From *Kierkegaard's Truth:The Disclosure of the Self* (Psychiatry and the Humanities, volume 5), edited by Joseph H. Smith, M.D. © 1981 by the Forum on Psychiatry and the Humanities of the Washington School of Psychiatry. Translated by David Pellauer.

with nothing outside itself. In the great debate between Kierkegaard and the system—which is to say, Hegel—the question of evil represents a touchstone beyond compare. . . . It is important to understand how Kierkegaard himself thought in the face of the irrational, the absurd. For he did not proclaim; he thought.

There is another reason for talking about evil. It is not only the touchstone for philosophy, it is also the occasion to take by surprise the quality of Kierkegaard's Christianity; I mean his Christianity of the Cross more than of Easter or of Pentecost. But above all, I want to attempt to show how Kierkegaard speaks and thinks about evil; that is, about what is most opposed to the system.

I shall begin with the following brief comment. Neither of these two books constitutes, in any way, a journal or a confession. You will find no trace in these two writings of the terrible confession his father made to him about that day in his youth when, shepherding his sheep on the Jutland heath, he climbed up on a rock and cursed God. Or anything about the precipitous marriage of the widower father to his servant mistress, or of all the deaths that struck the paternal home, as if in punishment for the earlier blasphemy, or of Søren's melancholy, or of the splinter in his flesh. We would be wasting our time if we took the short way of psychoanalytic biography and if we looked in these complicated and argumentative writings for the direct transposition of an emotional life weighed down by torments and remorse. This direct way, from the life to the work, is absolutely forbidden to us. Not that a psychoanalysis of Kierkegaard, or at least a fragmentary psychoanalytic approach, is impossible, but rather we must resolutely take the inverse way to him—that is, start with the exegesis of texts and perhaps return from them to the life, for there is more in these texts than the biographical odds and ends we might collect.

Thus, let us turn directly to the texts. These two treatises have in common that they are built upon the basis of two feelings or moods, more precisely, two negative feelings or moods whose object remains indeterminate: dread (or anxiety) and despair. Anxiety about what? Despair about what? Yet it is from these two that we must begin, for if we adopt as our starting point what we already know about evil, we will miss precisely what these two moods can teach us. To begin from known evil is to begin from a purely moral definition of guilt, as the transgressing of a law or as an infraction. On the contrary, the question is to discover a quality and a dimension of "sin" that only these profound emotions, ordinarily linked to melancholy or fear, can announce. Because the determination of evil occurs entirely within the orbit of these two moods, the resulting "concept" of evil is profoundly different in each treatise. The analysis of anxiety leads to a concept of sin as event or upheaval. Anxiety itself is a sort of slipping, of fascination wherein evil is circumscribed, approached from back and front. To the contrary, the *Treatise on Despair*—another name for *The Sickness unto Death*—takes place in the midst of sin, no longer as a leap, but as a state: despair is, if we may put it this way, the evil of evil, the sin of sin.

Let us successively consider these two approaches. To finish, we shall try to understand their conjunction.

The first is deliberately anti-Hegelian: leap, upheaval, event, are opposed to mediation, synthesis, reconciliation. In this way, too, the equivocal mixing of the ethical and the logical is broken off: "In logic this is too much, in ethics too little; it fits nowhere if it has to fit both places" (*The Sickness unto Death*). But who then will speak justly about sin? The metaphysician? He is both too disinterested and too comprehensive. The moralist? He believes too much in man's effort and not enough in his misery. The preacher? Well, perhaps, for he addresses himself to the isolated individual, one to one. But do not let him be a Hegelian minister! The dogmatician too, though he only explains sin by presupposing it: "The concept of sin does not properly belong in any science; only the second ethics"—the one that follows dogmatics and that knows the real and sin without "metaphysical frivolity or psychological concupiscence"—"can deal with its apparition but not with its origin." And yet it is as a psychologist that Kierkegaard is going to speak. To isolate the act's radical leap, the psychologist outlines its possibility, thereby in a way approaching the discontinuity of upheaval through the continuity of a sliding or slippage.

The paradox here is that of a beginning. How does sin come into the world? By a leap that presupposes itself in temptation. This is the "concept of anxiety": a psychology as close as possible to the event, a psychology that clings to the event as an advent, a psychology of the *durée* wherein innocence loses itself, is already lost, where it seesaws, totters, and falls. But we do not know innocence. We only know its loss. Innocence is something that "only comes into existence by the very fact that it is annulled, comes into existence as that which was before it was annulled and now is annulled." Hence I only know innocence as lost. I only know the leap of sin in its transition. This is something that is in between innocence that is lost and a leap that proceeds itself in anxiety.

What can be said about anxiety per se? It is the birth of spirit, of that spirit the Bible calls discerning of good and evil. But spirit is still a kind of dreaming. It is no longer innocence, nor yet good and evil. About what then does spirit dream? About nothing. Nothing at all. This nothing gives birth to anxiety. It is why "dread is freedom's reality as possibility for possibility." Nothing—possibility—freedom . . . One sees that ambiguity—the word is Kierkegaard's—is more enigmatic than the already too ethical "concupiscense." A "sympathetic antipathy and an antipathetic sympathy," the subtle Kierkegaard prefers to say. And he calls this ambiguity dialectical, but psychological, not logical. We will return to this point in our second encounter: "Just as the relation of dread to its object, to something which is nothing (language in this instance also is pregnant: it speaks of being in dread of nothing), is altogether ambiguous, so will the transition here from innocence to guilt be correspondingly so dialectical that the explanation is and must be psychological."

Will someone say that it is prohibition that awakens desire? Yet innocence does not understand prohibition. This is an explanation after the fact. We should rather say that prohibition is the *word*—the "enigmatic word"—that crystallizes anxiety. The decree alarms Adam because it awakens in him the possibility of freedom. Nothingness becomes the "possibility of the possibility of being able to do something." This is what Adam loves and what he flees.

We should not say that Kierkegaard delights in the irrational. He analyzes, he dissects, he abounds in words. He is the dialectician of the anti-dialectic. And this paradoxical dialectic culminates in the representation of human beings as a synthesis of soul and body, united in this third term: spirit—spirit that dreams about nothing, spirit that projects the possible. Spirit is the "hostile power" that constantly disturbs this relation, which, however, only exists through it. On the other hand, it is a "friendly power," which desires to constitute exactly this relation: "What then is man's relation to this ambiguous power? How is spirit related to itself and to its situation? It is related as dread."

Hence psychology comes too soon or too late. It recognizes either the anxiety of before, which leads to the qualitative leap—the anxiety of dreaming, of nothing—or the anxiety of afterward, which augments evil—the anxiety of reflection, about something, become in a way nature insofar as it henceforth has a "body." This is why anxiety permeates sex: not that it comes with it but because it comes to it. The anxiety of dreaming becomes flesh and extends an "inexplicable deep melancholy" over everything. It would be a mistake here to look for some kind of puritanical repugnance to sexuality. Before Max Scheler, Kierkegaard understood that anxiety does not come from sex but descends from the spirit into sexuality, from dreaming into the flesh. It is because man is disturbed in spirit that he is ashamed in his flesh. The spirit is uneasy in modesty and frightened over assuming sexual differentiation. Thus sin enters the world, becomes a world, and increases quantitatively.

Yet we do not know better what sin is through subsequent anxiety than through prior anxiety. It remains anxiety, closely circumscribed, yet empty at its center: "No science can explain how. Psychology comes nearest to doing so and explains the last step in the approximation, which is freedom's apparition before itself in the dread of possibility, or in the nothingness of possibility, or in the nothing of dread."

The Sickness unto Death, or *Treatise on Despair*, is also a psychological essay. More precisely, according to its subtitle, it is "A Christian Psychological Exposition for Edification and Awakening." Consequently, this treatise associates psychology, in the sense of *The Concept of Dread*, with edification in the sense of the *Edifying Discourses*. We have spoken [elsewhere] of the difference that separates these two treatises: the first speaks of evil as an event, a leap; the second speaks of it as a state of affairs. The substitution of despair for anxiety expresses this shift: anxiety tends toward . . . , despair resides in. . . . Anxiety "ex-ists"; despair "in-sists." What does this shift signify? It is impossible to understand *The Sickness unto Death* without referring back to an earlier essay, *Fear and Trembling*, which situates the meaning of faith and sin beyond the sphere of the ethical. Sin is not the contrary of virtue but of faith, which is a theological category. Faith is a way of being face to face with God, before God. This liaison is elaborated in *Fear and Trembling*, not by means of an abstract discussion about theological concepts, but by way of an *exegesis*. The new concepts are deciphered by means of the interpretation of a story, the story of Abraham. The *meaning* of the sacrificing of Isaac decides the meaning of the concepts of law and faith. Sacrificing Isaac would be a crime according to the moral law. According to faith, it is an act of obedience. To obey God, Abraham had to suspend the ethical. He had to become the knight of faith who moves forward alone, beyond the security of the universal law, or, as Kierkegaard puts it, of the universal. Hence *Fear and Trembling* opens a new dimension of anxiety, which proceeds from the contradiction between ethics and faith. Abraham is the symbol of this new species of anxiety linked to the theological suspension of the ethical.

The concept of despair belongs to the same nonethical but religious sphere as does Abraham's faith. Despair is the negative version of Abraham's faith. This is why Kierkegaard does not first say what sin is, then what despair is; instead he constructs and discovers sin in despair as its religious signification. From there on, sin is no longer a leap but a stagnant stage, a persisting mode of being.

Second consequence: the question is no longer, How did it enter into the world?—through anxiety; but, How is it possible to escape? Despair is thus comparable to one of the "stages on life's way" that Kierkegaard explores in another work. It is a sickness, a sickness one dies of without dying. It is the sickness "unto death," in the way that injustice, according to Plato, in book 10 of *The Republic*, is a living death and the paradoxical proof of immortality. Despair, according to Kierkegaard, is a greater evil than injustice according to Plato, which still refers to the ethical sphere. Yet because it is more grave, it is closer to recovery.

Now, how can we speak of despair? Structural analysis of *The Sickness unto Death* should bring us closer to our problem: What is Kierkegaard's mode of thinking? How is it possible to do philosophy after Kierkegaard? What is remarkable, is that Kierkegaard constructs the concept of despair. A quick look at the table of contents of this treatise reveals a tangle of titles and subtitles. The plan is even curiously didactic. The first part demonstrates this: "The Sickness Unto Death Is Despair." Its possibility, actuality, universality, and forms are carefully distinguished. Its forms are even elaborated in a rather systematic manner, from the point of view of a "lack of finitude" and a "lack of infinitude," from a "lack of possibility"—which is to say of imagination and dreaming—and a "lack of necessity"—which is to say of submitting to our tasks and general duties in this world. The same balancing is renewed with the appearance of new distinctions. The most subtle one is presented as follows: "Despair viewed under the aspect of consciousness," wherein it knows itself or does not know itself. Therefore, there is a despair over "not willing to be oneself" and over "willing to be oneself."

Then the second part, entitled "Despair Is Sin," elaborates all the characteristics of sin according to the model of despair and leads to the conclusion that "sin is not a negation but a position." I will stop with this conclusion, which I will oppose to the nothingness of anxiety.

But first I want to interrogate the strange structure of this treatise. It is impossible not to be impressed by the heavy and laborious aspect of its construction, which resembles an interminable and awkward dissertation. What does it signify? We are confronted by a sort of grimacing simulacre of Hegelian discourse. Yet this simulacre is at the same time the means of saving its discourse from absurdity. It is didactic because it cannot be dialectic. In other words, it replaces a three-term dialectic by a cut-off dialectic, by an unresolved two-term dialectic. A dialectic without mediation—this is the Kierkegaardian paradox. *Either* too much possibility *or* too much actuality. *Either* too much finitude *or* too much infinitude. *Either* one wants to be oneself *or* one does not want to be oneself. What is more, since each pair of contrary terms offers no resolution, it is not possible to construct the following paradox on the one that precedes it. The chain of paradoxes is itself a broken chain—hence the didactic framework, which is substituted for the immanent structure of a true dialectic. The rupture that threatens this discourse must constantly be conjured away or compensated for by an excess of conceptuality and rhetorical hability. From this, finally, comes the strange contrast that it is the most irrational term—despair—that sets into movement the largest mass of conceptual analyses. In my second encounter, we shall begin from this strange situation: a hyperintellectualism linked to a fundamental irrationalism.

Let us examine this somewhat forbidding construction a bit more closely. The kernel about which the great antinomies of despair are constructed is a definition of the self that *The Concept of Dread* prepared us for when it spoke of spirit as the third term—the spoilsport—in the tranquil relation between soul and body. This definition in its disconcerting abstraction runs as follows: the human self is "a relation which relates itself to its own self, and in relating itself to its own self relates itself to another" (*The Sickness unto Death*). Whether out of derision or loving vexation, . . . this definition bears the mark of the Hegelian dialectic. But as a difference from Hegel, this relation that relates itself to itself is more a problem than an answer, more a task than a structure. For what is given in despair is what Kierkegaard calls the "disrelation." This priority of the disrelation throughout the subsequent analysis rests on the structure's relation as an impossible task: the possibility of despair resides in the possibility of a disrelation—that is, in the fragility of the relation that relates itself to its own self, as the expression "and in relating itself to its own self relates itself to another" signifies. For this relation, to constitute oneself is to unmake oneself.

We can already understand what force this union of mood and analysis can give to the Kierkegaardian rhetoric of pathos. Despair exists—or as I have tried to say, insists—in the figures of disrelation. Consequently, everything will be more complicated than in *The Concept of Dread*. Dread or anxiety was fascinated by the nothingness of pure possibility; despair "is the disrelationship in a relation which relates itself to itself. But the synthesis is not the disrelationship, it is merely the possibility, or, in the synthesis is latent the possibility of the disrelationship. . . . Whence then comes despair? From the relation wherein the synthesis relates itself to itself, in that God who made man a relationship lets this go as it were out of His hand, that is, in the fact that the relation relates itself to itself." The latter remark allows us to further our explication of the strange expression about a relation that "in relating itself to its own self relates itself to another." In this abandonment, it is *related* to itself as to *another*. Dereliction is the reflective aspect of this abandonment by God, who lets go of the relation as though it escaped his grasp. Kierkegaard, prior to existentialism, discovered this identity of reflection and dereliction.

From here on, all of Kierkegaard's art consists in applying his psychological subtlety to the numerous possibilities offered by the dissociating of this relation that relates itself to its own self in relating itself to another. Kierkegaard's literary, psychological, philosophical, and theological genius seems to me to lie in this half-abstract, half-concrete way of presenting these artificially constructed possibilities, of making the *opéra fabuleux* of despairing states of the soul correspond to this conceptual game. The reader's astonishment, unease, admiration, and irritation depend on this incessant oscillating between the most pointed imaginary experimentation and the most artificial conceptual dialectic. Here are some examples: Man, we are told, is a synthesis of infinitude and finitude, of possibility and necessity. Despair springs up as soon as the will to become infinite is felt or experienced as a lack of finitude, and vice versa. This interplay between opposed concepts is fed by an extraordinary power to create human types, among whom we recognize the hero of fantastic possibilities, the Don Juan of the aesthetic stage, the seducer of the "Journal of a Seducer," Goethe's Faust, and also the poet of the religious stage, the explorer of the open according to Rilke; in brief, the imagination, the crucible of every process of infinitization. The self is reflection, says Kierkegaard, and imagination is the possibility of all reflection. This is why the loss of a place to stand, the endless distance from oneself, is felt or experienced as a loss, as despair. The abstract paradox becomes a concrete one: the "either/or" of the infinite and the finite is the "either/or" that confronts the seducer and, on his level, the hero who does his duty, depicted through the traits of Judge William. The lack of infinity, the narrowness of a mediocre life, the loss of a horizon, are very concrete possibilities, as anyone will discover who feels his own existence as that of a pebble on the shore or one number lost in the crowd.

Yet it is perhaps the last dialectic that clarifies all the others. The worst despair is "the despair that is unaware of being despair." The ordinary person is desperate, is in despair, but does not know it. Thus it is because despair may be unconscious that it has to be discovered, even constructed. The dialectic of the unconscious and the conscious unfolds inside of despair as if within the heart of an ontic possibility, of a mode of being. Consciousness does not constitute despair. Despair exists, or, as I have said, insists. This is why even consciousness attaches itself to despair. The great despair, despair over oneself, the despair of willing despairingly to be oneself, which Kierkegaard calls defiance, represents the final degree of "the constant heightening of the power of despair." Here, more than anywhere else, this possibility may only be tried out in imagination: "This sort of despair is seldom seen in the world, such figures generally are met only in the works of poets, that is to say, of real poets, who always lend their characters this 'demoniac' ideality (taking this work in the purely Greek sense)." In real life, this supreme despair can only be approached in the most spiritual despair, the despair that no longer has to do with some earthly loss, the despair of not wanting to be helped.

We may now confront *The Concept of Dread* and *The Sickness unto Death* on the point of sin, so circumscribed by two opposed approaches.

The two treatises agree that sin is not an ethical reality but a religious one. Sin is "before God." But while *The Concept of Dread* remains outside of this determination of sin as "before God," *The Sickness unto Death* stands within its heart. *The Concept of Dread* stays purely psychological; *The Sickness unto Death* "edifies and awakens," according to its subtitle. While anxiety was a movement toward . . . , despair is sin. To say this is no longer psychology: "There here may be introduced, as the most dialectical borderline between despair and sin, what one might call a poetic existence in the direction of the religious."

This "poetic existence in the direction of the religious" has nothing to do with a mystical effusion. It is, says Kierkegaard, "prodigiously dialectical, and is in an impenetrable dialectical confusion as to how far it is conscious of being sin." Everything that will be said from here on belongs to this reduplication of the dialectic when it passes from psychology to poetic existence in the direction of the religious. First, psychology designates sin through the experience of vertigo as a fall, then it designates it as a lack, consequently as "nothing." For poetic existence, sin is a state, a condition, a mode of being; further, it is a *position*.

Let us consider these new dimensions that could not appear in *The Concept of Dread*, first because this treatise stays purely psychological, next because it approaches sin as a leap.

That sin is a *state* is revealed by despair itself. We cannot say that anxiety *is* sin, we can say that despair *is*. In this way, the concept of sin is definitively transported from the ethical sphere of transgression into the religious sphere of unfaith. We may even say, from the sphere where sin is flesh to the sphere where it is spirit. It is the power of weakness and the weakness of defiance. Hence sin is no longer the contrary of virtue but of faith. It is an ontic human possibility, and not just a moral category according to a Kantian ethics or an intellectual defect comparable to ignorance according to the Socratic concept of evil. In other words, sin is our ordinary mode of being before God. It is existence itself as dereliction.

But we come to the final difference between *The Concept of Dread* and *The Sickness unto Death* when we say that "sin is not a negation but a position." This thesis—which Kierkegaard takes to be the orthodox Christian interpretation of sin—is directed against all speculative philosophy. To comprehend evil philosophically is to reduce it to a pure negation: weakness as a lack of force, sensuality as a lack of spirituality, ignorance as a lack of knowledge, finitude as a lack of totality. Hegel identified comprehension with negation or, better, with the negation of negation. It is here that Kierkegaard opposes his most vigorous protest against philosophy—that is, against Hegelian philosophy. If to comprehend is to overcome, that is, to pass beyond negation, then sin is one negation among others and repentance one mediation among others. In this way, negation and the negation of negation both become purely logical processes.

But, if we only comprehend when we negate negation, what do we *say* and *understand* when we say sin is a position! Here is Kierkegaard's response: "I am merely keeping a steady hold upon the Christian dogma that sin is a position—not, however, as though it could be comprehended, but as a paradox which must be believed."

"A paradox which must be believed." With these words, Kierkegaard poses the question of a genre of language suitable to poetic existence. It is language that must destroy what it says, a language that contradicts itself. In this way, Kierkegaard transfers the aim of negative theology to anthropology when it attempts to say, through the voice of contradiction, that God is a position—beyond being, beyond determinations. To believe and not understand. Of course, Kierkegaard does not refer to negative theology, or to the Kantian abolition of knowledge in favor of belief, but to Socratic ignorance.

It is within *this* situation of philosophical discourse that the question arises, How can we do philosophy *after* Kierkegaard?

STANLEY CAVELL

Kierkegaard's On Authority and Revelation

"I myself perceive only too well," Kierkegaard says in beginning a second Preface to his Cycle of Ethico-Religious Essays, "how obvious is the objection and how much there is in it, against writing such a big book dealing in a certain sense with Magister Adler." His first answer to this objection is just that the book is "about" Adler only in a certain sense, the sense, namely, in which he is a Phenomenon, a transparence through which the age is caught. But that is scarcely a serious answer, because what the objection must mean is: Why use the man Adler in this way? And Kierkegaard has an answer to this as well: it enabled him to accomplish something which "perhaps it was important for our age that [I] should accomplish and which could be accomplished in no other way." This is not a moral defense for his treatment; it does not, for example, undertake to show that an action which on the surface, or viewed one way, appears callous or wanton, is nevertheless justified or anyway excusable. Kierkegaard goes on to offer what looks like an aesthetic defense of his treatment of Adler—"without him [I] could not have given my presentation the liveliness and the ironical tension it now has." This moral shock is succeeded by another as we realize that the presentation in question is not offered for its literary merit, but for its value as a case study; it is the justification of a surgeon, whose right to cut into people is based on his skill and credentials and whose right to present his cases to others is based on his office and on the obligation to transmit his knowledge to his peers.

Why, on this ground, is the Adler case of profit? Of what is he a typical, and until now undiagnosed, case? He is a case of a particular and prevalent and virulent confusion, and an initial diagnosis is broached: "Disobedience is the secret of the religious confusion of our age." But what is the secret? Isn't this just what the case was widely known to be all about? Adler's claim to have had a revelation was certainly a case for the Church, and in particular a case of confusion; he was suspended on the ground that his mind was deranged and finally deposed after replying evasively to the ecclesiastical interrogatories. This seems patently a case of trying unsuccessfully to evade the Church's authority. But it seems Kierkegaard's view of the case is different: "the whole book is essentially . . . about the confusion from which the concept of revelation suffers in our confused age. Or...about the confusion involved in the fact that the concept of authority has been entirely forgotten in our confused age." The concept is *entirely forgotten*. This suggests not merely that Adler, for instance, was disobedient in this particular case; it suggests that Adler would not have known what obedience consisted in. And it implies that no one else would have known either, in particular not the Church. The concept of revelation, on the other hand, is not forgotten; it is confused. Adler suffers from this, but so do all men in our age, in particular men of the Church. When Bishop Mynster appealed to Adler's mental derangement as the ground for suspending him, he was evading the same thing Adler would come to evade, the claim to a revelation; and in this evasion the Church is disobedient to its divine command to preach and clarify, to hold open, the word of God.

So the case deepens. For it is not merely that the situations of the extraordinary preacher and the ecclesiastical authority are morally analogous, each suffering his own confusion and each falling into his own disobedience. The third Preface Kierkegaard composed seems to me to go farther, almost saying that they suffer identical consequences, the same confusion of mind, that they are both, as the age is, spiritually deranged. The political events of 1848, which called out this final Preface, are interpreted by Kierkegaard as an attempt to solve a religious problem in political terms, an attempt which will go on, and with increasing confusion and fury, until men turn back to themselves:

> Though all travel in Europe must stop because one must wade in blood, and though all ministers were to remain sleepless for ruminating [about constitutional amendments, votes, equality, etc.] and though every day ten ministers were to lose their reason, and every next day ten new ministers were to begin where the others left off, only to lose their reason in turn—with all this not one step forward is made, an obstacle to it is sternly fixed, and the

bounds set by eternity deride all human efforts. . . . Ah, but to get the conflagration quenched, the spontaneous combustion brought about by the friction of worldliness, i.e., to get eternity again—bloodshed may be needed and bombardments, *item* that many ministers shall lose their reason.

The book on Adler is about a minister who has lost his reason, and the flat ambiguity of Kierkegaard's "many ministers" registers exactly the ambiguity of concepts, the confusion of realms, which he finds the cause, and the content, of our sickness. Both political and religious ministers madly try to solve religious problems with political means, the one by "levelling" worldly differences into a horrible parody of what is, Christianly, already a fact; the other by trying to approach by reason what is always grasped by faith, or by trying to make a shift of emotion do what only a change of heart can do. This points to a second ambiguity in Kierkegaard's prediction, recorded in the phrase "shall lose their reason." To lose their reason, religiously understood as "[letting] the understanding go" is precisely what the ministers, what we all, should do; it is precisely because we are incapable of that "leap into the religious" (but equally incapable of letting go of religious categories, of "Christianity of a sort") that we are confused. This is one way Adler is seen by Kierkegaard as a Satire upon the Present Age, and one prompting, throughout the book, for Kierkegaard's recourse to his categories of the comic and ironic. Adler performed the one saving act, he lost his reason; only he did it the way he does everything else, the way things normally are done in our reflective age: he did it literally, not religiously. He went crazy. But just in this lies the real defense of Adler, the *moral* answer to the question "Why expose Adler?" The derangement of this minister is shared by all ministers. Of course in his case the derangement may have got out of hand, he went too far; but this, as Kierkegaard says in the concluding sections of his book, is to his "advantage" as a Christian, because it came from a real spiritual movement toward inner self-concern. Religiously considered, other ministers are in the same, or in a worse, state; so it is unjust that Adler should be singled out for deposition on the ground of derangement. And the Bishop should have considered it religiously. For the Church, Adler is not a transparent medium, but an opaque glass, a mirror. Perhaps this is a way of seeing why, while Kierkegaard calls Adler a satire on the present *age*, he calls him an epigram on the Christendom of our age—a terse and ingenious expression of it.

Of course this does not mean that there are no valid religious grounds on which to question and perhaps depose Adler. What it means is that providing these religious grounds, in our age, for our age, will require *overcoming the specific confusion* which has deprived us of religious ground altogether; hence the form of activity will be one of *regaining clarity*. (In this book, Kierkegaard characterizes our age in a few, very specific, and often repeated, ways; his task is to provide correctives specific to them. For example, he finds that we are absent-minded, so his task is to provide presence of mind; he finds us lightminded (lightheaded?), so his task is to inject seriousness and balance; he finds us *distrait,* so his task is to attract our attention.) In his first Preface Kierkegaard says he uses the Adler case "to defend dogmatic concepts," and in the second Preface he claims that from the book one will "get a clarity about certain dogmatic concepts and an ability to use them." By "defend dogmatic concepts" he does not mean "provide a dogmatic backing for them," but rather something like "defend them as themselves dogmatic"; as, so to speak, carrying their own specific religious weight—something, it is implied, theology now fails to do—and this is a matter of coming to see clearly what they mean. So his task is one of providing, or re-providing, their meaning; in a certain sense, giving each its definition. This definition is not to provide some new sense to be attached to a word, with the purpose of better classifying information or outfitting a new theory; it is to clarify what the word does mean, as we use it in our lives— what it means, that is, to anyone with the ability to use it. Now an activity which has the form of taking us from confusion to clarity by means of defining concepts in such a way has, from Socrates to Wittgenstein, signalled philosophical activity.

As I do not insist that philosophy is exhausted in this activity, so I do not insist that Kierkegaard is, in this book, exclusively philosophical. The question I want to turn to is, rather: How far is the book on Adler to be considered a book of philosophy? There are several reasons for pressing this question:

1. It recognizes that the *kind* of writing before us is problematic, and so keeps faith with Kierkegaard's own efforts, as an author and as a Christian, to write distinct kinds of works.

2. This book is itself about writing, about the differences between real and fake authors: our amnesia of the concept of authority is expressed by an amnesia of genuine writing and reading: speech, never easy, has now fully become talk. Adler's confused disobedience to religious authority is not merely analogous to, but is instanced by his disobedience, as an author, to the requirements of art. Adler's books are not only fake religion, they are fake books—and the one because of the other.

3. The emphasis on philosophy distinguishes Kierkegaard's effort here from other efforts with which it may be confused:

a) If one says he writes to defend Christianity and to reform Christendom, then one must know his differences from (say) Luther. "[Luther's] . . . day is over," Kierkegaard said in a work composed during the period in which he was reading and writing about Adler; "No longer can the individual . . . turn to the great for help when he grows confused." Luther saw the Church in bondage, Kierkegaard sees it in a position of false mastery and false freedom; Luther's problem was to combat a foreign institution motivated politically and economically, but Kierkegaard's problem is that the mind itself has become political and economic; Luther's success was to break the hold of an external authority and put it back into the individual soul, but what happens when *that* authority is broken? Luther's problem was to combat false definitions of religious categories, but Kierkegaard has to provide definition for them from the beginning; Luther could say, "The mass is not a sacrifice, but a promise," and now Kierkegaard's problem is that no one remembers what a promise is, nor has the authority to accept one.

b) The emphasis on philosophy serves as a corrective to calling it psychology. Kierkegaard is often praised in our age as a "profound psychologist," and while I do not wish to deny him that, it seems to me attractively misleading praise, especially about such efforts as the present book; because what is profound psychology in Kierkegaard's work is Christianity itself, or the way in which Kierkegaard is able to activate its concepts; and because the way he activates them, wherever else it is, is through philosophy, through attention to the distinct applicability of concepts—perhaps one could say, attention to the a priori possibility of applying the concepts in general: it is what Kant called Transcendental Logic, what Hegel called Logic, why Oxford philosophers are moved to speak of their attention to words as a question of logic; Wittgenstein called it "grammar." Take the originating concern of the book on Adler: "How far a man in our age may be justified in asserting that he had a revelation." This is the question the Church ought to have confronted—in order to confront itself, as it stands, with the fact that it cannot answer it. Because this question of being "justified in asserting" is not a matter of determining how likely it is, given a certain man's psychological make-up and given a particular historical condition, that he had or will have a revelation (it is always unlikely); nor a matter of determining whether one is religiously prepared to receive a revelation (for, religiously speaking, there is no human preparation possible); nor a matter of determining psychological variation and nuance in different instances of the experience of a revelation and tracing its antecedents and consequences in a particular man's worldly existence. The question is whether, no matter *what* occurs in a man's life, we are conceptually prepared to call it a revelation, whether we have the power any longer to recognize an occurrence as a revelation, whether anything any longer could conceivably count for us as a revelation—could, so to speak, *force us to assert* that what has taken place is a revelation. Of course, anyone can, and occasionally will, *use the word* "revelation," to refer perhaps to a striking or unexpected experience—this, as emerged in the interrogation of Adler, is what happened in his case. And quite generally: "every Christian term, which remaining in its own sphere is a qualitative category, now, in reduced circumstances, can do service as a clever expression which may signify pretty much everything." The serious issue, which is simultaneously the logico-philosophical and the Christian issue, remains: for a Christian church to be in a position in which it has to say that God is hidden or distant or silent, is one thing; for it to be in a position in which it would not find it conceivable that God should speak to us, is something else. In the latter case, the implication is, one should stop referring to such a thing as Christianity altogether.

Let me, then, call attention to two procedures characteristic of Kierkegaard's writing which I think of as philosophical, and philosophically correct:

1. He frequently wishes to show that a question which appears to need settling by empirical means or through presenting a formal argument is really a conceptual question, a question of grammar. (This is one way of putting the whole effort of the book on Adler.) Take the question John Stuart Mill raises in his essay on Revelation (part 4 of *Theism*): "Can any evidence suffice to prove a divine revelation?" Mill's answer, after careful consideration and reasoning is that "miracles have no claim whatever to the character of historical facts and are wholly invalid as evidences of any revelation"; but he adds to this the concession that if a certain sort of man" . . . openly proclaimed that [a precious gift we have from him] did not come from him but from God through him, then we are entitled to say that there is nothing so inherently impossible or absolutely incredible in this supposition as to preclude anyone from hoping that it may perhaps be true. I say from hoping; I go no further. . . . " From a Kierkegaardian perspective, Mill has gone nowhere at all, and indeed there is nowhere to go along those lines. For the answer to his question is just, No. The statement "A revelation cannot be proven by evidence" is not an empirical discovery, nor a sensible topic for an argument; it is a grammatical remark. (Religiously speaking, such a thing *is* "absolutely incredible.") One factor of Mill's hope is that there is a God through whom the gift can have come; and he regards someone as "entitled" to this hope because there is some evidence for his existence. For Kierkegaard, to hope for such a thing on such a ground is not an act of piety and intellectual caution; it is a hope for nothing: *hoping it* is as incoherent as *believing it firmly*. Other

grammatical remarks in, or to be elicited from, the book on Adler are, for example, "Religion only conquers without force"; "One must *become* a Christian"; "Christianity is not plausible."

2. The other philosophical procedure to be mentioned is what Kierkegaard calls "qualitative dialectic." Very generally, a dialectical examination of a concept will show how the meaning of that concept changes, and how the subject of which it is the concept changes, as the context in which it is used changes: the dialectical meaning is the history or confrontation of these differences. For example, an examination of the concept of *silence* will show that the word means different things—that silence is different things—depending on whether the context is the silence of nature, the silence of shyness, the silence of the liar or hypocrite, the short silence of the man who cannot hold his tongue, the long silence of the hero or the apostle, or the eternal silence of the Knight of Faith. And the specific meaning of the word in each of those contexts is determined by tracing its specific contrasts with the others—the way its use in one context "negates" its use in another, so to speak.

There is one dialectical shift which is of critical importance for Kierkegaard, that which moves from "immanent" to "transcendent" contexts. It is, I believe, when he is speaking of this shift that he characteristically speaks of a *qualitative* (sometimes he adds, decisive) difference in meaning. (This is the point at which his insistence on God as "wholly other" finds its methodological expression.) The procedure is this: he will begin with an immanent context, appealing to ordinary contexts in which a concept is used, for example, ordinary cases of silence, or of authority, or of coming to oneself, or of being shaken, or of living in the present, or of offense . . . ; and then abruptly and sternly he will say that these concepts are decisively or qualitatively different when used in a transcendental sense, when used, that is, to characterize our relationship to God. ("The situation is quite otherwise"; "It is quite another matter with") Sometimes he is *merely* abrupt and stern, and offers us no further help in understanding; as if to say, You know perfectly well what I mean; as if to rebuke us for having forgotten, or for refusing to acknowledge, something of the clearest importance. Sometimes, of course, he does go further; then he will describe what the life of a man will look like which calls for description, which can only be understood in terms of—which(he sometimes puts it) *is lived in*—Christian categories. A man's life; not a striking experience here and there, or a pervasive mood or a particular feeling or set of feelings. As if to say: in that life, and for that life, the Christian categories have their full, mutually implicating meaning, and apart from it they may have any or none. And contrariwise, a life which does not invite, require description in terms of (is not lived within) the mutual implications of these categories—no matter how religious it is in some sense, and however full it may be of sublime and intricate emotion—is not a Christian life.

When I said that I thought this procedure was philosophically correct, I did not mean to suggest that I found it philosophically clear. As an *account* of "qualitative differences of meaning" (in terms of "immanence," "transcendence," "qualitative," etc.), I find it all but useless. But it begins and ends in the right place, with the description of a human existence; and each difference in each existence makes what seems intuitively the right kind of difference. And it seems to me right that Kierkegaard should suggest that we *do* or could know, without explanation, what it means to say that a man "stands before God" or that "This night shall thy soul be required of thee"; know what they mean not just in *some* sense, but know what they mean in a sense which we may wish to call *heightened*. That we may not know this all the time is no proof against our knowing; this may only indicate what kind of knowledge it is—the kind of knowledge which can go dead, or become inaccessible. Nor would the fact that we cannot *explain* the (heightened) meaning of such utterances prove that we do not understand them, both because it is not clear what an explanation would consist in, and because knowing where and when to use an utterance seems proof that one knows what it means, and knowing where and when to use it is not the same as being able to give an explanation of it. It is true that in the religious case an explanation seems *called for;* but this may only mean, one might say, that we are perplexed about *how* we know its meaning, not whether we do; and even that not all the time. And, again, this particular situation may be characteristic of a particular kind of meaning rather than a situation in which meaning is absent. There might even be an explanation for the sense, as I wish to put it, that we are balancing on the edge of a meaning. And Kierkegaard's explanations, however obscure, are not obviously wrong. He does not, for example, say that religious utterances are metaphorical.

While Kierkegaard's account sometimes refuses explanations of meaning, sometimes seems to rebuke us for being confused about a meaning which should be clear with a qualitatively decisive clarity, sometimes seems to suggest a mode of explanation for that sense of "balancing on the edge of a meaning," he would nevertheless not be surprised at Positivism's claim, or perception, that religious utterances have *no* cognitive meaning. Indeed, he might welcome this fact. It indicates that the crisis of our age has deepened, that we are no longer *confused,* and that we have a chance, at last, to learn what our lives really depend upon. Utterances we have shared about our infinite interests no longer carry any cognitive meaning. Well and good; we have now completely forgotten it. Then it is up to each man to find his own.

"To imagine a language," says Wittgenstein in one of his best mottoes, "is to imagine a form of life." When a form of life can no longer be imagined, its language can no longer be understood. "Speaking metaphorically" is a matter of speaking in certain ways using a definite form of language for some purpose; "speaking religiously" is not accomplished by using a given form, or set of forms, of words, and is not done for any further purpose: it is to speak from a particular perspective, as it were to mean anything you say in a special way. To understand a metaphor you must be able to interpret it; to understand an utterance religiously you have to be able to share its perspective. (In these ways, speaking religiously is like telling a dream.) The religious is a Kierkegaardian Stage of life; and I suggest it should be thought of as a Wittgensteinian form of life. There seems no reason not to believe that, as a given person may never occupy this stage, so a given age, and all future ages, may as a whole not occupy it—that the form will be lost from men's lives altogether. (It would be a phenomenon like everyone stopping having dreams.)

It is Kierkegaard's view that this has happened to the lives of the present age. Wittgenstein, late in the *Investigations*, remarks that "One human being can be a complete enigma to another. We learn this when we come into a strange country with entirely strange traditions; and, what is more, even given a mastery of the country's language. We do not *understand* the people. (And not because of not knowing what they are saying to themselves.) We cannot find our feet with them." Toward the end of the book on Adler, Kierkegaard has this:

> Most men live in relation to their own self as if they were constantly out, never at home. . . . The admirable quality in Magister A. consists in the fact that in a serious and strict sense one may say that he was fetched home by a higher power; for before that he was certainly in a great sense "out" or in a foreign land . . . spiritually and religiously understood, perdition consists in journeying into a foreign land, in being "out."

One may want to say: A human being can be a complete enigma to himself; he cannot find his feet with himself. Not because a particular thing he does puzzles him—his problem may be that many of the puzzling things he does do *not* puzzle him—but because he does not know why he lives as he

does, what the point of his activity is; he understands his words, but he is
foreign to his life.

Other major writers of the nineteenth century share the sense of foreign-
ness, of alienation, Kierkegaard describes; and not merely their own alienation from their societies, but of self-alienation as characteristic of the lives
common to their time; which is perhaps the same as seeing their time as alienated from its past. They can be understood as posing the underlying concern
of Kierkegaard's book: "how it comes about that a new point of departure is
created in relation to the established order." Kierkegaard's answer is that it
comes "from ABOVE, from God," but the test of this answer depends on
confronting it with the major answers given it by (say) Marx, and Freud, and
Nietzsche (both the Nietzsche of the *Birth of Tragedy* and the Nietzsche of
Zarathustra). This should forcibly remind one how little of the complexity of
Kierkegaard's book I have brought out; for politics, psychology, art, and the
final break with God are all themes of the dialectical situation within which
The Book on Adler, like Adler himself, is produced. I began by indicating
some lines through which the religious plane intersects the psychological; let
me end with a word or two about its intersection in this book with the political and with the aesthetic.

The Introduction, written one year before the *Communist Manifesto,*
starts the imagery of the newspaper which recurs throughout the book—the
image of its gossip, of its volatilization of concepts, the universal (no-man's)
intelligence it wishes to be, the fourth estate which undermines the idea of
estates altogether with their recognized authority and responsibilities, pul-
verizes them into a gritty mixture called the public, from whom nothing but
violence and distraction can be expected. Four years earlier Marx had written
some articles for his newspaper against a rival editor who had raised the question: "Should philosophy discuss religious matters in newspaper articles?"
Marx despises the mind which could frame this question as passionately as
Kierkegaard would, and Marx responds to it by criticizing it, as Kierkegaard
would; that is to say, he responds dialectically. The point of application of
his criticism is evidently different, not to say opposite from Kierkegaard's,
but it clarifies for me a particular lack in Kierkegaard's "ethico-religious
investigation" of his age and of the way that determines its possibilities for a
new departure. He was deeply responsive with the "criticism of religion"
which Marx said is now (in 1844) complete in Germany (*Critique of Hegel's
Philosophy of Right*). Kierkegaard can be seen as attempting to carry its com-
pletion to the North, while at the same time one of his dominating motives
would be to criticize religion's criticizers. Nothing an outsider can say about
religion has the rooted violence of things the religious have themselves had it

at heart to say: no brilliant attack by an outsider against (say) obscurantism will seem to go far enough to a brilliant insider faced with the real obscurity of God; and attacks against religious institutions in the name of reason will not go far enough in a man who is attacking them in the name of faith. The criticism of religion, like the criticism of politics which Marx invented, is inescapably dialectical (which is, I take it, a reason Marx said it provided the origin for his criticism), because everything said on both sides is conditioned by the position (e.g., inside or outside) from which it is said. (This emerges in so differently conceived a work as Hume's *Dialogues,* in its outbreaks of irony.) Kierkegaard is fully dialectical where religious questions are concerned, as is displayed not merely in his long attention to different Stages of life, but in the many particular examples in which the same sentence is imagined to be said by men in different positions and thereby to mean differently. (On the recognition that they mean differently depends salvation, for the Gospel saves not because of what it says but because of who it is who has said it.) But his dialectical grasp is loosened when he comes to politics, where his violence does not see its own position and where the object he attacks is left uncriticized. He attacks newspapers and gossip and the public, as no doubt they deserve (on religious and on every other ground); but he does not consider, as it is Marx's business to consider, that what is wrong with them is itself a function of the age (not the other way around), and that a press which really belonged to the public (a public which belonged to itself) would reflect its audience otherwise than in gossip, and that its information would become, thereby, personal—existential in the relevant sense. We now know that this has not happened, but we should not therefore know that it is inevitable that it has not happened. I do not suggest that if it did happen Kierkegaard's problems would become solved, or irrelevant. But to the extent such a question is neglected, Kierkegaard's damning of society to perdition and his recourse to the individual, is suspect—it may be that a fear of the public is only the other side of a fearful privacy, which on his own ground would create the wrong silence and the wrong communication and provide no point for a new departure.

In our age, as yet an unknown distance from that of Kierkegaard, we are likely to read his books as aesthetic works, thus apparently denying his fervent claims that they are religious (even . . . ignoring his claim that it can be understood essentially only by theologians—a remark I choose to interpret ironically or aesthetically, as a rebuke to theologians for not attending to their job of defending the faith, in the categories of the faith, but instead help deliver it bound and gagged into the hands of philosophy). We read him running the risk, and feeling the pinch, of his damning outbursts against the merely curious, who translate the real terrors of the religious life into sublime spectacles of suffering with which to beguile their hours of spiritual leisure. I take heart from the realization that both his and our concepts of aesthetics are historically conditioned; that the concepts of beauty and sublimity which he had in mind (in deploring the confusion between art and religion) are ones which our art either repudiates or is determined to win in new ways; that, in particular, our serious art is produced under conditions which Kierkegaard announces as those of apostleship, not those of genius. I do not insist that for us art has become religion (which may or may not describe the situation, and which as it stands describes phenomena other than those I have in mind) but that the activity of modern art, both in production and reception, is to be understood in categories which are, or were, religious.

The remarkable Introduction is, in effect, an essay in aesthetics—or is something I wish aesthetics would become. Its distinction between "premise-authors" and "genuine authors" is drawn in a vital place—the place at which one must criticize a given work, perhaps the work of a given period, not as deficient in this or that respect, but dismiss it as art altogether. This kind of occasion is characteristic of the modern in the field of art. It does not arise as a problem until some point in the nineteenth century. I might call the problem "the threat of fraudulence," something I take to be endemic to modern art. One cannot imagine an audience of new music before Beethoven, or viewers of the paintings or spectators of the theater of that period, as wondering, or having the occasion to wonder, whether the thing in front of them was a piece of genuine art or not. But sometime thereafter audiences did begin to wonder, until by now we grow up learning and cherishing stories of the outrage and rioting which accompanied the appearance of new works, works *we* know to be masterpieces. At the same time, the advanced critics of the period in which this is becoming manifest (e.g., Matthew Arnold, Tolstoy, Nietzsche) were finding that it was precisely the work acceptable to the public which was the real source of fraudulence. It is characteristic of our artistic confusion today that we no longer know, and cannot find or trust ourselves to find occasion to know, which is which, whether it is the art or its audience which is on trial. Kierkegaard, who knew one when he saw one, defines the genuine author in terms of his moral relation to his work and to his audience: having a position of his own, the real author can give to the age what the age needs, not what it demands, whereas the fraudulent artist will "make use of the sickness of our age" by satisfying its demands; the genuine author "needs to communicate himself" whereas the false author is simply in need (of praise, of being in demand, of being told whether he means anything or not); the genuine is a physician who provides remedies, the false is a sick man, and contagious. Kierkegaard has other ways of capturing the experience of this difference (which he calls a qualitative difference), and when we find him saying that

> it is a suspicious circumstance when a man, instead of getting out of a tension by resolution and action, becomes literarily productive about his situation in the tension. Then no work is done to get out of the situation, but the reflection fixes the situation before the eyes of reflection, and thereby fixes (in a different sense of the word) the man.

we recognize that writers in our time, such as Georg Lukács and Sartre, have not deepened this definition of the problem of modernism. Adler is, of course, a premise-author, and Kierkegaard goes on in the body of his book to use the out-throw of imagery and contrasts which emerge in this Introduction to mark the features by which one knows that Adler is no better an apostle than he is an author; in both fields he lacks, in a word, the authority. I do not suppose Kierkegaard meant to suggest that a genuine author has to have, or claim, God's authority for his work, but his description of the apostle's position characterizes in detail the position I take the genuine modern artist to find himself in: he is pulled out of the ranks by a message which he must, on pain of loss of self, communicate; he is silent for a long period, until he finds his way to saying what it is he has to say (artistically speaking, this could be expressed by saying that while he may, as artists in former times have, begin and for a long time continue imitating the work of others, he knows that this is merely time-marking—if it is preparation, it is not artistic preparation— for he knows that there are no techniques at anyone's disposal for saying what he has to say); he has no proof of his authority, or genuineness, other than his own work (artistically speaking, this is expressed by the absence of conventions within which to compose); he makes his work repulsive, not, as in the case of the apostle, because of the danger he is to others but because mere attraction is not what he wants (artistically, this has to do with the various ways in which art has today withdrawn from, or is required to defeat, its audience); he must deny his personal or worldly authority in accomplishing what he has to do (artistically, this means that he cannot rely on his past achievements as securing the relevance of his new impulse; each work requires, spiritually speaking, a new step); art is no longer a profession to which, for example, a man can become apprenticed (religiously speaking, it is a "call," but there is no recognized calling in which it can be exercised); finally, the burden of being called to produce it is matched by the risk of accepting it (religiously speaking, in accepting or rejecting it, the heart is revealed). Art produced under such spiritual conditions will be expected to have a strange, unheard of *appearance*. Kierkegaard puts it this way:

> That a man in our age might receive a revelation cannot be absolutely denied [i.e., I take it, denying it would suffer the same confusion as affirming it], but the whole phenomenal demeanor of such an elect individual will be essentially different from that of all earlier examples.

All this does not mean (it is not summarized by saying) that the artist *is* an apostle; because the concept of an apostle is, as (because) the concept of revelation is, forgotten, inapplicable. So, almost, is the concept of art.

To the extent that one finds such considerations an accurate expression of one's convictions about the modern enjambment of the impulse to art and to religion, one will want to re-examine the whole question of Kierkegaard's own authorship—a task which could take a form related to Kierkegaard's book on Adler: for Kierkegaard is a "case" with the same dimensions, and no less a phenomenon than Adler, if harder to see through. In particular, in the light of our un-aestheticizing of aesthetics, what shall we make of Kierkegaard's famous claim for himself that he was, from the beginning, a *religious* author, that the Pseudonymous works were part of a larger design which, at the appropriate moment, emerged in directness? Since, presumably, he denied being an apostle, his claim says nothing about any special spiritual position he occupies as a Christian; he, like many others—like Adler—is a writer about religious matters. What the claim means, to our position, is that he is a *genuine* author, that he shares *that* fate. One fate of the genuine modern author is exactly his indirectness; his inability, somehow just because of his genuineness, to *confront* his audience directly with what he must say. Kierkegaard's claim to religious authorship sounds too much as though the Pseudonymous works were a strategy he employed for the benefit of others; whereas those works ought to be seen as a function of his inner strategy, as a genuine writer, to find ways of saying what he has it at heart to say. For it is very peculiar to us—in an age of Rilke, Kafka, Joyce, Mann, Beckett, non-objective painting, twelve-tone music—to hear an artist *praising* the strategy of indirectness, thinking to encompass its significance by acknowledging its usefulness as a medium of communication. What else have we had, in major art of the past hundred years, but indirectness: irony, theatricality, yearning, broken forms, denials of art, anti-heroes, withdrawals from nature, from men, from the future, from the past. . . . What is admirable in a work like *Fear and Trembling* is not its indirectness (which, so far as this is secured by the Pseudonym, is a more or less external device) nor its rather pat theory about why Abraham must be silent. What is admirable, exemplary, is its continuous awareness of the pain, and the danger, of that silence—of the fear of the false word, and deep wish that the right word be found for doing what one must: what, to my mind, Kierkegaard's portrait of Abraham shows is not the inevitability of his silence, but the completeness of his wish for directness, his refusal of anything less. Exemplary, because while we are stripped of Abraham's faith and of his clarity, it is still his position we find ourselves in. For certainly we cannot see ourselves in Kierkegaard's alternative, we are not Tragic Heroes: our sacrifices will not save the State. Yet we are sacrificed, and we sacrifice. Exemplary, because in our age, which not only does not know what it needs, but which no longer even demands anything, but takes what it gets, and so perhaps deserves it; where every indirectness is dime-a-dozen, and any weirdness can be assembled and imitated on demand—the thing we must look for, in each case, is the man who, contrary to appearance, and in spite of all, speaks.

JEAN-PAUL SARTRE

Kierkegaard: The Singular Universal

The title of our colloquium is "The Living Kierkegaard." It has the merit of plunging us to the very heart of *paradox*, and Søren himself would have appreciated this. For if we had gathered here today to discuss Heidegger, for example, no one would have dreamed of entitling our debate "The Living Heidegger." The living Kierkegaard, in other words, turns out to mean "the dead Kierkegaard." But not just this. It means that for us he exists, that he forms the object of our discussions, that he was an instrument of our thought. But, from this point of view, one could use the same expression to designate anyone who became part of our culture after he died. One could say, for example, "The Living Arcimboldo," since surrealism has allowed us to reappropriate this painter and cast him in a new light; but this would amount to making an *object* of him within what Kierkegaard called the *world-historical*. But, precisely, if Søren is in our eyes a sort of radioactive object, of whatever potency and virulence, then he can no longer be this living being whose subjectivity necessarily appears—in so far as it is lived—as other than what we know of it. In short, he sinks into death. The abolition of the subjective in a subject of History—the reduction of one who was an agent to an object—is an explosive historical scandal in the case of all who disappear from amongst us. History is full of holes. But nowhere is this more obvious than in the case of the "knight of subjectivity." Kierkegaard was a man who set out to pose the problem of the historical absolute, who emphasized the scandalous paradox of the appearance and disappearance of this absolute in the course of History. If we cannot revive this martyr of interiority other than in the form

From *Between Existentialism and Marxism.* © 1972 by Editions Gallimard, © 1974 by New Left Books. Pantheon Books, a division of Random House, 1975.

of an object of knowledge, a determination of his *praxis* will forever escape us: his living effort to elude knowledge through reflective life, his claim to be, in his very singularity and at the heart of his finitude, the absolute subject, defined in interiority by his absolute relationship with being. In other words, if death is historically no more than the passage of an interior to exteriority, then the title "The Living Kierkegaard" cannot be justified.

If we retain something of this life which, in its time and place, removed all traces of itself, then Kierkegaard himself is the scandal and the paradox. Unable to be understood as anything other than this immanence which for forty years never stopped designating *itself* as such, either he eludes us forever and the world rid itself, in 1856, of *nothing;* or else the paradox exposed by this dead man is that a historical being, beyond his own abolition, can still communicate as a non-object, as an absolute subject, with succeeding generations. What will attract our attention then will not be the religious problem of Christ incarnate nor the metaphysical problem of death, but the strictly historical paradox of survival: we shall plumb our knowledge of Kierkegaard in order to locate what in a dead man eludes knowledge and survives *for us* beyond his destruction. We shall ask ourselves whether the presence, that is the subjectivity of someone else, always inaccessible to cognition in its strict sense, can nevertheless be given to us by some other means. Either History closes back over our knowledge of this death, or the historical survival of the subjective ought to change our conception of History. In other words either Kierkegaard today, 24 April 1964, is dissolved by the enzymes of knowledge or he persists in demonstrating to us the still virulent scandal of what one might call the transhistoricity of a historical man.

He posed the fundamental question in these terms: "Can History act as the point of departure for an eternal certitude? Can one find in such a point of departure anything other than an historical interest? Can one base eternal happiness on a merely historical knowledge?"

And of course what he has in mind here is the scandalous paradox of the birth and death of God, of the historicity of Jesus. But we must go further; for if the answer is yes, then this transhistoricity belongs to Søren, Jesus' witness, just as much as to Jesus himself; and to us as well, Søren's grand-nephews. As he says himself, we are all contemporaries. In a sense, this is to explode History. Yet History exists and it is man who makes it. Thus posteriority and contemporaneity mutually imply and contradict each other. For the moment we cannot proceed further. We must go back to Kierkegaard and question him as a privileged witness. Why privileged? I am thinking of the Cartesian proof of the existence of God through the fact that *I exist with the idea of God.* Kierkegaard is a singular witness—or, as he says, the Exception—by virtue of a *redoubling* in himself of the subjective attitude: in our eyes he is an object of knowledge in so far as he is a subjective witness of his own subjectivity, that is to say, in so far as he is an existent announcer of existence by virtue of his own existential attitude. Thus he becomes both object and subject of our study. We should take this subject-object in so far as it demonstrates a historical paradox that transcends it; we shall question its testimony in so far in its historicity—he said such-and-such on such-and-such a date—transcends itself and makes the paradox of the object-subject burst within History. By integrating *his* words into our language, in translating him with *our* words, will the limits of knowledge be revealed? And by virtue of a paradoxical reversal of meaning, will this knowledge point to the signifier as its silent foundation?

In principle everything about him can be *known (connu)*. Doubtless he kept his secrets well. But one can press him hard and extract statements from him and interpret them. The problem can now be formulated: when everything is *known (su)* about the life of a man who refuses to be an object of knowledge and whose originality rests precisely in this refusal, is there an irreducible beyond this? How are we to seize it and think it? The question has two sides to it—prospective and retrospective. One can ask what it means to have lived when all the determinations of a life are *known*. But one can also ask what it means to live when the essential core of these determinations has been foreseen? For the singularity of the Kierkegaardian adventure is that, as it unfolded, it revealed itself to itself as known in advance. Thus it lived within and in spite of knowledge. It must be borne in mind that this opposition between foreseen and lived experience was made manifest around 1850 in the opposition between Hegel and Kierkegaard. Hegel had gone, but his system lived on. Søren, whatever he did, acted within the limits of what Hegel had called the unhappy consciousness—that is to say he could only realize the complex dialectic of the finite and the infinite. He would never be able to surpass it. Kierkegaard knew that he already had his place within the system. He was familiar with Hegel's thought, and he was aware of the interpretation it conferred *in advance* on the movements of his life. He was trapped and held in the beam of the Hegelian projector; he either had to vanish into objective knowledge or demonstrate his irreducibility. But, precisely, Hegel was dead and this death pronounced his knowledge as dead knowledge, or as knowledge of death. While Kierkegaard showed by the simple fact of his life that all knowledge concerning the subjective is in a certain sense false knowledge. Foreseen by the system, he disqualified its legitimacy by not appearing *in it* as a moment to be surpassed and at the site assigned to him by the master, but on the contrary, emerging quite simply as a survivor of the system and its

prophet, as one who, despite the dead determinations of an anterior prophecy, had to live this foreseen life as if it were indeterminate at the outset and
as if its determinations had arisen of their own accord within free "non-
knowledge."

The new aspect of the problematic that Kierkegaard reveals to us is the
fact that in his personal life he did not contradict the content of knowledge
but illegitimized knowledge of any content. By negating the concept through
the very fashion in which he realized its prescriptions in another dimension,
he was traversed through and through by the light of knowledge—for others
and also for himself, as he was acquainted with Hegelianism—but at the
same time remained utterly opaque. In other words, this pre-existent knowledge revealed a being at the heart of future existence. Thirty years ago, the
contradictions of colonialism constituted, in the eyes of the generation of col-
onized born into it, a being of misery, anger, blood, revolt and struggle; a few
amongst the best-informed of the oppressed and of the colonialists themselves were aware of this. Or to take a quite different example, a vacancy
created high up or low down on the social scale creates a destiny, that is to
say a future but foreseeable being for the person who will fill it, even though
this destiny remains for each candidate, if there is more than one, no more
than a *possible being*. Or, in the narrow particularity of private life, the structures of a specific family (seen as a local example of an institution produced
by the movement of History) permit the psychoanalyst, in theory at least, to
foresee the future destiny (to be lived and undergone) that will be a particular
neurosis for a child born into this milieu. Kierkegaard *foreseen* by Hegel is
but a privileged example of such ontological determinations which pre-date
birth and allow themselves to be *conceptualized*.

Søren identified with the problem because he was conscious of it. He
knew that Hegel, in pointing to him as a moment of universal History vainly
posed for itself, attained him in the being which he suffered as a schema to be
accomplished in the course of his life, and which he called his Untruth, or the
error that he was at the start of his life, as a truncated determination. But this
was the point: Hegel's designation attained him like the light from a dead
star. The untruth *had to be lived*; it too belonged to his subjective subjectivity.
And so he could write, in the *Fragments*: "My own Untruth is something I
can discover only by myself, since it is only when I have discovered it that it
is discovered, even if the whole world knew of it before." But when it is discovered, my Untruth becomes, at least in the immediate, my Truth. So subjective truth exists. It is not knowledge (*savoir*) but self-determination; it can
be defined neither as an extrinsic relation of knowledge (*connaissance*) to
being, nor as the internal imprint of a correspondence, nor as the indissoluble

unity of a system. "Truth," he said, "is the act of freedom." I would not know how to *be* my own Truth even if its premises were given in me in advance: to reveal it means to produce it or to produce myself as I am; to be for myself what I have to be.

What Kierkegaard highlighted was the fact that the opposition between non-knowledge and knowledge is an opposition between two ontological structures. The subjective has to be what it is—a singular realization of each singularity. One would have to go to Freud for the most illuminating commentary on this remark. In fact psychoanalysis is not knowledge nor does it claim to be, save when it hazards hypotheses on the dead and thus allows death to make it a science of death. It is a movement, an internal labour, that at one and the same time uncovers a neurosis and gradually makes the subject capable of supporting it. With the result that at the term (actually an ideal) of this process, there is a correspondence between the being that has developed and the truth it once was. The truth in this case is the unity of the conquest and the object conquered. It transforms without teaching anything and does not appear until the end of a transformation. It is a non-knowledge, an effectivity, a placing in perspective that is present to itself in so far as it is realized. Kierkegaard would add that it is a decision of authenticity: the rejection of flight and the will to return to oneself. In this sense *knowledge* cannot register this obscure and inflexible *movement* by which scattered determinations are elevated to the status of being and are gathered together into a tension which confers on them not a signification but a synthetic meaning: what happens is that the ontological structure of subjectivity escapes to the extent that the subjective being is, as Heidegger has put it so well, in question in its being, to the extent that it never *is* except in the mode of having to be its being.

From this point of view, the moment of subjective truth is a temporalized but transhistorical absolute. And subjectivity is temporalization itself: it is *what happens to me*, what cannot be but in happening. It is myself in so far as I can only be a random birth—and, as Merleau-Ponty said, in so far as I must, no matter how short my life, *at least* experience the occurrence of death; but it is also myself in so far as I try to regain control of my own adventure by assuming—we shall come back to this point—its original contingency in order to establish it in necessity. In short, in so far as *I* happen to myself. Dealt with in advance by Hegel, subjectivity becomes a moment of the objective spirit, a determination of culture. But if nothing of lived experience can elude knowledge, its *reality* remains irreducible. In this sense, lived experience as concrete reality is posed as *non-knowledge*. But this negation of knowledge implies the affirmation of itself. Lived experience recognizes itself as a projection into the milieu of meaning, but at the same time it fails to recognize itself there since, in this milieu, an ensemble is constituted which aims randomly at objects and since, precisely, it is itself not an object. Doubtless, one of the principal concerns of the nineteenth century was to distinguish the being of an object from one's knowledge of it, in other words to reject idealism. Marx attacked Hegel not so much for his point of departure, as his reduction of being to knowledge. But for Kierkegaard, as for ourselves today when we consider the Kierkegaardian scandal, the question is one of a certain ontological region in which being claims at once to elude knowledge and to attain itself. Waelhens has rightly written: "With the advent of Kierkegaard, Nietzsche and Bergson, philosophy ceased to be *explanation at a distance*, and claimed to be henceforth *at one* with experience itself; it was no longer content to throw light on man and his life, but aspired to become this life in its full consciousness of itself. It seemed that for the philosopher this ambition involved an obligation to renounce the ideal of philosophy as a rigorous science, since the basis of this ideal was inseparable from the idea of a detached . . . spectator."

In short, the determinations of lived experience are not simply heterogeneous to knowledge, as the existence of thalers was heterogeneous for Kant to the concept of thaler and to the judgement that combined the two. It is the very way in which these determinations attain themselves in the redoubling of their presence to themselves that reduces knowledge to the pure abstraction of the concept and, in the first moment at least (the only one Kierkegaard described) turns an object-subjectivity into an objective *nothing* in relation to a subjective subjectivity. Knowledge (*savoir*) itself has a being; bodies of knowledge (*connaissances*) are realities. For Kierkegaard, even in his lifetime, the being of knowledge was obviously radically heterogeneous to that of the living subject. Thus we can designate the determinations of existence with words. But *either* this designation is nothing but a place-marker, a set of references without conceptualization, *or else* the ontological structure of the concept and of its links — i.e. objective being, being in exteriority—is such that these references, grasped as notions, cannot but yield a false knowledge when they present themselves as insights into being in interiority.

In his life, Kierkegaard lived this paradox in passion: he desperately wanted to designate himself as a transhistorical absolute. In humour and in irony, he revealed himself and concealed himself at the same time. He did not refuse to communicate, but simply held on to his *secrecy* in the act of communication. His mania for pseudonyms was a systematic disqualification of *proper names*: even to *assign* him as an individual before the tribunal of others, a welter of mutually contradictory appellations was necessary. The more he becomes Climacus or Virgelin Hufnensis, the less he is *Kierkegaard*, this Danish citizen, this entry in the registers of the civil authorities.

This was all very well so long as he was alive: by his life he gave the lie to a dead man's predictions which were a knowledge of death. That is to say he ceaselessly fabricated himself by writing. But on the 11th of November 1855 he died, and the paradox turned against him without ceasing to be scandalous *in our eyes*. The prophecy of a dead man condemning a living being to exist as an unhappy consciousness, and our knowledge of this living being once he has died, reveal their homogeneity. In fact in our own time Käte Nadler—to cite but one example—has applied to the late Kierkegaard the prediction of the late Hegel. A dialectical pair is formed, in which each term denounces the other: Hegel foresaw Kierkegaard in the past, as a superseded moment; Kierkegaard gave the lie to the internal organization of Hegel's system by showing that superseded moments are conserved, not only in the *Aufhebung* that maintains them as it transforms them, but in themselves, without any transformation whatever; and by proving that even if they arise anew, they create, merely through their appearance, an anti-dialectic. But, once Kierkegaard died, Hegel regained possession of him. Not *within the System*, which visibly crumbled in so far as it was a finished totality of Knowledge which, as a system, was subsequently totalized by the onward movement of History itself—but simply by virtue of the fact that the late Kierkegaard has become *in our eyes* homogeneous with the descriptions that Hegelian knowledge gives of him. The fact remains, of course, that he contested the whole system by appearing in a place that was not assigned to him: but since the system itself is an object of knowledge and as such is contested, this anachronism provides us with nothing really new. By contrast, the Knowledge that *we* have of him is knowledge of a dead man and thus knowledge of death; as such it rejoins the Hegelian intuition which produced and conceptualized a future death. In ontological terms, Kierkegaard's pre-natal being was homogeneous with his post-mortem being and his existence seemed merely to be a way of enriching the first so that it could equal the second: it was no more than a provisional *malaise,* an essential means of getting from one to the other, but, in itself, an inessential fever of being. The notion of the unhappy consciousness became Søren's insurpassable destiny as well as the generality enveloping our most particularized items of knowledge concerning his dead life. Or if you like, to die meant to be restored to being and to become an object of knowledge. That at least is the recurrent lazy conception whose aim is to close a breach. Is it true? Should we say that death terminates the paradox by revealing that it is nothing more than a provisional appearance, or on the contrary, that it pushes it to the extreme and consequently, since we die, the whole of History becomes paradoxical—an insurmountable conflict between being and existence, between non-knowledge and knowledge? It was Kierkegaard's merit that he formulated this problem *in the very terms of his life*. Let us come back to him.

Let us note at the outset that between him and us, History has *taken place*. No doubt it is still going on. But its richness puts a distance, *an obscure density* between him and us. The unhappy consciousness will find other incarnations, and each of them will contest this consciousness by his life and confirm it by his death, but none of them will reproduce Kierkegaard by virtue of a kind of resurrection. Knowledge has its foundations in this instance in noncoincidence. The poet of faith left texts behind. These writings are dead unless we breathe our life into them; but if revived they bear the stamp of thoughts committed to paper long ago, somewhere else, with the means to hand—they only partially answer to our present requirements. Unbelievers will pronounce *the Kierkegaardian proof to be unconvincing*. Theologians, in the name of dogma itself, may declare themselves unsatisfied and find the attitude and declarations of the "poet of Christianity" insufficient and dangerous. They may reproach him in the name of his own admission, through the very title of *poet* that he gave himself, with not having got beyond what he himself called the "aesthetic stage." Atheists will *either*—a formula dear to him— reject any relationship with this absolute and opt firmly for a relativism, *or else* define the absolute in History *in other terms*—and regard Kierkegaard as the witness of a false absolute or a false witness of the absolute. Believers, on the other hand, will declare that the absolute Kierkegaard aimed at is certainly that which exists, but that the relation of historical man to transhistoricity which he tried to establish, was involuntarily deflected and lost by him in the night of atheism. In each case, his attempt is pronounced a *failure*.

There is more: the failure is *explained*. In different ways, it is true, but by convergent approximations. Mesnard, Bohlen, Chestov and Jean Wahl are all agreed in stressing the psychosomatic significance of the "thorn in the flesh." This means that, in the case of this dead man, lived experience itself is contested. Later conceptual judgement renders the life itself inauthentic. Kierkegaard lived out badly—in the sense of obscurely, disguisedly—determinations that we can perceive better than he. In short, in the eyes of historical knowledge, one lives to die. Existence is a mild surface ripple that is soon stilled in order to allow the dialectical development of concepts to appear; chronology dissolves into homogeneity and in the end, into timelessness. Every lived venture ends in failure for the simple reason that History continues.

But if life is a scandal, failure is even more scandalous. First we describe and denounce it by collections of words that aim at a certain object named Kierkegaard. In this sense the "poet of faith" is a signified—like this table, like a socio-economic process. And it is true that death first presents itself as the fall of the subject into the realm of absolute objectivity. But Kierkegaard in his writings—today inert or living with our life — proposes a usage of words that is the converse of this: what he seeks is a dialectical regression from signified and significations to signifier. He presents himself as a signifier, and at a stroke refers us back to our transhistoricity as signifiers. Should we reject this regression *a priori?* To do so is to constitute ourselves as relative— relative to History if we are unbelievers, relative to Dogmas and mediated by the Church if we believe. Now if such is the case, then everything should be relative, in us and in Kierkegaard himself, *except his failure.* For failure can be *explained* but not *resolved:* as non-being it possesses the absolute character of negation. In fact historical negation, even at the heart of a relativism, is an absolute. It would be a negative absolute to declare that at Waterloo *there were no* fighter planes. But this negative declaration remains a formality: as the two adversaries were equally without air power and were both incapable of missing it, this ineffectual absence is no more than a formal proposition devoid of interest, that merely registers the *temporal distance* from Waterloo to the present. There are, however, other negative absolutes and these are concrete: it is correct to state that Grouchy's army *did not* link up with the Emperor; and this negation is historical in the sense that it reflects the frustrated expectation of the head of an army, and the fear turned to satisfaction of the enemy. It is effective in the sense that Grouchy's delay in all probability *settled* the outcome of the battle. It is thus an absolute, an irreducible but a concrete absolute. Similarly in the case of the failure: the fact that an ambition is not realised in objectivity means that it returns to subjectivity. Or, more precisely, the interpretations of such a failure aim via moderate negations (he didn't consider . . . , he couldn't be aware at the time, etc.) to reduce it *to the positive,* to erase it before the affirmative reality of the Other's victory, whatever it may be.

But at once this relative positivity slips back and reveals what no knowledge could ever transmit directly (because no historical advance could recuperate it): failure lived in despair. Those who died of anguish, of hunger, of exhaustion, those defeated in the past by force of arms, are so many gaps in our knowledge in so far as they existed: subjectivity constitutes *nothing* for objective knowledge since it is a non-knowledge, and yet failure demonstrates that it has an absolute existence. In this way Søren Kierkegaard, conquered by death and recuperated by historical knowledge, triumphs at the very moment he fails, by demonstrating that History cannot recover him. As a dead man, he remains the insurpassable scandal of subjectivity; though he may be known through and through, he eludes History by the very fact that it is History that constitutes his defeat and that he lived it in anticipation. In short, he eludes History because he is historical.

Can we go further? Or must we simply conclude that death irrevocably filches the agents of past History from the historian? Here it is necessary to question *what remains* of Kierkegaard, his verbal remnants. For he constituted himself in his historicity as an absolute contesting the historical knowledge that would penetrate him after his death. But the kind of interrogation with which we are concerned is of a particular type: it is a paradox itself. Kant situated himself in the realm of cognition in order to test the validity of our knowledges. We, the living, can approach him through the realm of cognition, question his words with words, and cross-examine him on concepts. But Kierkegaard stole language from knowledge in order to use it against knowledge. If we approach him, as we are compelled to do, through the realm of cognition, our words encounter his and are disqualified by disqualifying them. The fact is that his use of the Word and our own are heterogeneous. Thus the message of this dead man is scandalous through the very fact of its existence, since we are incapable of considering this residue of a life as a determination of knowledge. On the contrary, the paradox reappears since his thought expressed in words constitutes itself within knowledge as irreducible non-knowledge. Our interrogation must then either disappear without trace, or be transformed and itself become non-knowledge questioning non-knowledge. That is to say, the questioner is called into question in his very being by the questioned. Such is the fundamental virtue of the pseudo-object called the works of Kierkegaard. But let us push our examination to the very moment of this metamorphosis.

This philosopher was an anti-philosopher. Why did he reject the Hegelian system and, in a general way, the whole of philosophy? Because, he says, the philosopher seeks a first beginning. But why, one may ask, did he who rejected beginnings take as his point of departure the Christian dogmas? For to accept them *a priori* without even testing their validity is tantamount to making them the uncontested principles of thought. Is there not a contradiction here? Did not Kierkegaard, having failed to establish a solid beginning himself, take the beginning of others as the origin and foundation of his thought? And as he failed to test it through criticism, and as he neglected to doubt it to the point where it could no longer be doubted, did it not retain for him, even in his most intimate thought, its character of otherness?

This is, indeed, the unfair question that knowledge puts to existence.

But, in Kierkegaard's pen, existence replies by rejecting knowledge's case. To deny dogma, it says, is to be mad and to proclaim the fact. But to prove dogma is to be an imbecile: while time is wasted proving that the soul is immortal, living belief in immortality withers away. At the absurd limit of this logic, the day would come when immortality was finally proved irrefutably—except that no one would believe in it any more. There is no way we could better understand that immortality, even if proven, could never be an object of knowledge: it is a particular absolute relationship between immanence and transcendence that can only be constituted in and through lived experience. And of course this is sufficient for believers. But for the non-believer that I am, what this means is that the real relation of man to his being can only be lived, in History, as a transhistorical relationship.

Kierkegaard replies to our question by rejecting philosophy or rather by radically changing its end and aims. To seek the beginning of knowledge is to affirm that the foundation of temporality is, precisely, timeless, and that the historical individual can wrench himself free of History, de-situate himself and relocate his fundamental timelessness by a direct vision of being. Temporality becomes the means of intemporality. Naturally Hegel was aware of the problem since he placed philosophy at the end of History, as truth-that-has-come-into-being and retrospective knowledge. But this is the point: History is never finished, so this atemporal reconstitution of temporality, understood as the unity of the logical and the tragic, becomes in turn an object of knowledge. From this point of view, there is no being at all at the beginning of Hegel's system, but only the person of Hegel, such as it had been fashioned, such as it had fashioned itself. This is the sort of ambiguous discovery that can lead, from the point of view of knowledge, only to scepticism.

To avoid this, Kierkegaard took as his point of departure the *person* envisaged as non-knowledge, that is to say in as much as he both produces and discovers, at a given moment in the temporal unfolding of his life, his relation to an absolute which is itself inserted in History. In short, far from denying the beginning, Kierkegaard testified to a beginning that is lived.

How is it possible that, in the context of History, this historical situation does not contest the claim of the thinker to have disclosed the absolute? How can a thought *that has appeared* testify on its own behalf after its *disappearance?* This is the problem Kierkegaard set himself in the *Philosophical Fragments*. Of course, this paradox was first and foremost a religious one. What was at stake was the appearance and disappearance of Jesus. Or equally, the transformation of one sin—Adam's—into original and hereditary sin. But it was just as much the personal problem of Kierkegaard the thinker: how could he establish the transhistorical validity of a thought that had been produced within History and would disappear into it? The answer lay in "reduplication": the insurpassable cannot be knowledge, but must be the establishment in History of an absolute and non-contemplative relation with the absolute that has been realized in History. Rather than knowledge dissolving the thinker, it is the thinker who testifies on behalf of his own thought. But these ideas are obscure and can appear to be merely a verbal solution so long as one has not understood that they proceed from a novel conception of thought.

The beginning of the thinker's existence is analogous to a birth. This is not a rejection but a displacement of the beginning. Before birth there was non-being; then comes the leap, and the moment they are born to themselves, the child and the thinker find themselves immediately situated within a certain historical world that has produced them. They discover themselves as a particular adventure, whose point of departure is a set of socio-economic, cultural, moral, religious and other relations, which proceeds with whatever means are to hand, that is to say within the limits of these relations, and which gradually becomes inscribed in the same set. The beginning is reflective—I saw and touched the world, and so see and touch myself, this self who touches and sees the surrounding things; in this way I discover myself as a finite being, one that these same objects I touched and saw condition invisibly in my very sense of touch and sight. As against the constant and non-human beginning that Hegel postulated, Kierkegaard proposed a start that is in flux, that is conditioned and is conditioning, whose foundation approximates to what Merleau-Ponty called *envelopment*. We are enveloped: being is behind us and in front of us. He-who-sees is visible, and sees only by virtue of his visibility. "My body," said Merleau-Ponty, "is caught in the fabric of the world, but the world is made from the stuff of my body." Kierkegaard knew he was enveloped: he saw Christianity and in particular the Christian community in Denmark with the eyes that this community had given him. This is a new paradox: I see the being that fashioned me. I see it as it *is* or as it made me. "Overview thought" has an easy solution to this: having no qualities, the understanding grasps the objective essence without its own nature imposing particular deviations on it. Idealist relativism has an equally simple solution: the object fades away; what I see, being the effect of causes modifying my vision, contains no more than what these latter determine me to be. In each case, being is reduced to knowledge.

Kierkegaard rejects both solutions. The paradox, for him, is the fact that we discover the absolute in the relative. Kierkegaard was a Dane, born at the beginning of the last century into a Danish family, and conditioned by Danish history and culture. He came across other Danes as his contemporaries, people who were formed by the same History and cultural traditions. And at the same time, moreover, he could *think* the historical traditions and circumstances that had produced them all and produced himself. Was there either deviation or appropriation? Both. If objectivity has to be unconditioned knowledge, then there can be no true objectivity: to see one's surroundings, in this instance, would be to see without seeing, to touch without touching, to possess in oneself an *a priori* intuition of the other and, at the same time, to grasp him on the basis of common presuppositions that can never wholly be uncovered. Even in broad daylight my neighbour is dark and impenetrable, separated from me by his apparent resemblances; and yet I sense him in his underlying reality when I penetrate deeper into my own inner reality and attain its transcendental conditions. Later, much later, the presuppositions inscribed in things will be correctly deciphered by the historian. But at this level, the mutual comprehension that takes the existence of a communal envelopment for granted will have disappeared. In short, contemporaries understand each other without knowing each other, whereas the future historian will know them but his greatest difficulty—a difficulty bordering on the impossible—will be to understand them as they understood each other.

In fact—and Kierkegaard was aware of this—the experience which turns back upon itself, after the leap, comprehends itself more than it knows itself. In other words, it sustains itself in the milieu of the presuppositions that are its foundation, without succeeding in elucidating them. Hence a beginning that is a dogma. A particular religion produced Kierkegaard: he could not pretend to emancipate himself from it so that he could rise above it and see it as historically constituted. Note however that other Danes, from the same society, from the same class, became non-believers: but even they could do nothing to prevent their irreligion questioning or challenging *these* dogmas, this particular Christianity which had produced them — and hence their past, their religious childhood and finally themselves. Thus whatever they did, they remained wedded to their faith and their dogmas while vainly attempting to negate them by using other words to express their demand for an absolute. Their atheism was in fact a Christian *pseudo-atheism*. As it happens, one's envelopment determines the limits within which real modifications are possible. There are times when disbelief can only be verbal. Kierkegaard doubted as a youth, and hence was more consequential than these "free-thinkers": he recognized that his thought was not free and that whatever he might do or wherever he might go his religious determinations would follow him. If in spite of himself he saw Christian dogmas as irreducible, then it was perfectly legitimate for him to locate the beginning of his thought at the moment when it retraced its steps to them to get at its roots.

Such a thought was doubly embedded in history: it grasped its envelopment as a conjuncture, and it defined itself as an identity between the beginning of thought and thought of the beginning.

If such was the case, what then was to become of the universality of historical determinations? Must we deny in absolute terms that there is any social sphere, with structures, pressures and developments of its own? Not at all. We shall see that Kierkegaard testified to a double universality. The revolution consisted in the fact that historical man, by his anchorage, turned this universality into a particular situation and this common necessity into an irreducible contingency. In other words, far from this particular attitude being, as in Hegel, a dialectical incarnation of the universal moment, the anchorage of the individual made this universal into an irreducible singularity. Did not Søren say to Levin one day: "How lucky you are to be a Jew: you escape Christianity. If I had been protected by your faith, I would have enjoyed a quite different life"? This was an ambiguous remark, for he often reproached Jews with being inaccessible to religious experience. There could be no doubt that dogma was truth, and the Christian who was not religious remained inauthentic, outside himself, lost. But there was a sort of humble birthright which meant, in the case of a Jew, a Moslem or a Buddhist, that the chance occurrence of their birth in one place rather than another was transformed into a statute. Conversely, Kierkegaard's deepest reality, the fabric of his being, his torment and his law appeared to him in the very heart of their necessity as the accidental outcome of his facticity. Again this contingency was common to all members of his society. He came across others which belonged only to him. In 1846 he wrote: "To believe is to lighten oneself by assuming a considerable weight; to be objective is to lighten oneself by casting off burdens . . . Lightness is an infinite weight, and its altitude the effect of an infinite weight." He was clearly alluding to what he called elsewhere the "thorn in the flesh." Here we are confronted with pure contingency, the singularity of his conditionings. Søren's unhappy consciousness was the product of random determinations which Hegelian rationalism did not take into account: a gloomy father who was convinced that he would be struck by a divine curse on his children; the mournings that seemed to bear out these expectations and ended by persuading Søren that he would die by the age of thirty-four; the mother, mistress and servant, whom he loved in so far as she was *his* mother and whom he reproved in so far as she was an intruder in the household of a widower and testified to the carnal lapses of his father, and so on. The origin of singularity is the random at its most radical: if I had had a different father . . . if my father had not blasphemed, etc. And this pre-natal accident reappears in the individual himself and in his determinations: the thorn in the flesh was a complex disposition whose inner secret has not yet been unearthed. But all authors are agreed in seeing a sexual anomaly as its kernel. A singularizing accident, this anomaly *was* Kierkegaard, it *made* him; it could not be cured, and hence could not be surpassed; it produced his most intimate self as a pure historical contingency, which might not have been and in itself meant nothing. Hegelian necessity was not negated, but it could not be embodied without becoming a singular and opaque contingency; in an individual the rationality of History is experienced irreducibly as madness, as an inner accident, expressive of random encounters. To our questioning, Kierkegaard replies by revealing another aspect of the paradox: there can be no historical absolute that is not rooted in chance; because of the necessity of anchorage, there can be no incarnation of the universal other than in the irreducible opacity of the singular. Is it Søren who *says* this? Yes and no: to tell the truth he *says nothing* if "to say" means the same as "to signify," but his work refers us back, without speaking, to his life.

But here the paradox has a twist to it, for to experience original contingency means to surpass it. Man, irremediable singularity, is the being through whom the universal comes into the world; once fundamental chance starts to be lived, it assumes the form of necessity. Lived experience, we discover in Kierkegaard, is made up of non-significant accidents of being in so far as they are surpassed towards a significance they did not possess at the beginning, and which I will call the singular universal.

To gain more insight into this message, let us come back to the notion of sin which lies at the centre of Kierkegaard's thought. As Jean Wahl has noted correctly, Adam exists in a pre-Adamite state of innocence, i.e. of ignorance. Nevertheless, although the Self does not yet exist, this being already envelops a contradiction. At this level, the spirit is a synthesis which unites and divides: it brings body and soul together and, in doing so, engenders the conflicts which oppose them. Dread makes its appearance as the interiorization of being, that is to say its contradiction. In other words, being has no interiority prior to the appearance of dread. But since the spirit can neither flee nor fulfil itself, since it is a dissonant unity of the finite and the infinite, the possibility of choosing *one* of the terms — the finite, the flesh, in other words the Self which does not yet exist — makes its appearance in the form of dread, at the moment when God's Thou Shalt Not resounds. But what is this prohibition? In actual fact, communication is not possible — no more than it was possible between Kafka's Emperor and the subject he wanted to touch but whom his message does not reach. But Kierkegaard gave his Shalt Not its full value when he deprived the Serpent of the power to tempt Adam. If the Devil is eliminated and Adam is not yet Adam, who can pronounce the prohibition and at the same time suggest to the pre-Adamite that he *turn himself* into Adam? God alone. A curious passage from the *Journal* explains why:

> Omnipotence . . . should make things dependent. But if we rightly consider omnipotence, then clearly it must have the quality of so taking itself back in the very manifestation of its all-powerfulness that the results of this act of the omnipotent can be independent. . . . For goodness means to give absolutely, yet in such a way that by taking oneself back one makes the recipient independent. . . . Omnipotence alone . . . can create something out of nothing which endures of itself, because omnipotence is always taking itself back. . . . If . . . man had even the least independent existence (in regard to *materia*) then God could not make him free.

The pre-Adamite state of innocence is the final moment of dependence. At any moment God will withdraw from his creature as the ebbing tide uncovers a piece of flotsam; and by this movement alone he creates dread— as the possibility of independence. In other words, God becomes at once the Prohibiter and the Tempter. Thus dread is the abandonment of being to the forbidden possibility of choosing finitude by a sudden retreat of the infinite. Dread is the internalization of this forsaken condition and it is completed by the free realization of the sole possible future of Adam abandoned—the choice of the finite. The moment of sin is defined by the restitution of original being as *meaning*. Being was the contradictory unity between the finite and the impalpable infinite, but this unity remained in the indistinction of igno-rance. Sin as *re-exteriorization* makes the constituent contradiction reappear. It is the determination of it: the Self and God appear. God is infinite with-drawal but yet immediate presence, in so far as sin bars the way to any hope of return to Eden. The Self is chosen finitude, nothingness affirmed and delim-ited by an act; it is determination conquered by defiance; it is the singularity of extreme estrangement. Thus the terms of the contradiction are the same and yet the *state* of ignorance and sin are not homogeneous: the finite is now constituted as loss of the infinite, freedom as the *necessary* and irremediable foundation of the formation of the *Ego*. Good and Evil make their appear-ance as the meaning of this exteriorization of the interiority that is sinful free-dom. Everything happens as though God *needed sin* in order that man might produce himself in front of him, as if he had solicited it in order to bring Adam out of his state of ignorance and *give* meaning to man.

But we are all Adam. Thus the pre-Adamite state is one with the contin-gency of our being. For Kierkegaard, what produces it is a disunited unity of accidents. In this sense, sin becomes the *establishment* of Kierkegaard as a surpassal of these scattered data *towards a meaning*. The contingency of our being is the beginning; our necessity only appears through the act which assumes this contingency in order to give it a *human meaning*, in other words to make of it a singular relationship to the Whole, a singular embodiment of the ongoing totalization which envelops and produces it. Kierkegaard was well aware of this: what he called sin is, as a whole, the supersession of the (pre-Adamite) *state* by the advent of freedom and the impossibility of retreat. Thus the web of subjective life—what he called passion, and Hegel called *pathos*—is nothing other than the freedom that institutes the finite and is lived in finitude as inflexible necessity.

If I wished to summarize what Kierkegaard's non-signifying testimony has to offer to me, a twentieth-century atheist who does not believe in sin, I would say that the state of ignorance represents, for the individual, being-in-exteriority. These exterior determinations are interiorized in order to be re-exteriorized by a *praxis* which *institutes* them by objectifying them in the world.

This is what Merleau-Ponty was saying when he wrote that History is the milieu in which "a form burdened with contingency suddenly opens up a cycle of the future and commands it with the authority of the instituted." The cycle of the future is a *meaning*: in the case of Kierkegaard, it is the Self. Meaning can be defined as the future relation of the instituted to the totality of the world or, if you like, as the synthetic totalization of scattered chance occurrences by an objectifying negation, which inscribes them as necessity freely created in the very universe in which they were scattered, and as the presence of the totality—a totality of time and of the universe—in the determination which negates them by posing itself for itself. In other words, man is that being who transforms his being into *meaning*, and through whom *meaning* comes into the world.

The singular universal is this meaning: through his *Self*—the practical assumption and supersession of being as it is—man restores to the universe its enveloping unity, by engraving it as a finite determination and a mortgage on future History in the being which envelops him. Adam temporalizes himself by sin, the necessary free choice and radical transformation of what he is —he brings human temporality into the universe. This clearly means that the foundation of History is freedom in *each man*. For we are all Adam in so far as each of us commits on his own behalf and on behalf of all a singular sin: in other words finitude, for each person, is necessary and incomparable. By his finite action, the agent alters the course of things—but in conformity with what this course itself ought to be. Man, in fact, is a mediation between a transcendence behind and a transcendence in front, and this twofold transcendence is but one. Thus we can say that through man, the course of things is deviated in the direction of its own deviation. Kierkegaard here reveals to us the basis of his own paradox and of ours—and the two are the same. Each of us, in our very historicity, escapes History to the extent that we make it. I myself am historical to the extent that others also make history and make me, but I am a transhistorical absolute by virtue of what I make of what they make of me, have made of me and will make of me in the future—that is, by virtue of my historiality (*historialité*).

We still need to understand properly what the myth of sin holds for us: the *institution* of a man is his singularity become law for others and for himself. What is Kierkegaard's body of work but himself in so far as he is a universal? But on the other hand the content of this universality remains his contingency—even if elected and surpassed by his choice of it. In short, this universality has two sides to it: by virtue of its meaning it raises contingency to the level of concrete universality. This is its luminous and yet unknowable *recto* side—to the extent that knowledge refers to the "world-historical" by the mediation of an *anchorage*. Its *verso* side is in darkness, and refers back to the contingent set of analytical and social data which define Kierkegaard's being before his *institution*. Two errors in method are thereby denounced. The first of them, the world-historical, would define Kierkegaard's message in its abstract universality and as the pure expression of general structures; thus Hegelians would categorize it as the unhappy consciousness, incarnation of a necessary moment in universal History, or interpreters like Tisseau would view it as a radical definition of faith, an appeal by a true Christian addressed to all Christians.

The other error would be to deem his work a simple effect or translation of original chance occurrences: this is what I would call psychoanalytical scepticism. Such a scepticism is founded on the fact that the *whole* of Kierkegaard's *childhood* is present in his work and forms the basis of its singularity, and that in a sense, there is nothing more in the books he wrote than the life he instituted. Søren's works are rich in Freudian symbols, it is true, and a psycho-analytical *reading* of his texts is quite possible. The same holds good for what I would call sceptical Marxism, that is to say bad Marxism. Although its truth here is mediate, there is no doubt that Kierkegaard was radically conditioned by his historical environment: his disdain for the masses, and aristocratic demeanour, his attitude to money, leave no trace of doubt as to his social origins or his political position (for example his liking for absolute monarchy), which, though well concealed, surface time after time and obviously form the basis of his ethical and religious opinions.

But this is the point: Kierkegaard teaches us that the Self, action and creation, with their dark side and light side, are absolutely irreducible to the one or to the other. The shadow is wholly in the light because it is *instituted*: it is true that every act and every text expresses the whole of the Self, but this is because the Self-as-institution is homogeneous with action-as-legislator. It is impossible to make the general conditions the *basis of it*: this would be to forget that they are general in a "world-historical" sense—for example the relations of production in Denmark in 1830—but that they are lived as non-significant chance by each individual, who is inserted in them fortuitously. By virtue of the fact that the individual expresses the universal in singular terms, he singularizes the whole of History which becomes at once *necessity*, through the very way in which objective situations take charge of themselves, and *adventure*, because History is forever the general experienced and instituted as a particularity which at first is non-signifying.

In this way the individual becomes a singular universal by virtue of the presence within himself of agents defined as universalizing singularities. But conversely, the side in shadow is already in light because the same individual is the moment of interiorization of exterior contingency. Without this pre-instituting unity, the person could lapse into scattered disorder; too frequently psychoanalysis reduces meaning to non-meaning because it refuses to acknowledge that dialectical stages are irreducible. But Kierkegaard was perhaps the first to show that the universal enters History as a singular, in so far as the singular institutes itself in it as a universal. In this novel form of historiality we encounter paradox once again: here it acquires the insurpassable appearance of ambiguity.

But as we have seen, the *theoretical* aspect of his work, in the case of Kierkegaard, is pure illusion. When we *encounter* his words, they immediately invite us to another use of language, that is to say of our own words, since they are the same as his. Kierkegaard's terms refer to what are now called, in accordance with his precepts, the "categories" of existence. But these categories are neither principles nor concepts nor the elements of concepts: they appear as lived relationships to a totality, attainable by starting with the words and following their trajectory back from speech to speaker. This means that not a single one of these verbal alliances is *intelligible*, but that they constitute, by their very negation of any effort to know them, a reference back to the foundations of such an effort. Kierkegaard made use of irony, humour, myth and non-signifying sentences in order to communicate indirectly with us. This means that if one adopts the traditional attitude of a reader to his books, their words engender a series of pseudo-concepts which are organized under our eyes into false knowledge. But this false knowledge denounces itself as false at the very moment of its formation. Or rather it is constituted as knowledge of something which pretends to be an object but in fact cannot be other than a subject. Kierkegaard made *regressive* use of objective and objectifying ensembles in such a way that the self-destruction of the language necessarily unmasked he who employed it. In this way the surrealists were later to think that they could unmask being by lighting fires in language. But being was still, they believed, *in front of their eyes*; if the words—whatever they were—were burned, being would be unveiled to infinite desire as a surreality, something which was also ultimately a non-conceptual sur-objectivity. Kierkegaard by contrast constructed his language in such a way as to reveal within his false knowledge certain lines of force which allowed the possibility of a return from the pesudo-object to the subject. He invented regressive enigmas. His verbal edifices were rigorously logical. But the very abuse of this logic always gave rise to contradictions or indeterminacies which implied a complete reversal of our own perspective. For example, as Jean Wahl has pointed out, even the title *The Concept of Dread* is a provocation. For in Kierkegaard's terms dread could never be the object of a concept. To a certain extent, in so far as dread is the source of a free and temporalizing choice of finitude, it is the non-conceptual foundation of all concepts. And each of us ought to be able to understand that the word "dread" is a universalization of the singular, and hence a false concept, since it awakens universality in us to the very extent that it refers to the Unique, its foundation.

It is by turning his words upside down that one can understand Kierkegaard in his lived and now vanished singularity, that is to say in his instituted contingency. His finitude, excluded, corrupted and ineffective, victim of the curse that he believed his father had brought on the whole family, could be described as impotence and as alterity. He is *other* than *all* others, other than himself, other than what he writes. He institutes his particularity by his free choice to be singular, that is to say he establishes himself at that ambiguous moment when interiorization, pregnant with future exteriorization, suppresses itself so that the latter may be born. Kierkegaard, who was afraid of being alienated by inscribing himself in the transcendence of the world, opted for identification with this dialectical stage, the perfect *locus of the secret*. Of course, he could not refrain from exteriorizing himself, as interiorization can only be objectification. Yet he did his best to prevent his objectification from defining him as an object of knowledge, in other words to ensure that the inscription of his person in the realm of reality, far from condensing him into the unity of ongoing History, should remain *as such* indecipherable, and refer back to the inaccessible secret of interiority. He performs brilliantly at a social function, laughing and making others laugh, and then notes in his journal that he wishes he could die. He could make people laugh because he wanted to die, and he wanted to die because he made people laugh. In this way his exteriority—a sparkling wit—was deprived of meaning, *unless* it is to be seen as the intentional contestation of every action reduced to its objective result, *unless* the *meaning* of any manifestation is not precisely incompletion, non-being, non-signification, forcing he who wishes to decipher it to return to its inaccessible source, interiority. Kierkegaard instituted his accidents by choosing to become the knight of subjectivity.

Now that he is dead, Søren takes his place in knowledge as a bourgeois who came to Denmark in the first half of the last century, and was conditioned by a specific family situation, itself an expression of the movement of history in its generality. But he takes his place in knowledge as unintelligible, as a disqualification of knowledge as a virulent lacuna, that eludes conceptualization and consequently death. We have now gone full circle and can reconsider our initial question. We asked what it was that prevented the late Kierkegaard from becoming the object of knowledge? The answer is that he was not such while he was alive. Kierkegaard reveals to us that death, which we took to be the metamorphosis of existence into knowledge, radically *abolishes* the subjective, but does not change it. If Kierkegaard, in the first instance, can appear to be an assemblage of items of knowledge, the reason is that the *known* is not contested in any immediate fashion by *lived experience*. But at the next moment it is knowledge which radically contests itself in the pseudo-object that this dead man is to us. It discovers its own limits as the object of study, impotent to become an autonomous determination of the exterior, escapes it.

The paradox, at this level, can be seen in a new light: can the contestation of knowledge by itself be surpassed? Can it be surpassed in the face of the living being who bears witness to his secret? Can it be surpassed when this living being has utterly disappeared? To these questions, Kierkegaard has but one reply, and it is always the same: the regression from signified to signifier cannot be the object of any act of intellection. Nevertheless, we can grasp the signifier in its real presence through what Kierkegaard calls *comprehension*. But the knight of subjectivity does not define comprehension, and does not conceive it as a new action. However, through his work, he offers his life to us *to be comprehended*. We encounter it in 1964, in History, fashioned as an *appeal to our comprehension*.

But is there anything left to be understood if death is utter abolition? Kierkegaard replied to this with his theory of "contemporaneity." In relation to the dead man Søren, there remains one thing to be understood, and that is ourselves. Søren, alive in his death, is a paradox for us: but Søren had already himself encountered the same paradox in relating to Jesus, in starting from Adam. And his first solution was to say that one comprehends what one becomes. To comprehend Adam is to become Adam. And certainly if an individual cannot become Christ, at least he can comprehend his unintelligible message without any temporal mediation by becoming the man to whom this message was destined—by becoming a Christian. Thus Kierkegaard lives on if it is possible for us to become Kierkegaard or if, conversely, this dead man is ceaselessly instituted by the living—borrowing their life, flowing into their life, and nourishing his singularity with our own. Or if, in other words, he appears at the heart of knowledge as the perpetual denouncer, in each of us, of non-knowledge, of the dialectical stage in which interiorization turns into exteriorization; in short, of existence.

Yes, says Kierkegaard; you may become myself because I may become Adam. Subjective thought is the reflective grasp of my being-an-event, of the adventure that I am and which necessarily ends in my becoming Adam—that is, in recommencing original sin in the very movement of my temporalization. Sin in this case is choice. Every man is at once himself and Adam renewed, precisely to the extent that Kierkegaard was at once himself and his father, the blasphemer whose blasphemy he took upon himself through his own sin. Every sin is singular in so far as it institutes, in particular conditions, a unique individual and, at the same time, it is sin in general in so far as it is the choice of finitude and blasphemous defiance of God. In this way the universality of sin is contained in the singularity of choice. By virtue of it, every man always becomes all man. Each individual moves History forward by recommencing it, as well as by prefiguring within himself new beginnings yet to come. From this point of view, if Kierkegaard could become Adam, it was because Adam was already at the heart of his sinful existence the premonition of a future Kierkegaard. If I can become Kierkegaard it is because Kierkegaard was in his being already a premonition of us all.

If we take up the question again in the initial terms in which we posed it, it comes to this: Kierkegaard's words are our words. To the extent that, within the framework of knowledge, they are changed into non-knowledge and are referred back via the paradox from the signified to the signifier, we are the signifier they regressively disclose. Reading Kierkegaard I reascend back to myself; I seek to grasp Kierkegaard and it is myself I hold; his non-conceptual work is an invitation to understand myself as the source of all concepts. Thus the knowledge of death, by discovering its own limits, does not issue into sheer absence, but comes back to Kierkegaard. I discover myself as an irreducible existent, that is to say as freedom that has become my necessity. I understand that the object of knowledge *is* his being in the peaceful mode of perennity and by the same token that I am a non-object because I have to be my being. In fact my being is a temporalizing and hence suffered choice—but the nature of this sufferance is to be *freely* suffered, and thus to be sustained as a choice.

Kierkegaard is restored as my adventure not in his unique meaning but at the level of my being-as-adventurer, in so far as I have to be the event that happens to me from outside. In so far as History, universalized by things— the bearers of the seal of our action—becomes, through each new birth of man, a singular adventure within which it enfolds its universality, Søren could continue to live after his death as my forerunner before birth, when I begin anew in different historical conditions. Curiously, this relationship of reciprocal interiority and immanence between Kierkegaard and each of us is established, not in the relativity of circumstances, but rather at the very level where each of us is an incomparable absolute. And what can demonstrate to us the reality that is common to all and yet in each case is singular, but words? Words are signs turned back on themselves, tools of indirect communication referring me to myself because they refer uniquely to him.

Kierkegaard lives on because, by rejecting knowledge, he reveals the transhistorical contemporaneity of the dead and the living. In other words, he unmasks the fact that every man is all man as a singular universal or, if you like, because he shows temporalization, in opposition to Hegel, to be a trans-historical dimension of History. Humanity loses its dead and begins them absolutely anew once more in its living. Kierkegaard is not myself, how-ever—I am an atheist. Nor is he the Christian who will reproach him tomor-row for his negative theology. Let us say that he was, in his own time, a unique *subject*. Once dead he can be revived only by becoming a *multiple subject*, that is to say an inner bond linking our singularities. Each of us *is* Søren in our capacity as adventure. And each of our interpretations, contesting the others, nevertheless subsumes them as its negative depth. Just as each of them, conversely, is contested but subsumed by the others to the extent that, refus-ing to see in it a complete reality or knowledge concerning reality, they con-ceive of its possibility by referring to the susceptibility of Kierkegaard to several different interpretations: in fact, divergence, contradiction and ambi-guity are precisely the determinate qualifications of existence. Thus it is today's Other, my real contemporary, who is the foundation of Kierkegaard's profundity, his way of remaining *other* within myself, without ceasing to be mine. Conversely he is, in each of us, the denunciation of ambiguity in himself and in others. Kierkegaard, comprehensible in the name of each ambiguity, is our link, a multiple and ambiguous existential relation between existent contemporaries, themselves lived ambivalences. He remains within History as a transhistorical relation between contemporaries grasped in their singular historiality. Within each of us he offers and refuses himself, as he did in his own lifetime; he is my adventure and remains, for others, Kierkegaard, the other—a figure on the horizon testifying to the Christian that faith is a future development forever imperilled, testifying to myself that the process of *becoming-an-atheist* is a long and difficult enterprise, an absolute relationship to these two infinites, man and the universe.

Every enterprise, even one brought to a triumphant conclusion, remains a *failure*, that is to say an incompletion to be completed. It lives on because it is open. The particular failure, in Kierkegaard's case, is clear. Kierkegaard demonstrated his historicity but failed to find History. Pitting himself against Hegel, he occupied himself over-exclusively with transmitting his instituted contingency to the human adventure and, because of this, he neglected *praxis*, which is rationality. At a stroke, he denatured *knowledge*, forgetting that the world we know is the world we make. Anchorage is a fortuitous event, but the possibility and rational meaning of this chance is given by general structures of envelopment which found it and which are themselves the universalization of singular adventures by the materiality in which they are inscribed.

Kierkegaard is alive in his death in as much as he affirms the irreducible singularity of every man to the History which nevertheless conditions him rigorously. He is dead, within the very life that he continues to lead within ourselves, in as much as he remains an inert interrogation, an open circle that demands to be closed by us. Others, in his own time or shortly thereafter, went further than him and completed the circle by writing: "Men make history on the basis of prior circumstances." In these words there is and is not progress beyond Kierkegaard: for this circularity remains abstract and risks excluding the human singularity of the concrete universal, so long as it does not integrate Kierkegaardian immanence within the historical dialectic. Kierkegaard and Marx: these living-dead men condition our anchorage and institute themselves, now vanished, as our future, as the tasks that await us. How can we conceive of History and the transhistorical in such a way as to restore to the transcendent necessity of the historical process and to the free immanence of a historicization ceaselessly renewed, their full reality and reciprocal interiority, in theory and practice? In short, how can we discover the singularity of the universal and the universalization of the singular, in each conjuncture, as indissolubly linked to each other?

BERTEL PEDERSEN

Fictionality and Authority:
A Point of View for
Kierkegaard's Work as an Author

Toward the end of *Repetition* (1843) Constantin Constantius writes, in a critical letter to "the real reader of this book," a passage in which the whole preceding fiction is questioned:

> I think, then, that it might well be worth the trouble to let such a [poet] exist [*blive til*]. The young man, whom I have let exist, he is a poet. More I cannot do, since at the most I can get so far that I can think a poet and through my thought bring him forth; I cannot become a poet myself, as my interest also lies in another area. My task has occupied me purely aesthetically and psychologically. I have included myself [*anbragt mig selv med*], but when you, my dear reader! Look closer you will easily see that I am merely a serving spirit [*Aand*] and far from being, what the young man fears, indifferent toward him. This was a misunderstanding which I have caused, in order to bring him out in this way as well. Each movement I have made is merely to illuminate him; I have constantly had him in mind, every word by me is either ventriloquism or said in relation to him.... For that reason all movements take place in a purely lyrical manner, and what I say one must understand darkly in him, or by what I say one must better understand him. Thus I have done for him what I could, *just as I now attempt to serve you, dear reader, by being still another.*

From *MLN* 89, no. 6 (December 1974). © 1974 by The Johns Hopkins University Press, Baltimore/London.

We see here an unusual complication of the assumptions that generally govern our ideas about fiction. A fiction normally supports itself by means of reference to a geographical/historical set of exterior circumstances. In this particular case we have a curious relationship between two characters and narrators. Constantin and the Young Man, who have been interacting and exchanging communications in a well-defined "reality" that stretches from Copenhagen to Berlin. But now we suddenly discover that all previous formations and movements have been held in a very deliberate state of illusion. In this letter to the real (*virkelige*) reader—who is then immediately called a "poetic person(ality)" ("you [are] actually a poetic personality"—we learn that the young man is a psychological experiment, created by and within the consciousness of Constantin. This in itself is not an unusual practice—pointing out the fictionality of a text, ironically destroying its governing assumptions, or laying bare a given procedure—especially if we place *Repetition* against the background of the writings of Fr. Schlegel, Tieck, and other German Romantics who are important for an understanding of Kierkegaard. Such procedures are frequently used to invoke a supreme fiction which far transcends traditional and more "naive" modes of writing, both in its ironic play between the construction and destruction of patterns of meaning and in its deliberately arabesque and self-commentating organization (and *Repetition* certainly partakes of this characteristic). But Constantin goes further; he includes and changes himself and not merely the status of his characters in the fiction when he writes, "I have included myself; but when you, my dear reader! look closer, you will easily see that I am only a serving spirit." Constantin, the narrator, has in fact employed a purely strategic "personality" because of the young man and, what is more important, because of the reader. "Thus I have done for him what I could, just as I now attempt to serve you, dear reader, by being still another."

In this last illusionist's trick we see Constantin dissolve and change completely, forcing the reader—here a very real and necessary part of the text—out of the fiction, back upon himself and his own resources. The play upon fictionality and modes of writing is therefore radically different from the German writers just mentioned, for whom the text and its ironical play are sufficient ends in themselves. For Kierkegaard sees such moves as part of an attempt to go beyond any fiction in the name of a pedagogic task, or perhaps even *Truth*. The very fact that the pseudonym functions as an "author" who negates both openly and by implication his central authority over the text, as well as the structure of the text itself (*Repetition* is a most imperfect demonstration of its own central concept and its significance), both tend to support this textual movement.

Such writing procedures are most frequently discussed within the limits of Kierkegaard's own theories of communication, more specifically in terms of what he calls "indirect communications." But when we invoke Kierkegaard and accept his later explanations, most extensively set forth in *The Point of View for My Work as an Author* [*POV*] (written 1848, published posthumously 1859), we should be well aware of the dangers. In the extremely ironical structure of *Repetition* and the other texts we do not merely have the textual procedures negated, as we already saw in Constantin's letter, but the negations themselves are ironical, for these "breaks of illusion" purporting to be "explanations" always threaten to lead to new illusions and entrapments. We should hardly read Kierkegaard himself less ironically than we do his pseudonyms. His own set of ground rules, laid out in the texts and in their extensive commentaries (either by other, later pseudonyms or by Kierkegaard himself), only lead us to a critical problem similar to the one that Erich Heller discusses in connection with Thomas Mann's *Doktor Faustus:* "There is no critical thought which the books do not think *about themselves* . . . it has made criticism either too easy or impossible and maneuvered the critic into a position where he is bound to plagiarize the object of his critique." It is this difficulty which accounts in part for the tendency in the critical literature on Kierkegaard to rely on the paraphrase or to extend and repeat the values and assumptions which Kierkegaard himself outlines in his reflections on earlier texts.

Another difficulty arises when we take into account the unique character of Kierkegaard's Authorship: it consists of the pseudonymous texts (1843–48), the religious edifying discourses published in his own name and running concurrently with the pseudonyms, various polemics in newspapers and periodicals (the feud with *Corsaren* and later with the Danish Church establishment), and finally the twenty volumes of *Papirer* which he left unpublished at his death. Considering this variety of genres or modes it is hardly surprising that Kierkegaard can be, and has been, put to many uses. But regardless of which position a critic takes on Kierkegaard he is bound to encounter contradictions in other Kierkegaard texts, because several of these, particularly the pseudonymous series, embody principles of contradiction which refuse to be mediated. In the case of Kierkegaard the *locus* of any utterance is of primary importance, and before accepting and relying upon it, the critic ought to unfold the implications of its status. If the statement is pseudonymous, who has authorized it and how is it situated strategically? If it carries Kierkegaard's own name, is it a published or an unpublished statement?

Therefore, rather than entering into any internal Kierkegaard debate by participating in the hermeneutic attempt to determine what Kierkegaard really means, this essay will attempt to outline under what conditions the writing (and hence its "meaning") takes place. It assumes that the more interesting (that is formally significant) works are pseudonymous and that Kierkegaard's own explanations of his writings exhibit the critical polarities of blindness and insight which Paul de Man has discussed. The problem, then, is to investigate the genre of these texts and to "deconstruct" Kierkegaard's own explanations and theories of writing in an attempt to gain a critical perspective not defined in Kierkegaardian terms.

The movement toward "authorial" effacement in *Repetition*, with which we began, is not an isolated instance in Kierkegaard but is part of a pattern found from the first textual arrangements to the last (or what he provisionally thought was the conclusion of his work as an author)—from *Either/Or* (1843), with its system of editor and main and sub authors (A, Johannes the Seducer, and B, the minister from Jutland), to Johannes Climacus' *Concluding Unscientific Postscript* (CUP) (1846). In each of these pseudonymous texts, there are several explicit or implicit references by its "author" to previous pseudonyms, most extensively in Climacus' long essay "A Glance at a Contemporary Effort in Danish Literature" in *CUP*. It is characteristic that all these discussions are conducted from the position of a reader: "Whether my perception of the pseudonymous authors corresponds to what they themselves have intended I cannot decide, since I am merely a reader . . . but that they have a relation to my thesis is clear enough." This is, in a sense, a consequence of accepting and extending the fiction, that Climacus enters into a dialogue with earlier pseudonyms as their reader and critic (and the situation outside the fiction is not without irony when we take into account that with minor exceptions, notably "Diary of the Seducer" from *Either/Or*, the pseudonymous texts had been largely ignored or, at best, thoroughly misunderstood by the contemporary Danish critics). But when Kierkegaard comments upon the pseudonyms in a "direct" explanation in his own name in *My Activity as a Writer* (written 1849, published 1851 as a pamphlet), he maintains the same position. "I prefer to consider myself as a *Reader* of the books, not as an *Author*." Before then Kierkegaard had already acknowledged himself responsible for the pseudonymous texts in an appendix to *CUP* (which also had Søren Kierkegaard on the title page as editor). "A First and Last Explanation" is in fact the second part of the appendix and follows Climacus' comment which "recalls" this book in full understanding with an "imagined reader." We find here that Kierkegaard's formal acknowledgment of the whole series paradoxically supports his own separation from them.

From my reader, if I dare speak about such a person, I would request a forgetful memory *en passant*, a sign that it is I he remembers, because he remembers me as irrelevant to the books, demanded by the relation, just as the appreciation for this is offered sincerely here at this moment of parting, when in addition I am obliged to thank everyone who has been silent, and with deep veneration the firm Kts [Bishop Mynster's journalistic signature]—that it has spoken.

On the other hand Kierkegaard writes in his *Papirer* that it would be overstepping his given limits to publish any "explanation," which did not prevent him from publishing *My Activity as a Writer* two years later while he kept his *POV* out of public sight. So again we confront these contradictions between the various texts as well as the problematics of status.

Given these circumstances, it is easiest to describe negatively some of the rules which the various texts already mentioned utilize. Kierkegaard's own "explanations" are all anti-biographical and indicate the difference between the existence ("I," Kierkegaard) and the writings, rather than any "beautiful correspondence with the affairs of the excellent [person]." Even the most explicit and pathetic—hence, perhaps, unpublished—biographical text, *POV*, merely introduces biographical material (often in the form of hidden riddles under the names of Guidance and *Factum*) to support a given reading/writing of the published works. Thus, in the first (and last) explanation we read:

My pseudonymity or polynymity has not had an *accidental* reason in my *personality* (certainly not out of fear of punishment by the laws, concerning which I am not aware of having violated anything, and the publisher, as well as censor *qua* official, has always been informed at the time of publication who the author was), but [is] an *essential* in the *production* [*Frembringelsen*] itself, which required, because of the psychologically varied individuality-difference, that ruthlessness in good and evil, in dejection and exuberance, in despair and arrogance, in suffering and exultation, etc., which is limited ideally only by the psychological consequences which no actual, real person within the limitation(s) of reality dare allow himself or might wish to allow himself. Thus the written [material] is surely mine, but only to the extent that I have put into the mouth of the producing individuality, who is poetically real, the *Weltanschauung* by means of the audibility of

his lines [*Replikkens Hørlighed*]. For my relationship is more
external than that of the *author* who creates persons and who
himself is the author in the relationship. I am impersonally or per-
sonally in the third person a *souffleur* who poetically has produced *authors* whose prefaces, yes even their names, in their turn
are their own production. Thus there is not in the pseudonymous
books a single word by me, myself; I have no opinion regarding
them except as a third person, no knowledge of their significance
except as a reader, not the slightest private relationship to them,
since this is impossible in a doubly-reflected communication.

Such a description of the conditions governing the writing of the pseudonymous works is perhaps less puzzling to a late twentieth-century reader,
who can draw upon a rather large and differentiated corpus of theories of
writing, than it must surely have been to our "imagined reader" of 1850. But
the problem is further complicated by the important strategy of mystification
which we find in the texts: revealing by hiding, hiding by revealing. In this
quotation, Kierkegaard first moves his explanation from an accidental biographical set of circumstances to an essential condition for the production.
Then the mode of production is distinguished from other writing projects by
introducing a distancing agency to the second degree ("a doubly-reflected
communication"). The situation in which the "explanation" takes place is
one which has become increasingly popular in modern criticism: writing as
theater. But it is significant that in this theater Kierkegaard does not see himself as the powerful director (the omniscient author), but as a *souffleur* who
remains invisible and inaudible to the audience and who, at most, assists the
actors (who, in their turn, are authors) to perform. But whose is the script?
Not Kierkegaard's apparently. This kind of writing, this script, effectively
hides and obliterates any connection between the writing "self" and the written, in contrast to "ordinary" fiction in which we can establish such an interpretative relationship between self and text, what Kierkegaard's one-page
letter calls "a beautiful [*skjøn*] correspondence"—*skjøn*, here, having definite literary connotations.

We have then, on the one hand, a certain kind of writing in which a
biographical relationship can be established, or rather, in which the simple
transformation of "I" into "he" and "she" is contained within the consciousness of the writer: he has authorized his characters in the fiction and under-
written them in or through his "preface." Goethe provides a good example
of such literary procedures. In his narrative and dramatic works we find sym-

pathetic bonds extending from author to characters and, through the fiction, involving the reader in a process of integration and development. It is one of the assumptions in the *Bildungsroman* that an ordinary young man can gradually learn to incorporate and mediate the conflicts which he encounters during his *Lehrjahre*. It is by no means a guarantee that the integration is successful, and a certain awareness of the irony involved in such an assumption might well be present in the text, but in spite of, or behind, such problems remains an awareness of *Bildung*—a process of resolving conflicts, overcoming oppositions, or coming to terms with desires. Such structures or processes are often considered in a psychobiographical context: it is the author's *Bildung*, too, which is at stake in his novel.

Thus, Edith Kern summarizes Kierkegaard's admiration for Goethe: "it is not surprising that Kierkegaard greatly admired Goethe for his ability to establish not merely an external relationship to his work but to make each of his poetic productions a moment in his own development. Kierkegaard considered Goethe's achievement to be a result of 'mastered irony.'" But it is important to add that in spite of his admiration Kierkegaard writes in terms radically different from those of Goethe (and other authors working toward a "beautiful correspondence"). In contrast to this mode of writing, his fictional texts bring a much more complex series of transformations into play, going through an "impersonal" distancing which in its turn produces the "persona" that allows for a certain text. Here we see clearly how the writing self, through the writing process, becomes another. Kierkegaard is thus, from our perspective, quite consistent when he claims his own relationship to the texts is that of a reader or secretary since this claim guarantees the otherness of the other and constitutes the autonomy of the persona.

As soon as the "otherness" of the pseudonym is established, however, we find an additional difficulty at work. For example, the "author" of *Repetition* disrupts his fiction at the end by dissolving his identity as narrator (as we already saw in Constantin's letter), and although *Repetition* is the clearest example of this movement, we find similar operations, which "dissolve" or qualify the text, in the prefaces and postscripts to the other pseudonymous works. The effect of this method is to remove each text further from the writer who wrote it, emphasizing a distance as well as an ironical structure and status. In *POV*, under the general concept of "deceit," Kierkegaard discusses and comments on this problem of the function of the pseudonymous fictions which he had published. (And it is worth noting that here he is less clearly positioning himself as a reader of the books than as someone who can certify their significance.)

> But from the complete viewpoint of the entire author-activity, the aesthetic productivity is a deceit, and in this [lies] the deeper significance of the "Pseudonymity." However, a deceit is something nasty. To this I would answer: do not be deceived by the word "deceit." One can deceive a person for [the sake of] truth, or one can, recalling old Socrates, deceive a person into truth. Yes, fundamentally one can only in this manner bring a person who is in [a state of] illusion into the truth by deceiving him.

This shifting of perspective from that of reader without a privileged position to that of privileged author is one of the difficulties in *POV*. It brings into focus two of the levels of description in the text: one at which the rules and conditions for the individual texts are discussed, and another at which the total design, the significance of the entire production, is explained. But if we take seriously the first position, that an author can only discuss his texts as a reader—which means, in fact, that we accept the distance or otherness of the text—we must be suspicious of this second level in *POV* and read it, perhaps, more as another fiction than as a direct explanation. It may "explain" a good deal in the pseudonymous texts, but at the same time it involves a Kierke-gaardian myth of writing, his (self-) justification and *apologia sua vita* in and through the act of writing, guided (quite literally or scripturally) by "God." Kierkegaard's refusal to publish this text, which at moments approaches the pathetic or pathological in its explanation, might well indicate his own awareness of the "theoretical" difficulties involved. The short pamphlet *My Activity as a Writer,* which he did publish, avoids or reduces the explanatory fiction.

However, the reference to Socrates and the maieutic method is rather interesting and goes far beyond the status which Kierkegaard's argument suggests. An entire genre and a tradition are involved here (aside from any Idealistic *philosopheme*), that of the literary anatomy or Menippean satire. With slight reservations, it is possible to inscribe Kierkegaard's pseudonymous texts in this tradition, which also includes Plato's *Symposium* and (elements of) a number of other dialogues. Certainly it would not be too difficult to demonstrate the applicability of Frye's descriptions of the anatomy to Kierkegaard's texts. In fact, Frye refers to both *Either/Or* and *Repetition* in his discussion of the genre, and his observation—"At its most concentrated the Menippean satire presents us with a vision of the world in terms of a single intellectual pattern. The intellectual structure built up from the story makes for violent dislocations in the customary logic of narrative"—is a particularly apt formula for *Repetition,* where this concept is brought into play in an astonishingly large number of ways, from cryptic philosophical polemics to parodic anecdotes.

But the anatomy is such a diffuse genre that a formal description or definition *per se* might be of very limited use. Rather more useful would be the attempt to see its *écriture* as possessing a polemical orientation toward other forms, whether literary or philosophical, which it tries to oppose or displace. In this context Bakhtin's studies of Dostoevsky and Rabelais are important, for aside from specific problems of genre in the most limited sense, Bakhtin sees exemplified in the Menippean satire a general problem of transforming and transcending other established norms into what he describes as a polyphonic or dialogic ambivalence. The concept of the dialogic or polyphonic word (*slovo*—in her introduction to the French translation of the Dostoevsky study, Kristeva suggests the double translation *mot/discours*) is developed by Bakhtin in an attempt to outline a typology of prose discourses and is opposed to the monologic word. In a very schematic form we can summarize his discussion by saying that in a monologic discourse we find a single dominant voice; the word is either directly oriented toward its object or is an expression of a single intent or point of view ("en tant qu'expression de la dernière instance interprétative du locuteur"). Thus, in a monologic novel we might well find dialogues, reflections, and conflicts between characters, but these words are all ultimately directed by or contained within the consciousness of the Author. Bakhtin's examples of these types are found in the tradition of the novel particularly represented by Tolstoy, and these procedures correspond, in our discussion of Kierkegaard's distinctions, to the "beautiful" mode of writing for which we have offered Goethe as a possible example. Similarly, the discourse in (Hegelian) dialectic can be characterized as monologic since each "opposing view," each antithesis, is merely a negative moment which will be relieved in the process of mediation. In contrast and opposition we find the dialogic discourse with a "mot orienté sur le mot d'autrui (mot bivocal)," which is characteristic of Dostoevsky and, we might add, of Kierkegaard.

There seem to be at least two major elements in the dialogic discourse. It implies an awareness of the integral function of the reader in a text, and it incorporates, with domination, an Other discourse. Hence, it is particularly appropriate to describe the strategies of such writing as intertextual, since each text is a reading/writing of another. In her essay on Bakhtin, Kristeva suggests that intertexuality is the condition of any text; monologic discourse merely suppresses or limits the other voice: "le mot (le texte) est un croisement de mots (de textes) où on lit au moins un autre mot (texte). Chez Bakhtine d'ailleurs, ces deux axes, qu'il appelle respectivement *dialogue* et ambivalence, ne sont pas clairement distingués. Mais ce manque de rigueur est plutôt une découverte que Bakhtine est le premier à introduire dans la théorie littéraire: tout texte se construit comme mosaïque de citations, tout texte est absorption et transformation d'un autre texte." The term "inter-textuality" cannot, therefore, be translated into the traditional problem of "sources" and "influences," but indicates a decisive shift in the critical approach from a psychological orientation (in which the writing easily becomes an *indicium* of authorial intentions and Meaning) to an examination of textual elements in their functions (in which the sense of dominant Meaning is surmounted).

A "word" (and, by amplification, a text) is always written into a given place and context: it is (re)structuration of other texts and rules, involving both writer and reader at a given time. Kierkegaard is well aware of these circumstances, as he always insists upon the reader as a necessary element in the situation of communication. Bakhtin, writing in an explicitly revolutionary context, tends to emphasize the historical conditions in which the importance of the dialogic becomes the refusal to submit to one single, dominant ideological system, and he sees Dostoevsky's writing as a confrontation of equally strong opposing forces which are not centrally controlled. Kierkegaard, on the other hand, is at pains to find a dimension outside and above the historical/political where his communication can find its proper place. He attempts, therefore, to oppose his ideal "reader" as "the individual" (*"hiin enkelte"*) to "the crowd" or "the masses" (*"mængden"*).

> For "masses" is the untruth [*Usandheden*]. Eternally, in godly and Christian terms, it holds, as Paul says, that "only one attains the goal," not in a comparative sense, since in the comparison "the others" are included.
>
> "The masses" is to be understood as a purely formal definition of the concept, not as what otherwise is understood by "the masses" when it apparently shall be a qualification as well, insofar as human selfishness, in an irreligious manner, divides human beings into "the masses" and the nobility . . . No, "the masses" is the number, the numerical, a *Numerus* of nobles, millionaires, grand dignitaries, etc.—as soon as it is a matter of action in accord with the numerical, it is "masses," "the masses."

We see here that "the masses" is not primarily a concept written into a class structure but rather the lack of a necessary dimension in the act of communication. If we compare this description of "the masses" with a passage on the press, where Kierkegaard indicates his opposition to the anonymity of the writing in newspapers—"That the press—representing the abstract impersonal communication, especially the daily press, purely formally disregarding whether it is true or false, what it states—contributes enormously to demoralizing, because everything impersonal, which is also more or less irresponsible and unrepenting, is demoralizing; that anonymity, the highest expression for abstraction, impersonality, unrepentance, irresponsibility, is a basic source of modern demoralization"—we see again that Kierkegaard's writing is opposed to a situation in which the individuality of the reader, as well as that of the writer, is disregarded. What Kierkegaard writes against, then, is the mode of discourse which Bakhtin calls monologic and which sets forth a single anonymous point of view in order to dominate the field. In fact, it would be possible to discuss Kierkegaard's concept of public morality as one particular kind of monologic textual circulation which attempts to swallow up all differences. The counterproposal in his *mode* of writing is an insistence upon the necessity of the reader as an individual, and upon the text as an arena, a place of confrontation, without mediation, for different values and points of view.

This, of course, does not make a revolutionary (in Bakhtin's terms) of "the individual." Kierkegaard's descriptions designate a religious dimension which makes possible this other mode of apprehension opposed to the anonymous (monologic). And his concept of truth is written into the same complex where it first finds its *locus* in the individually qualified reader (a qualification guaranteed and controlled by "God").

> The truth can neither be communicated nor received except as it were in front of God's eyes, not without God's help, not without God going along, who is the middle term [*Mellembestemmelsen*], just as he is truth. It can therefore only be communicated or received by the individual [*den Enkelte*], who for that matter could be each and every human being alive. The definition is simply that of truth in contrast to the abstract, phantastic, impersonal, "masses"—"public" which excludes God as a middle term (the *personal* God cannot be the middle term in an *impersonal* relationship), thereby also [excludes] the truth, for God is the truth and the middle term.

If we translate this argument into our language of communication theory, it is clear that "God" is the instance, the guarantee, which limits "noise" and makes "proper" communication possible. As well as enforcing and guaranteeing certain codes, "God" excludes others.

One might object that this "dialogic modality," which brings writer and reader together in the act of communication without domination, is merely a relative element in the total design of Kierkegaard's writings, a necessary and deliberate strategy to force the reader "to become aware" ("*blive opmærksom*"—a frequent phrase in *POV*); that behind the dialectical movements of the individual texts, we find Kierkegaard in central control. But such objections ignore the fact that there are several contradictions in the texts (as well as in individual explanations) which fail to cohere for, or "guide," the reader, and they pre-suppose that Kierkegaard's explanation in *POV* is an accurate description, a critical deconstruction of his own previous texts. However, a more careful reading of this text will reveal its dominant theme as another fiction whose fictionality is perhaps most clearly visible in the description of the very neat and amazingly symmetrical relationship between the aesthetic and edifying productions, between his "life" and "work" with their proper tragicocomical reversals (see especially part 1 and chapter 2 of part 2 in *POV*). The text exhibits all the traditional literary entrapments of a confession and the fictions of an autobiography. But more important, such objections ignore the initial set of writing conditions which Kierkegaard had described in "A First and Last Explanation" and which are still evident, though weakened, in *POV*. If Kierkegaard's first description of his own separation from the text is accurate, he cannot be invoked as a primary source for their meaning—even if he later rewrote himself into the texts as their Author.

When Kierkegaard *post facto* reflects upon the production in ethical terms, as well as in terms of the writing conditions, he subordinates the first moral demands to the *écriture:* "The *production required* that ruthlessness in good and evil, in dejection and exuberance, in despair and arrogance, in suffering and exultation, etc., which is limited ideally only by the psychological consequences which no actual, real person within the limitation(s) of reality dare allow himself or might wish to allow himself" (my italics). Here is acknowledged what is required for the production (*Frembringelsen*), as well as what is permissible for the "actual, real person in reality." But in *POV* the problems of writing (which disregard otherwise binding restrictions within the polarity of Good and Evil, a polarity which in its turn controls other oppositions related to various modalities of "existence" from ecstasy to despair) are at times subordinated to existential concerns, even if the life seems to be justified only by and through writing. The correlation of the two spheres of life and writing, after their initial separation, then constitutes (or is constituted in) a fiction, a deceit which finally threatens to include Kierkegaard himself when he tries to account for his own life *in writing*. The two terms "writing" and "life" here tend to replace one another rapidly as nodal points: each presupposes the other as a "fiction."

Such "explanations" and "fictions" in the text can also be related to the second implication of a dialogic discourse, which involves the relationship of the text to other texts. Any notions of a *tabula rasa* upon which the text is immediately and unproblematically inscribed are very far from Kierkegaard's theories of writing. The act of writing always takes place in a given social-historical context (although Kierkegaard would like to see this situation outside the political sphere), so that rather than considering the new Kierkegaardian text as an addition, a "positive" act of communication, we must see it as a negation, written against other texts, trying to replace them and, if possible, destroy the illusions (*Sandsebedrag*) they have caused. Thus we find in *POV* Kierkegaard's ingenious argument against the given Christian state of affairs. His whole production, which he summarizes as dealing with one problem, "to become a Christian," can be seen as an attempt to destroy the assumption that *this* (his time and morality) is Christian, hence the Socratic, maieutic method—his production is another "deceit." "One can deceive a person for [the sake of] truth or one can, recalling old Socrates, deceive a person into truth." And he develops in the same paragraph a theory (and a justification) for these procedures by distinguishing between two possible receivers of a communication:

> One who is ignorant and is given knowledge, thus he is like an empty vessel to be filled or like the clean sheet to be written—and one who is in an illusion which first must be removed; likewise there is a difference between writing on a clean piece of paper—and by means of an acid bringing forth a writing [*Skrift—écriture*] hiding behind another writing. Now suppose that someone is in an illusion, thus properly understood the first [task] of the communication is to remove the illusion—if I do not begin by deceiving then I begin with direct communication. But direct communication presupposes, with regard to the receiver, everything is in order for the reception: but this is exactly not the case here, here an illusion is interfering [*til Hinder*]. That means here an acid must first be used, but this acid is the negative, but the negative in relation to communication is precisely deceit.

This passage is closely related to his conclusion in "A First and Last Explanation," in which he marks the "significance" of the completed pseudonymous works *in opposition* to other projects.

> The significance [of the pseudonyms] (regardless of what *in reality*
> it might be) does not, under any circumstances, lie in making any
> new proposal, any unheard-of discovery, or establishing a new
> party and going further, but precisely in the opposite, in wanting
> no significance, in wanting, from a distance which is the remote-
> ness of a double reflection, to read through, *solo*, the Ur-writing
> of the individual human existence-relationship—the old, well-
> known [writing] inherited from the fathers—one more time in a
> deeper [*inderligere*] manner if possible.

In this quotation the allusions are, as usual, condensed, but they do give a
clear sense of the displacement of other "texts." Thus the "new proposal"
and the call for a new (political) party refer to the political debates about a
parliamentary constitution which were "news" in Denmark in the 1840s; the
"unheard-of discovery" is a reference to N. F. S. Grundtvig, whose many loud
proclamations of a "marvelous discovery," based upon inspirational revela-
tions of the Living Word, Kierkegaard regarded with distrust (he refers on
occasion to Grundtvig as "The Living Word's Abracadabra"); and finally the
phrase "going further" identifies the Hegelians who were always "relieving"
problems.

    In contrast, Kierkegaard's own attempt or project can best be described
as a rediscovery of an Original Script inherited from the fathers (a sense of
the Tradition is clearly implied in his formulations). So while the tendencies
to which Kierkegaard's writing is opposed can be clearly identified and
described (and this passage is far from unique), the "positive" elements
remain unspecified except as the *qualification* of something given (but perhaps forgotten), as the process of making visible, in an act of submission, the
Writing (*Urskrift*) behind the writings. But this whole procedure of discovering another writing before and behind the visible *écriture* has become
highly problematical for us. What is there to guarantee that the *texte retrouvé*
does not give way to another (and another), or that the removal of one illusion is not merely its replacement by another? Although contemporary writing has accepted and is beginning to explore this limitless intertextual play,
Kierkegaard's texts are limited and regulated in their intertextuality by the
notions of "Guidance" ("*Styrelse*") and "God" (and in a suspicious reading
of Kierkegaard's own "explanations," we should take note that a third term
frequently appears at these moments: the father). We have now finally arrived
at a "center" in these texts which reconfirms Johannes Sløk's statement:
"[Kierkegaard's] Anthropologie hat ihr Zentrum in Gott, erst der Gottesbe-

griff verleiht den Bestimmungen einen Sinn." What applies to Kierkegaard's "anthropology" applies *ad fortiori* to his *écriture*. Whatever else "God" might be and mean in his texts (and Climacus, at least, has radically denied the possibility of any direct, immediate God-relationship through "authorized" texts, the Bible, or institutions, the Church), "God" is also an instance, a factor in the situation of communication, which regulates and guarantees Kierkegaard's whole writing project.

This is already evident in the "First and Last Explanation" in which "Guidance" is mentioned together with the father, but the theme is most completely written out in *POV* (in the chapter "The Part of Guidance in my Authorship"). In this chapter we can find the authorization for the preceding two chapters (which "explain" the significance of the whole writing project and its relationship to its author) and, by amplification, all that Kierkegaard had written. Again, he distinguishes between two modalities or conditions of writing when he discusses the possibilities for speaking about his relationship to God. The one is poetic, ecstatic—here we see the temptations of "the living word," writing as a *plenum* which calls for erotic imagery, fulfillment to the point of death—and it is prohibited.

> I wanted, more determined than the king who cried "my kingdom for a horse," and joyously determined as he was not, to give everything including my life in order to find what is more joyous for the thought to find than the lover the beloved: the "expression," and then die with this expression on my lips. And look, it is offered, the thoughts, as enchanting as the fruits in the garden of fairy tales, so rich, so warm, so intense; expressions so soothing to the need of gratitude in me, so cooling to the hot yearning—it seems to me as if I had a winged pen, yes had I ten, still I would not be able to follow in relation to the riches offered. But just as I take my pen in hand, at that moment I cannot move it, just as one speaks about not being able to move his foot; in this condition I do not get a line on the paper regarding this relationship.

Is there not indicated here a desire for mythologizing, even if in the service of God? One can, perhaps, see behind Kierkegaard's writing an awareness of Oehlenschläger's *Aladdin,* which has become in Danish literature the primary symbol of the integrated writer and text, made possible in and through a *Märchen.* But this desire is immediately checked, and at the moment of interdiction we find a reversal to the other (guided) writing. It is noteworthy that Kierkegaard describes the change as caused by a voice from the outside—

as an order or a compulsion which supports itself by an appeal to obedience (invoking Samuel 15:22). In the same transition the metaphors of "speech" and "voice" are replaced by those of "writing."

> And then I can do it, then I dare not do otherwise, then I write each word, each line almost ignorant of the next word and next line. And afterwards when I read through it, then it satisfies quite differently. For even if it were the case that some glowing expression escaped me, the production [of it] is another, is not that of the passion of a poet or thinker, but that of the fear of God, and [is] for me a worship of God.

This is "Guidance" (a term which in this context has an almost grammatical or linguistic sense), writing as penitence and self-denial "guided" by "God." Whatever might escape him (the "glowing expression") is only authorized through "Guidance"/"God." This agency functions almost as a grid or a "Watching Institution" which *limits* the writing and imagination ("I have needed God every day to protect me against *the richness of my thoughts*" [my italics]); later the aesthetic writing is interpreted as a "necessary purgation." Thus, if "God" is considered as "self-denial," as the limitation of desire which requires an act of submission, we can begin to see how problematic writing must be insofar as it is an imitation, a verbal displacement of desire. But the writing is also Kierkegaard's only fulfillment and justification, the *telos* of his existence. "Guidance" or his God-relationship offers a planned coherence which had escaped him by himself. "When I, like a quite ordinary man, followed the impulses determined by my nature, that this which for me had a purely personal significance bordering on the accidental, that this then proved to have a quite different, ideal significance when it afterwards was viewed in the activity as an author . . . I did not understand myself, became melancholy—and look, out of this was developed a mood and exactly the one which I should use in relation to the work preoccupying me at the time, and exactly in that place."

But in this confession, which pretends to explain, we most clearly see (self-) deceptions at work. There can be no doubt that the posited coherence is established *post facto* and through the act of writing. Thus we see in *POV* a curious combination of truly penetrating insights and a pathetic blindness. Perhaps the self-mystification is the necessary complement of the awareness, allowing (and at the same time limiting) a dialogic discourse.

It is difficult, perhaps impossible, to order the contradictions and paradoxes which have been the occasion for this essay into a unified theory or structure. What we have attempted here, instead, is to indicate certain levels in those texts where Kierkegaard reflects upon his own writing project, especially *POV*, not in order to find an explanation which will enable us to decode the large labyrinth which is his pseudonymous texts, but rather in order to indicate some registers in which the texts move. Schematically and initially we have distinguished between two levels in the explanatory texts: one at which a theorizing about the writing process takes place and which insists upon the alterity of the texts, and another at which the total design or orientation of the pseudonymous series is interpreted. While the second level implies a Meaning which the first would disqualify, we nevertheless can not favor one over the other but must see the paradoxes and contradictions involved in their confrontation—in the self-interpretation on conditions which have negated any relation between self and text—as the condition of a complex "writing machine."

In this perspective an opening, rather than a closure (a conclusion), should have been established by the possibility of (re)examining the pseudonymous texts in terms of genre and literary function. The notion of a double-oriented dialogic discourse makes it possible to play out Kierkegaard's texts (particularly the pseudonymous ones) against the dominant literary, philosophical, and theological discourses which constitute the textual space into which he wrote. The "pseudonymity" is therefore not primarily an attempt at "psychological" mystification (a popular *topos* in Kierkegaardian criticism), nor is it sufficient to see it as a "device," a maieutic deceit (as Kierkegaard himself explains) which, in a carefully controlled program, leads the reader into a state of awareness, but it is rather the necessary condition for a transformation of existing texts and structures of domination. As the example of *Repetition* bears out, the fiction does not carry or control a philosophical idea, nor does the "philosophy" utilize the fiction as an example, but each discourse dissolves the other and, in the process, poses the problem of the relationship between "literature" and "philosophy" as well as that of the insufficiency of posing the problem of repetition in these established modes of discourse. Kierkegaard's texts then do not, in turn, seek to dominate a textual field openly or by secret erosion, but are directed primarily at those instances and places where textual dominations or ideologies are generated.

SYLVIANE AGACINSKI

On a Thesis

IRONY AS A SUBJECT?

Not in any case that it is subject *to* anyone, rather it subjects (but whom?) because it seduces, at the risk of sweeping away the ironist himself.

Irony, then, seems rather to be a withdrawal of the subject, indeed a void. But it is a void so vain and disquieting that it immediately calls for some kind of positivity—perhaps philosophy—to unmask, or manifest itself. What thus appears afterwards rushes in to master retrospectively a certain vertigo, and to reappropriate this nothingness for itself in the form of *its* beginning. Socrates, since he's going to be this subject of irony, becomes a founder for philosophy.

But is it possible, even at the beginning, to *place* irony, which is perhaps displacement "itself"? And if philosophy claims to have no other beginning than *itself*, allowing for no preamble, then Socrates risks ending up in a position of instability (as is evident in Hegel)—should we even be able to speak of such a subject in terms of "position"? For from the Hegelian perspective, it is not yet a question of philosophy with Socrates, nor even of some "need for philosophy," but merely a question of what "aims at bringing forth" this necessity by means of a certain dialectical practice: one that allows the internal contradictions of the (still absent) Idea to appear, that allows its manifold determinations to develop and cancel one another in their reciprocal opposition. Socrates would have had the idea of the dialectic, but not the dialectic

From *Aparté: Conceptions and Deaths of Søren Kierkegaard.* © 1987 by Florida State University Press. Translated by Kevin Newmark.

of the Idea. His dialectic leads to nothing, it only stirs up consciousness and destroys certitudes, so it is only negative. But this is not yet the negativity that is posited as such at the heart of dialectical movement. Socrates never makes it as far as speculation. For this reason his "position" will remain constantly ambiguous, in particular within the Hegelian interpretation to which Kierkegaard is inextricably bound by a debate that is sometimes complicitous, sometimes critical.

If Hegel can be said to have perfectly understood Socrates' negativity (Kierkegaard borrows most of his analysis from him), he also wanted to find a "positive aspect" in Socrates that would have made him assimilable to the history of philosophy. This leads Hegel to "divide" Socrates, and finally to relegate irony, or the "questioning attitude," to a secondary status by distinguishing it from its *goal:* the positing by subjectivity of the Idea as such. But this goal itself *is not* reached by Socrates. Since the Idea is still entirely abstract, it has no content whatsoever.

In brief: Kierkegaard refuses to grant Socrates any kind of positivity; Socrates has no point of view outside of irony, his attitude is infinitely subjective and infinitely negative regarding every positivity; he is incapable of "positing" anything, at least as long as he sees his *point de vue* to the bitter end. Socrates himself is thus (nothing but) this infinitely ironic point of view. On the other hand, the Kierkegaardian interpretation is not for all that an *objection* to Hegel's. All the negativity of Socrates' dialectic, when pushed to its limit, can already be found in Hegel.

But who do we mean when we say "Socrates"? The interpretation is bound to be ambiguous given the diversity of the texts in which "Socrates" appears: Xenophon, Aristophanes, Plato. And under this last name, how many "Socrates'" are there? In this regard, Hegel is a bit lax since he picks things out willy nilly from the various texts. On the contrary, Kierkegaard isolates the specifically "Socratic" dialogues in Plato (the so-called "aporetic" dialogues), and he unhesitatingly dismisses Xenophon for having portrayed Socrates with a "shopkeeper's mentality," devoid of even the slightest trace of irony. Xenophon, for instance, sees in Socrates' death the "advantage of having escaped from the woes and worries of old age." Xenophon is much too *dull* to have understood the least little thing about irony. For this reason, we can expect nothing from him. Hegel, who had not thought of this argument, makes reference to Xenophon whenever he wants to illustrate the "positive side" of Socrates. (We can assume that the plurality of Socratic figures is an effect of Socratic irony. Only a Socrates of negativity, of dissimulation, could have endangered so many doubles. There were several "conceptions" of Socrates for the reason that Socrates himself did not have any. The gods, he liked to say, had failed to grant him "the power to beget.")

Is irony a fit subject for a *thesis*? Is it possible to set something up on the basis of that which pokes fun at every tenable position? What position is to be taken with respect to (that) which posits nothing? Does an ironist write a "thesis"? Did Kierkegaard?

> He was not like a philosopher lecturing upon his views, wherein precisely the lecture constitutes the presence of the Idea itself (*selve Ideens Tilstedevaerelse*), on the contrary, what Socrates said meant something 'other.'

Irony is an "interrogation" (*eirōnia*). In reference to Socrates it would have also had the connotation of a *feigned* ignorance and indeed even a jesting, "in which what is said is the opposite of what is to be understood." Socrates is supposed to have questioned his listeners so that by *pretending* to be ignorant he showed just how real their own ignorance was. Socrates *knew*, but he simulated, or played at being ignorant. Such is the traditional conception of simulation or ruse as dissemblance, indeed as deception. Irony would thus border on hypocrisy in the sense that *hypocritēs* has always had: at once "actor" and "hypocrite." This conception is as traditional as it is reductive: if Socrates "knew," then his method would be nothing more than a pedagogical tool (still recommended to teachers today). For philosophy properly speaking, then, it becomes a most curious prelude to speculation. Such a method is useless for speculation per se, from whose point of view it could hardly ever have had any use.

This is not Kierkegaard's point of departure, though, and when he speaks of simulation it is in another sense. In fact, if irony is not a simple "pretending," then it consists in the interrogation itself, in the questioning—provided we make a distinction here between two forms of questioning. In the first case, the question takes place in view of an answer that will complete the question with its own (meaning)fulness—in the second, it is only a matter of letting the question draw out the apparent and contradictory contents of the "answers," letting it hollow them out and leaving behind "a void." It is in this second form of interrogation that we recognize the celebrated Socratic method, which has no other aim, or in any event, no other result, than to let in a "slight draught" well-suited to clearing out the clutter of opinions. But if this is the case, then Socratic dialectic is purely negative. It has no conclusion, but is merely satisfied with negating (neither-nor). To any given question the answer is *neither* this, *nor* that. If, by means of negation, this method is able to indicate the Idea itself, it is only in the form of *allusion*. This negative dialectic at work in certain Platonic dialogues would thus be a dialectic devoid of synthesis and progress, unless we can speak of progress with reference to an Idea or an essence indicated in an allusive way, but also completely "hollowed out" or evaporated. Such is the case in the *Protagoras:*

> "Socrates' argumentation essentially aims at reducing the relative dissimilarity among the various virtues in order to preserve their unity. . . . But what I must call particular attention to is the fact that this unity of virtue becomes so abstract, so egotistically terminated in itself, that it becomes the very crag upon which all the individual virtues are stranded and torn asunder like heavily laden vessels."

The Idea appears only in its withdrawal, hollowed out.

The Idea would thus be related to the words of Socrates as the image of Napoleon is to the picture of his tomb: "There is an engraving that portrays the grave of Napoleon. Two large trees overshadow the grave. There is nothing else to be seen in the picture, and the immediate spectator will see no more. Between these two trees, however, is an empty space, and as the eye traces out its contours Napoleon himself suddenly appears out of the nothingness. . . . It is the same with Socrates' replies. As one sees the trees, so one hears his discourse; his words mean exactly what they sound like . . . just as there is not a single brush stroke to suggest Napoleon. Yet it is this empty space, this nothingness, that conceals what is most important."

We should ask ourselves about the pertinence of such an "image." Why is an ironic practice of discourse compared to an empty picture? Why this strange painting—unless it is because the metaphor of painting (though only its metaphor) has always been used to depict the imitation essential to "thought" itself? Unless it is because this *logos* has always been "the faithful image of the *eidos* of what is," producing it as "a sort of primary painting, profound and invisible." "Whether one conceives it in its 'Cartesian' or its 'Hegelian' modification, the Idea is the presence of what is" (Jacques Derrida, *Dissemination*).

According to the metaphysical conception of the Idea as the presence of what is, Napoleon should have been in the picture, a true likeness, truly painted and truly present. Metaphysics, just as painting in principle, has no use for "allusions"—in any sense of the word. Kierkegaard had already pointed out in his introduction that, "he was not like a philosopher lecturing upon his views, wherein precisely the lecture constitutes the presence of the idea itself." So Socrates would have posited nothing, exposed nothing. He would have engaged in only *allusive* discourse, never expressing the Idea as such, never claiming to coincide with it. For this reason, the possibility of a painting which would itself be allusive (something which for metaphysics would perhaps be either repugnant or inconceivable) is decisive. Painting no longer functions here as an image, or in other words, as a faithful imitation of what is. This painting no longer makes *visible*, just as the discourse of Socrates does not express "the presence of the idea itself," but only hints at it. Could it be, then, that the Socratic practice of interrogation, its allusive link to the Idea, does not belong to metaphysics? Yes and no. If we have recourse to those texts of Plato in which a Socratic conception of "the true" is worked out (the last pages of the *Cratylus*, for example), then it is obvious that Socrates defines as true that which resembles the thing in itself, even if such a resemblance occurs in a non-sensory mode. For the thing in itself is endowed with the status of an ultimate model, to which both thought and word ought to align themselves, and toward whose recovered presence they ought to strive. Thus, there can be no question here of seeing anything but a metaphysical definition of the Idea. Recalling this definition forces Socrates' metaphysics out into the open, and certain passages would justify such a procedure. But with respect to the *Cratylus* as a whole, the ending seems scanty and rather negative. We should not start out from names, but rather from things . . . at which point the dialogue breaks off; there is nothing to be learned from it. Socratic metaphysics is always failed or aborted—it is hardly a program. It is more common for Socrates to indicate where truth is *not* than it is for him to *tell* us where it is. He indicates where we have to start out from, but as Kierkegaard puts it, "where the inquiry should begin, there he stops." Socrates did away with non-truths in the name of a certain idea of Truth (the thing in itself, what *is* originally). He does *not* pronounce the truth, even less so in the *Cratylus* than elsewhere, since it is there that he is so wary of words and shows how they can be made to say contradictory things. In other words, even if he refers his listener to the Idea, conceived metaphysically as the presence of what is, he himself is never able to make the Idea *present* in his discourse: whence a practice that remains ironic. He always says "something other" than what he says, he does not pronounce "Truth" as such. From this point of view it could be said that irony does not simply belong to metaphysics. Kierkegaard does not put the question precisely in these terms. Nonetheless, as someone who is so obviously preoccupied by Hegelianism, he gives his reader ample notice when he declares that Socrates does *not* expose his views within a discourse that constitutes "the presence of the Idea itself":

Don't think that irony can be understood, or accommodated by philosophy, there is "something 'other' " at issue here—not, of course, another content or truth—perhaps another mode of discourse, another manner of speaking.

This whole interpretation is made possible only by isolating the specifically Socratic dialogues in Plato. Moreover, Hegel admits, but only in passing and without really paying much attention to it, that such dialogues do exist. They are characterized by a lack of dialectical progress, or synthesis. Kierkegaard, for instance, refers to the *Symposium*, where the various speeches are in no way moments that could coalesce in a final conception. It is not even possible to speak of any final "conception" here; Socrates has simply shown that Eros possesses none of those things he seeks (neither the beautiful nor the good): "Hence we see how Socrates gets at the nut not by peeling off the shell but by hollowing out the kernel." Still, we should remember that it was necessary to have had the idea of the "kernel" in the first place, in other words, the Idea. For it is only possible to hollow it out insofar as we go looking for it.

Socrates thus liberates empirical determinations from the contingency of concrete existence (and in so doing undermines the empirical), but he does this merely to indicate the Idea in its "most abstract determination." As a result, love becomes nothing but pure longing, or pure desire. This is something like a delivery without the birth. An interminable dialectic leads only to an indeterminate Idea.

Socratic dialectic can therefore be considered doubly negative: it negates without positing anything. "In its overall effort," it destroys and negates concrete positivity (Socrates as the one who "delivers Greece," "purifies the temple," etc.), and it does *not* go beyond this negativity, this pure polemic, unless by indicating abstract, in other words, hollow Ideas. Like the engraving of the grave. But by assimilating the abstract to the negative, are we not already within the Hegelian critique of the abstract, already considering the abstract part of the category of the *not yet* ("still abstract," Kierkegaard says)?

Hegel can get Socrates into philosophy (in a way that remains ambiguous, in the mode of the *not yet*) only by separating irony, or the *via negativa*, from a positing of the Idea, no matter how abstract. If, following Kierkegaard, we interpret Socrates from the standpoint of infinite irony alone, then no basis, no positivity whatsoever can be attributed to it. Conversely, if Socrates is to *posit* something, then he will have to go *beyond* irony. Hegel hesitates, then, and is forced to make a distinction between two dialectics, or two interrogations in Socratic *eirōnia*. On the other hand, irony is simulation or ruse—Socrates asks questions in an "apparently naive manner"—this irony being merely "a way of getting along with others." So much for the subjective aspect of the dialectic. On the other hand, there is dialectic properly speaking, which "deals with the ultimate reasons for things . . . . Out of every determinate proposition or out of its development, he developed the opposite of what the proposition stated: he did not affirm it against the proposition or definition in question, rather he took up this or that determination and showed how, even in itself, it contained its own opposite."

These two aspects of dialectic, sometimes simple simulation, sometimes manifestation of the dialectic *of* the Idea, are not easily reconciled with what Hegel goes on to say in these same lectures. Socrates actually knew nothing ("It may actually be said that Socrates knew nothing, for he did not reach the scientific construction of a systematic philosophy.") Socrates' results were purely formal and unsatisfactory; all he did was throw consciousness into a state of confusion. From this perspective, the Hegelian distinction between an irony that simulates and a dialectic properly speaking becomes rather tenuous. Otherwise, it would have been necessary to distinguish two Socrates'—something Hegel does not do—as a function of the particular dialogue in question. Kierkegaard will "retain" only the negative Socrates, but is this any more legitimate, since to do so he will have to dismiss numerous other texts?

SOCRATIC IRONY—PURE NEGATIVITY

Kierkegaard's dissertation was preceded by fifteen "theses," written in Latin. The ninth declared: "Socrates drove all his contemporaries out of substantiality as if naked from a shipwreck, undermined actuality, envisaged ideality in the distance, touched it but did not acquire it."

Socrates does not beget, nor does Theaetetus.

Were it a question of substantiating Kierkegaard's thesis, I would cite the ending of the *Theaetetus*, where, once the "pregnancy" has come to term, there is nothing to be known about knowledge except perhaps what it is *not*. No (philosophical) conception has taken place.

> SOCRATES: So then, all those fruits which we have borne here today, doesn't our midwife's skill pronounce them to be mere wind and not worth the rearing?
>
> THEAETETUS: Why, yes, it's just as you say.

A negative dialectic is an abortive dialectic. And yet, something does happen in it, something that provides irony with its double valorization: "For irony is a healthiness inasmuch as it rescues the soul from the snares of relativity: and it is an illness inasmuch as it is not able to maintain the absolute except in the form of nothingness."

THE DOUBLE VALORIZATION OF NEGATIVE DIALECTICS

Negatively, irony prompts thought to "cut loose from the purely empirical sand banks and to set sail for the open sea." Therefore, it is "liberating." It would seem that there is no image violent enough to express the destructive character of Socrates, and Kierkegaard depicts him by turns as an underminer, a warrior, a cannibal. First, he is the quiet underminer of the Sophists; he unmasks and confounds them by opposing their loquaciousness and pedantry with the silence of his own ignorance. He seems to efface himself before them, thus allowing their contradictory propositions to develop and cancel one another. At this point he rises above them, and in the deliberately ambiguous formula of Aristophanes he becomes their *master* (*maître:* master, schoolmaster, mentor). The formula is remarkable for the very reason of its own profound irony: "For it certainly would be an irony worthy of Aristophanes to conceive Socrates, the Sophists' most spiteful enemy, not as their antagonist, but rather as their schoolmaster (*laeremester*), which in one sense he certainly was. And the *curious confusion* that one who combats a particular movement may himself be conceived as its representative . . . conceals in itself so much intentional or unintentional irony that it should *not entirely* be lost sight of." Socrates brings sophistry to its term, so to speak, to the point where it exhausts and dissolves itself. He alone is "equipped and fitted out to do battle with the Sophists." He is also a warrior, then, who "in the infinite exaltation of his freedom" wielded irony like a brand or a sword: "the two-edged sword which he wielded over Hellas like a destroying angel." Isn't it in the *Apology* (30e) that Socrates compares himself to a gadfly or a goad sent by the gods to stimulate the Greek state?

The ironist talks—at least this one did not write—but he is not for all that a *voice;* he carries on a battle in which silence is both the means and the end of the combat. Even when he talks, the ironist does not *say* anything, he effaces himself in the questioning and allows the answers to become manifest in their apparent positivity. He is pure solicitation, provocation, although he himself remains hidden. And when at last all the answers have canceled themselves out, the ironist imposes silence on his distraught and befuddled interlocutors. Socrates is without a voice because he is not, or is not yet, the voice of Truth ("there's just nothing to be heard; a profound silence reigns"). Irony is nothing but pause or suspense: "Truth demanded silence before lifting up its voice, and it was Socrates who had to impose this silence. Thus he was *exclusively negative*. Had he possessed a positivity of his own, he would never have been so unmerciful, never so cannibalistic as he was." A strange image; the extreme case will crop up later, when the ironist gets swept away by his own negativity, as though he were in the process of devouring himself. One last image to show irony "opening up a vacuum," delivering its disciples of their fragile certitudes: the ironist not only strips his student clean, he actually skins him alive. For in *The Clouds*, Socrates is able to talk Strepsiades right out of the coat on his back. This is an apt way of symbolizing, according to Kierkegaard, that the disciple is also relieved of his now antiquated thought processes. Strepsiades, speaking of his vanished cloak, is thus fully justified when he says: "I haven't really lost it, I've just become dis-pensive about it." Socrates does not give anything, he only disencumbers, and just as Charon, "divesting his passengers of the manifold determinations of concrete existence," he leads only into a void. "*Actuality became nothingness* by means of the absolute; but this *absolute* was in turn a *nothingness*."

This "nothingness" is the *abstract* universal. Socrates brings to light the universality that, in Hegel's words, was "sunken in materiality." But for Hegel, it is a *moment*, necessary but unique, and it will not have to be repeated; it is a *moment* (in a sense which Kierkegaard will later take up without ever fully admitting it as such). After having considered the Sophists, Hegel begins his lecture on Socrates in the following way: "Consciousness had reached this point in Greece when Socrates appeared in Athens—the great figure of Socrates." At that point, consciousness is able to separate the universal from the concrete and to understand that whatever is, "is mediated by thought." This moment *will have been* necessary, but at a given time and once and for all. *We* no longer need Socrates, neither his method nor his irony, nor even *his* dialectic. As far as Hegel is concerned, what manifested itself in Socrates (the interiorization of consciousness) "would later become a matter of habit." Today, *we* are already "trained in representing to ourselves what is abstract," "*our* reflection is already accustomed to the universal." For *us*, then, "the Socratic method of so-called deference, the development of the universal from out of so many particulars, that verbosity of exemplification, all this has something about it that is often tiresome, boring (*taediositas*)." In other words, the Socratic point of view and method are totally *outmoded*.

This is where Kierkegaard's resistance is located. We could put this in a somewhat programmatic way by saying that for Kierkegaard irony will always be what eludes Hegelian sublation (*Aufhebung*), to the extent that irony—and this may seem paradoxical—also represents, and in a perhaps inevitable fashion, the writer's point of view. "Perhaps"—since the question remains whether Kierkegaard was ever able to get beyond what he called the author's ironic relation to his work. In his thesis and well afterwards, Kierkegaard "re-works" the Hegelian concepts of moment, stage, station, and development. But just as in the conclusion to his thesis, it is in order to resituate them on the level of "private life," of "individual existence." Now irony turns out to be necessary from the start as a *moment* in poetic creativity: "the poet must maintain an ironic relation with his work." In fact, the author is able to conceive only finite works; every "conception" depends on a certain point of view and remains particular. An author thus gives free rein in his work, in each of his works, to this "positive element," but without ever identifying himself with this positivity (just as Socrates lets the Sophists go on talking)—all this with profound irony. An author is thus always, and in advance, detached from the work with which he entertains a merely indirect relationship. Should he go further, should he become a philosopher, he will discover in each of his works a "moment" in his own development. Were this only possible, it would imply some final recuperation by the author, after the fact and outside every work, of his entire production.

Kierkegaard's thesis seeks to elaborate an interpretation of Socrates on the basis of irony as a negative dialectic. For this reason he must criticize the Hegelian reading, which attributes to Socrates a "positive aspect." But the arguments Hegel uses to distinguish a positive Socrates and a negative Socrates are not clear. On the one hand, it should be recalled that Hegel pushes the analysis of Socratic negativity just about as far as it will go. The result of the "dialectical" method is to throw "consciousness into a state of commotion," to startle it, surprise it, unsettle it, bewilder it, and finally to arrive at this point: "what we used to know has refuted itself." And again: "The main tendency of the dialogues was to provoke bewilderment." Such a result really isn't one for Hegel. On the basis of the *Meno* and the *Lysis* he shows that, "in reference to the result (the content) the dialogues leave us totally unsatisfied." But "this negative side is what is essential." It is of no use for Hegel to admit at first that such is the "essence" of Socratic dialectic, it is immediately apparent that such is *not* the essence for him, G. W. F. Hegel. What is essential is what Socrates makes possible, the beginning that he is (without really being this beginning, though, since neither philosophy nor the need to philosophize is actually there yet, it's just that now they *could* come into being). "Whence *ought to arise* the *need* for a *more strenuous effort after* knowledge" (emphasis added). The vexation apparent earlier, due to the tiresome "loquaciousness" of the dialogues, returns here in the form of a "more strenuous" effort. It would seem, then, that at the moment Hegel asserts the purely negative character of the Socratic dialectic, he dismisses it philosophically and relegates it to a point *short of* the beginning properly speaking. Nonetheless, Socrates remains a "founder," but for another reason and only to the extent, "on the other hand," as it were, that he has been constructive. The constructive element here is the idea of the Good posited as a universal. This is only the idea of some abstract good, and yet it is "no longer quite as abstract," says Hegel, since it is "produced by thought." Morality—the only real interest of Socrates—took the form of "the conviction of the Individual in his own unique consciousness." Immediacy no longer has its own validity, rather it must justify itself in the eyes of thought. This is the "return into oneself" and the isolation of the individual—who also separates himself from the State.

However, when Hegel wants to show in what manner Socrates at once represents the "two sides" of the universal—the negative that undercuts the particular, and the positive—he calls on Xenophon. In the *Memorabilia*, Socrates had been depicted "with much more precision and fidelity than in Plato." How could Xenophon have been more accurate? We can judge from the following passage: In the fourth book (4:2, 40), Xenophon wants partly to show how Socrates had attracted the youth to him and had led them to the realization that they *needed instruction (Bildung)*—something which we have already discussed—*on the other hand,* though, he *also* recounts how Socrates himself actually did instruct them and what they learned by frequenting him, "who no longer bewildered (tortured) them through subtleties, but rather taught them the Good in a clear and open (unequivocal) manner. He showed them the Good and the True in concrete determinations, which he always came back to so as not to stay in the merely abstract." In order to confirm the interpretation of this Socrates who left behind the "subtleties" of his dialectic and led his auditors onto firmer ground (a Socrates, that is, who finally gives up his irony), Hegel makes reference to the conversation with Hippias recorded by Xenophon. Socrates asserts there that the just person obeys the laws even if individual laws change, thereby making them seem contingent. Why is this obedience necessary? For the simple reason that "the best and happiest state is that in which the citizens are of one mind and obey the laws." Hegel: "Thus, Socrates closes his eyes to the contradiction and lets stand the law and its institutions, just as they are conceived by the man on the street. Here we can see an affirmative (constructive) content." Undoubtedly so, but does it have anything to do with the Socratic dialectic? Hegel explains this positive aspect in two ways: Socrates has understood the necessary movement in which laws are *sometimes* valid "just as they are to be found in the State," and "sometimes susceptible to being revoked inasmuch as they are particular laws." Socrates himself asks, "Aren't those who wage war the same ones who contract peace once again?" In this case, Socrates would not only be the one who brings to light contradictions and undercuts certitudes, but also the one who *already* comprehends the dialectic of the Concept. That is why, faced with the contradiction, he "looks the other way" and recommends obedience. The second argument, already referred to, occurs thanks to an unexpected coalition: "In a word, Socrates says that the best and happiest State is that in which the citizens are of one mind and obey the laws." If Kierkegaard remains puzzled by this interpretation it is not without reason, then, and it is precisely because it completely drops the "negative" dialectic to which Hegel himself will return in the following pages. If "Socrates exhibits something positive here," remarks Kierkegaard, "it is because he *does not carry through his standpoint (son point de vue)* . . . hence it is not a positivity following upon his infinite negation but a positivity *preceding it*" (emphasis added).

This whole discussion shows how Hegel tried to rescue Socrates from what he called the "dangerous side" of abstraction and purely negative upheaval. Still, chances are that no one has done more to reveal this negative risk than Hegel himself, no one pushed so far the analysis of negativity, an analysis that at this point leaves the "moral" and positive Socrates of Xenophon in order to outdo even the portrait left by Aristophanes. It is in this oscillation between Xenophon and Aristophanes that the ambiguity of the Hegelian interpretation can be read.

But Hegel couldn't agree with us more. No one understood Socratic negativity better than Aristophanes: "he was perfectly right in his *Clouds*." He was able to capture Socrates' philosophy with "precision," and the profundity of *The Clouds* lies precisely in its capacity to show how the Socratic method ends up suppressing whatever truth may be in naive consciousness and affirming in its stead the freedom—without content—of Spirit. In other words, and nearer the play itself, this dialectic allows a son, Phidippides, to behave most insolently toward his father, Strepsiades, and finally to give him a drubbing! Strepsiades, not having gotten much profit from the time he himself had spent with Socrates, decides to send his son to him. He regrets it, of course, and eventually curses dialectics and burns down Socrates' residence, the "Thoughtery." "We must admire," says Hegel, "the depth of Aristophanes in having recognized the dialectical side in Socrates as being something negative." Even if they don't come right out and say so, it seems that for Hegel, just as for Kierkegaard, the image of a son beating his father is both a subtle and accurate representation for the liberation of Spirit. Having once learned his p's and q's from Socrates, Phidippides not only succeeds in getting rid of the creditors who pester his father by demanding payment for debts runup by Phidippides himself, but beyond that, "*Filial respect* and obedience to his father fare no better than the due date under this dialectic." The comic side of dialectics is at the same time its healthiness.

For Kierkegaard, the Aristophanic reading of the Socratic dialectic goes even further; its every detail becomes significant. As such, the clouds themselves (the chorus) become a symbol of vacuousness, a reflection of Socrates' vacuous interior. Here the irony belongs to Aristophanes, and it consists in having shown the absence of content that is specific to Socratic irony by putting it in the form of the clouds invoked by Socrates in the play. The clouds ("haze," "fog," "mist," "smoke") represent the end, the "result" of negative dialectics. Aristophanes would have thus hinted at an analogical link between Socrates and the clouds on the one hand, and Socrates and the Idea on the other. The Socratic Idea would be nothing but haze and smoke, "which have fallen silent before the splendor of the Idea." As Kierkegaard puts it: "For what remains when one allows the various shapes assumed by the clouds to disappear is nebulosity itself, which is an excellent description of the Socratic Idea."

The fickle shapes in which actual clouds appear are related to the "essence" of clouds in the same way that every predicate is related to the Idea. Like clouds, "the True never *is*." Clouds (nothingness) and an eloquent tongue: that is all you have to believe in according to Socrates. *Nothingness* and the tongue's *Language*. Which is enough to imply that the tongue with which the dialectician speaks wags like the clapper in a bell and merely *resounds* like one: "Socrates impresses upon Strepsiades that instead of believing in the gods he must believe in nothing but wide empty space and the tongue, a condition describing perfectly all the obstreperous talk about nothing, and which reminds me of a passage in Grimm's *Irish Fairytales* where he speaks of people with an empty head and a tongue like the clapper in a church bell." (In Danish, *tunge* means not only language and tongue, but also bell clapper). The basket in which Socrates is *suspended* is also an "excellent image." Like Mohammed's casket hovering between two magnets, Socrates' basket is balanced between the earth and the clouds. In more ways than one, the ironist incarnates a subjectivity that is left "hanging."

Finally, Aristophanes' projection is correct inasmuch as it is *comical*. If Socrates is entirely negative, if the ironist "is extremely lighthearted about the idea . . . since for him the absolute is nothingness," then he achieves a high degree of the comical by means of this levity. "Aristophanes was wholly correct insofar as he was prompted to conceive [Socrates' activity] comically." Hegel had already demonstrated the relevance of a comic representation of

Socrates. "The comical," he said, "consists in showing how men or things bring about their own dissolution by making a show of themselves." In order for something to be comical it must contain its own contradiction; lacking this, the comical remains superficial. Socrates qualifies for the comical insofar as there is contradiction between the effort he expends and the result he achieves—"Socrates brings forth in his moral endeavor the opposite of what he intends." This is not only true in *The Clouds*. It would be possible to suggest that Socrates is comical because he makes a habit of shortchanging us (*à force de décevoir*), and this would conform to an entirely negative conception of Socrates. Negativity and the comical go hand in hand, and when Hegel lends his approbation to Aristophanes, he necessarily gives up his positive conception of Socrates. Kant, to rely on those rather sorry "jokes" he tells on the only page of the *Third Critique* devoted to the comical, did not have much of an opinion of the comical and did not see much use for it in art (the fine arts). Nonetheless, he says enough to make us wonder about his apparent lack of appreciation of comedy, or the value of the comical. That of Aristophanes and/or Socrates, for instance. What he actually writes is: "Laughter is an affection arising from the sudden transformation of a strained expectation into nothing." The understanding, "which does not find what it was expecting, suddenly relaxes itself and the effect of this slackening is felt throughout the body." This is laughter. An expectation that is frustrated makes us laugh; not of course that it is pleasing, nor is it enjoyable in itself (to the first edition Kant adds, "as in the case of a man who gets the news of a great commercial success"), but merely because the play of representations brings about a kind of "equilibrium of the vital forces in the body." This sudden movement of body and mind has a beneficial influence upon the health . . . At this point, and leaving aside his "jokes" for a while, Kant would have been able to analyze the comical aspect in Socratic irony, unless this very aspect belongs to philosophy itself.

But if the act of shortchanging (*la déception*), i.e., producing an expectation that is forever deferred, engenders the comical, it is equally certain that it is also capable of arousing love. Socrates' negativity is at the same time his seduction. The erotic nature of the disturbance caused in his disciples seems to have escaped Hegel. On the contrary, Kierkegaard was to see in Socrates a demon of a seducer, a master eroticist.

APOLOGY FOR A SEDUCER

Socrates' handsome boyfriend Alcibiades complains of having been one of the many victims of a seducer who lets himself be loved but who remains

unapproachable, who takes without giving anything in return, who maintains himself at a distance and *keeps himself* from loving: "And he has fooled
not only me, but Charmides, son of Glaucon, and Euthydemus, son of
Diocles, and many others in the same way—he starts out as though he is the
lover, but in fact he ends up being the beloved." Socratic coyness is not
derivative with respect to seduction, it is its cause. Alcibiades is thus "unable
to tear himself away," says Kierkegaard. By "never expressing the Idea as
such" (by never pronouncing the "Truth"), the ironist produces turmoil and
makes a romantic attachment "not only possible but necessary." Irony is
troubling, unsettling, disturbing, it has no other effect than to initiate a "love
affair" between the ironist and his listener. That Kierkegaard qualifies this
love affair as "intellectual" should not mislead us. What is at issue here is
passion and the *erotic* relationship that, barring evidence to the contrary and
no matter what form it takes, has always been of an "intellectual" order.
"When I hear his voice," says Alcibiades, "my heart leaps within me more
than that of any Corybantian reveller." "He is like one bitten by a serpent,
yet bitten by something even more painful and in the most painful place: in
the heart and soul." This "power of seduction and enchantment" is irony's
sole effect, inasmuch as it causes pure turmoil. In other words, irony does not
produce the "third term" in which the lover could find appeasement. The
ironist never comes out onto the field of exchange; no mediation intervenes
in order to guarantee communication. After having been skinned alive and
torn out of his immediate existence, the other is to receive nothing.

Giving away none of what he makes it seem as though he has, the ironist
stays in control of things and continues to be an object of desire. Showing
nothing, except by allusion, never expressing the Idea as such, he retains his
mastery over the relationship—"it pertains to the essence of the ironist . . . to
possess the Idea as his personal property." After having relieved the disciple
of his cloak (*The Clouds*) and his certitudes, after having excited his curiosity
and his desire, the ironist leaves him in the lurch.

The conveyance of a knowledge would never "have given rise to this
kind of passionate turmoil . . . But as it pertains to the essence of irony never
to unmask itself, and since it is equally essential for irony to change masks in
Protean fashion, it follows that it must necessarily cause the infatuated youth
much pain."

Love is thus the effect of an indirect relation, or "communication," from
afar, based on *allusion*, which the disciple can *never* be certain of having
understood. Prisoner of his own doubt, this is why he remains tied to the
person of the ironist: "The disguise and mysteriousness which it entails, the
telegraphic communication which it initiates, inasmuch as the ironist must

always be understood at a distance, the infinite sympathy it assumes, the elusive and ineffable moment of understanding immediately displaced by the anxiety of misunderstanding—all this captivates with indissoluble bonds." The ironist, a moment ago an underminer, now becomes a *vampire*—the delight which Kierkegaard apparently finds in developing these images is a good indication that they are not meant to denigrate the Seducer. Characterizing the seducer in such a way serves only to reinforce his power—"The ironist is a vampire who has sucked the blood out of the lover and fanned him with coolness, lulled him to sleep and tormented him with turbulent dreams." If this seducer is able to get himself paid in the bargain (as in *The Clouds*), then his vampirism becomes total. All the same, there is no law that says that someone who pays to get himself seduced can't make a profit on it, even if he is not, as the saying goes, paid back in kind. The ironist, the questioner who keeps himself out of sight, who stays behind a mask, is thus all the more seductive insofar as *he does not respond*, and this in more ways than one. He leaves the question, the disciple, and even himself "up in the air." Just as he admits in the *Apology*, Socrates is nothing but a goad sent to stimulate the Athenians. "An eroticist he certainly was to the fullest extent . . . in short, he possessed all the seductive gifts of the spirit. But communicate, fill, enrich, this he could not do. In this sense one might possibly call him a *seducer*, for he deceived the youth and awakened *longings* which he *never satisfied*, allowed them to become inflamed by the subtle pleasures of anticipation, yet never gave them solid and nourishing food." Then the youth which he "deceived"(?), "felt the deep pangs of unrequited love." Such is irony's mastery: it awakens desire just as it dominates and maintains it, all the while holding itself back—"Alcibiades' growing impetuosity always met its master in Socrates' irony."

Now for Kierkegaard—and this could be verified elsewhere—there is no mastery other than that of seduction, never. This seduction, which he first finds in Socrates, also belongs to Johannes. Moreover, it is the seduction of God himself. Is it not true that one of the most excruciating dilemmas is always to have to choose between the pleasure of seducing and that of being seduced?

Such is the dilemma of the fiancé who also wants to be an "author," and of the author who also wants to be a Christian. For the fiancé or the "writer" (the "poet") chooses seduction, while the Christian chooses passion. *Philosophical Fragments* develops the theme of divine seduction (a veritable rapture), which it is necessary to distinguish from the simply human seduction of Socrates. Sent on a mission of divine inspiration, "a midwife subject to examination by the God himself," Socrates represents only an "occasion" for the disciple to discover his ignorance in a relationship "between man and man." But the God will not permit Socrates to beget: "Heaven has debarred me," he says, "from giving birth." He who begets, for Kierkegaard, can only be the God himself. But this God, what does he do, if not "teach"man all over again that he is a man, that is, a non-truth, and that the unknown something colliding with the passion of his reason is the God? By which, according to this teaching, God is master. It is easy to see at what price, in what sort of panic, the mind is carried away. We need only recall Alcibiades. The God ravishes the mind and deals it a mortal blow; such is love. This is God's irony with respect to human intelligence.

But the *thesis* hasn't gotten that far. Kierkegaard still believes in speculation and in speculative knowledge. It could be that his own understanding of irony has him a little frightened. Even though it seems to be only in passing, he still makes a point of limiting its effects. Alcibiades is a most inflammable tinder since he is "rash, sensuous, and highspirited," but Plato, conversely, is strong enough to avoid getting taken in. *"Naturally*, for *more gifted* natures this realization [of the deceptive character of the ironist] could have been neither so noticeable nor so distressing" (emphasis added). Plato will learn to turn his gaze inward and to gain access to the Idea, though he also knows that, in a certain sense, he owes none of this directly to Socrates. Here is one of those numerous points where Kierkegaard joins Hegel and endeavors to go beyond irony. From this point of view, since he eludes the torments of love and moves toward authentic speculation, Plato is by far the best disciple. But it is not possible to say that Kierkegaard himself follows Plato. His model remains Socrates.

Indifference: such is the other name for ironic negativity. All the relations of the ironist—to his lovers, to the State, to death itself—are marked by indifference. This is what gives Socrates that haughty freedom, that attitude which could also seem "aristocratic." The lofty "ironic freedom," which elevates Socrates above empirical facticity, which produces Alcibiades' torments, and which will eventually cause Socrates' death, is not without a certain sensuous enjoyment. The ironist *delights* in his indifference and in his infinite detachment. Hegel does not miss the opportunity to condemn this sensuous enjoyment of subjectivity, which indulges itself in a lamentable vanity at the very moment (which in itself is necessary) that it becomes conscious of itself as absolute: "I am the master of the law and the world alike, I simply play with them as befits my caprice. My consciously ironic attitude lets even the highest things perish, and I merely delight in myself at the thought." Kierkegaard does not pick up on this condemnation, but before returning to the Hegelian point of view on "authentic freedom" in the life of the State, he treats himself to a moment's pause over the link between the delight of ironic enjoyment and the delight of cynical enjoyment. In its own way, each is to be understood as "negative enjoyment." This curious notion obviously does not mean—contrary to what has sometimes been suggested—that Socrates (like Diogenes) would have simply liberated himself from sensuous enjoyment, supposing he could have done this in the first place. Diogenes seems actually to have enjoyed the specific pleasure (negative enjoyment) of finding satisfaction in a lack, without in any case having been unacquainted with desire: "[Cynicism] seeks its satisfaction *in not surrendering to* [*this desire*] . . . instead of issuing in desire it turns back into itself at every moment and *enjoys the lack of enjoyment*—an enjoyment vividly suggesting what ironic satisfaction is in the intellectual sphere." How is it possible to enjoy the absence of enjoyment? It would be necessary here to distinguish between negative (ironic) enjoyment and "*happiness*," "that enjoyment possessing absolute content." This happiness—let's call it positive enjoyment—has to do with "possession." Obviously, the ironist possesses nothing; if he enjoys (it), it is perhaps because he knows that positive enjoyment can never quite be a sensuous enjoyment. Possession implies involvement and a dependence on the "content" in possession, something which always deprives the possessor of his mastery, therefore of his possession, and at the same time of his enjoyment. There is no such thing as a simple positive enjoyment. The desire to possess always hands itself over for possession. The ironist, thanks to the distance he maintains with respect to his own sensuous enjoyment (his hovering, the suspension of his desire, his detachment) is free to *not* enjoy sensuously; in which he delights. "Whereas the Sophist runs about like a harassed merchant, the ironist moves proudly as one terminated in himself—enjoying."

POLITICALLY BLAMEWORTHY IRONY

It remains to connect Socrates' politically negative attitude, a negativity that is in no way separable from negative dialectics in general, to the pure negativity of Socrates' irony. Insofar as dialectics is without a result here (except a "negative" one) and that it leads to indetermination, insofar as it is pure emancipation with respect to every positivity and that it denies every "established order" without ever establishing anything of its own, it is emancipation with respect to stability *par excellence*—that is, to the Institution of institutions, to the State. Corresponding to the non-positing of the Idea would be the Socratic wariness of any position, in particular a political position. There is neither Idea, nor stability, nor establishment, nor institution without posit(ion)ing. Now irony "establishes nothing," even more importantly, it "leaves nothing standing." Irony does not oppose itself to the State, rather it is not capable of entering into a relationship with the State: "For [Socrates] *was incapable* of contracting *any real relation* to the established order."

Socrates is in *ignorance* of the State; therein lies his irony. And his crime. The irony is double: there is the private individual's simple ignorance, and then there is the (ironic) claim that is made upon this ignorance before the people's tribunal. Socrates *boasts* of having never bothered about "acquiring money, nor about the management of his household, about military, civic, or other offices." "Now this can scarcely be regarded as so praiseworthy from the standpoint of the State," remarks Kierkegaard judiciously. If, when it comes to particular instances, Socrates can excuse himself on the basis of his ignorance, he is not able to do this with respect to the overall issue, for it is precisely this ignorance that renders him guilty in the eyes of the State, and of the people. "This non-acceptance of the gods of the State stems essentially from his whole standpoint theoretically designated by himself as ignorance."

Whoever is not with the State is against it; the death sentence will quite aptly label the ironist a "revolutionary" in spite of himself, negatively. "World history must adjudicate the case. But if it is to judge fairly, it must also admit that the State was within its rights in condemning Socrates. In a certain sense he was revolutionary, yet not so much by what he did as by what he omitted to do."

Ironic negativity, both in its reserve and its non-position, is interpreted by the State *ipso facto* as opposition. Whether we call it revolutionary or counterrevolutionary, we are equally correct. In its subjective vanity, irony is always a threat to institutions, established order, and to the power of the State. Persecution, indeed the death sentence itself, that is its destiny: Antigone, Socrates, Christ. By this means irony is not destroyed, but rather fulfilled.

Christianity, for Kierkegaard, can never have anything but an ironic relationship with the political order. The *extremely* ironic religious attitude, carried far enough, would consist in *defending* the powers that be, *no matter which ones*, out of indifference.

THE NON-TRAGIC DEATH OF SOCRATES

The death of Socrates is neither an unfortunate accident nor the result of a tragic confrontation; irony necessarily ends up by getting carried away with itself. The ironist seduces (himself) and holds (himself) back according to the logic of his point of view. Ironic negativity runs amuck: "totally, in its complete infinity . . . it finally swept away even Socrates himself." Death, that "next to nothing," was undoubtedly well-suited to the ironist's taste. Once again, though, it is especially his ignorance concerning death that makes death the one punishment that is possible for the ironist, since *it really isn't one.* Socrates chooses his own sentence; "whatever is no punishment at all." For he is ignorant of whether it will turn out to be a good or an evil.

Socrates is in ignorance about death, and this last ignorance sweeps him away. To the ironist death would be what the "negative result" was to his questioning: self-destruction. "Irony, on the other hand, like the old witch, constantly makes the tantalizing attempt first to devour everything in sight, then to devour itself too, or as in the case of the old witch, her own stomach." A witch has nothing of the hero about her. If, faced with death, Socrates maintains his point of view right up to the bitter end, this is not because he is a hero—for the hero always posits or defends something. Kierkegaard does not say exactly why he refuses to see in Socrates a hero. Quite simply, he does not bother to find out if the verdict of guilty is "fair" or "unfair." He gives short shrift to the "erudite mourners, that insipid host of tearful philanthropists, whose weeping and wailing over the fact that such a noble creature, such an honorable man, a paragon of virtue . . . became a sacrifice to the meanest of envies." Then he also dismisses in passing "recent philosophic investigators"—by which we are to understand Hegel—who sketch Socrates as a "tragic hero." All of that with no further explanation: "these things we need not discuss further here."

What prevents Kierkegaard from following Hegel at this point? For the thesis easily concedes that *from the point of view of the State* and the Greek populus, "Socrates actually perpetrated evil," just as it also concedes that the Socratic point of view is different from that of the State; it is one of subjectivity, of an interiority that reflects itself into itself. So far, nothing would prohibit seeing in the death of Socrates the effect of a confrontation between two equally justified claims, in other words, the very condition for the appearance of tragic destiny according to the Hegelian analysis. Nothing, that is, but the structure of opposition and the reference to an historical necessity according to which, at a certain *moment,* two prerogatives *oppose* one another. Hegel says, "They were right, but so was he." How could Socrates have been *right,* and how could he have opposed himself to the State, since he is ignorant of it and *posits* nothing? In order for there to be tragedy, in the Hegelian sense, it is necessary for the negative to posit itself and oppose itself to something: "Tragedy consists, then, in the fact that within such a conflict, each of the opposed sides has *justification*: while each can establish the true and positive content of its own aim and character only by denying and infringing the equally justified power of the other. The consequence is that in its ethical life, and because of it, each nevertheless becomes guilty." The interpretation of tragedy is part and parcel of the dialectical "System." It is less the notion of the "hero" that is being rejected here than the system that posits it only in order more effectively to do away with it. As tragic hero, the ironist would become a combatant and join in the dialectic. Once irony is sublated, it disappears. "Ordinarily," writes Kierkegaard, "irony is made into an ideal concept; its place in the system becomes that of a moment which vanishes." "Doubt, too, effaces itself within the system." The question, for Kierkegaard, will always be to find out whether subjectivity's and irony's point of view, as an existential category, can ever be surpassed, whether it is true that subjectivity never gets beyond itself and thus always remains *the* particular point of view of an empirical existence. Kierkegaard could have said that there is no point of view of all the points of view. That is why he could never understand Hegel and why, for instance, he wrote in his thesis: "in the System . . . but in reality," always conceiving "reality" as existential subjectivity. Ironic subjectivity (was Kierkegaard ever able to get beyond that?) is defined as an oscillation "between the ideal self and the empirical self."

Socrates has no philosophy; he only has a point of view. For Kierkegaard—but for Nietzsche too—this is what resists philosophy, in other words, the System. Obviously, we have to say "resists" and not "opposes."

IRONY: NON-DIALECTIZABLE NEGATIVITY

The system, to put it quite simply, and if that's even possible, consists in internalizing every negativity, in making it immanent to some positivity. Hegel: "We have to think this absolute concept of difference in its radicality as an immanent difference (*als innerer Unterschied*)." "But *who*," Kierkegaard would ask, "can do such thinking?" Can simple infinity, or that absolute concept which Hegel also calls "the simple essence of life," "the universal blood, whose omnipresence is neither disturbed nor interrupted by any difference" can this simple infinity ever be "thought" by a living, existing subjectivity, insofar as such a subjectivity never has more than just one point of view? Is it not a paradox to speak of a "point of view" of the absolute, or infinity? The system actually ought to *lose* all the particular points of view, all the differences, and that is perhaps why it must give the absolute all those names which designate difference: Subjectivity, Interiority, Life—marking them off at the same time, as is evident in their translation, with a capital letter.

But what resists the system does not oppose it from the *outside*. Between Hegel and Kierkegaard what we have is not contradiction. What resists the system is found inside it without disturbing it, without upsetting it. More specifically, this also means that it is to be found in Hegel's text. But does that which is in the text necessarily belong to the system? There is no need to insist further on the nature of that which resists systematization, or the Hegelian *Aufhebung:* it is clear that what is at stake here is existence in its singularity, its difference, etc. What is remarkable, though, is the mode in which this resistance is expressed, we might say its *style*. Kierkegaard does not put his criticism in the form of opposition but in what is perhaps the only form left open to him, irony, taken here as a rhetorical figure and described in the chapter of the thesis called, "For Orientation." With this figure, the ironist "goes along with" what he actually considers a foolishly inflated wisdom and *outdoes* the very thing he is belittling: "In relation to an insipid and inane enthusiasm it is ironically correct to *outdo* this with ever more and more elated exultation and praise, although the ironist is himself aware that this enthusiasm is the greatest foolishness in the world." Such is Kierkegaard's own method. He seems to relate the Hegelian "oversights" to the system's grandeur and the haughty superiority of its perspective. It is as though the cogency of the Hegelian interpretation depended on the very thing that makes it suspect: as such, his lack of attention to "details," and also the way Hegel, for instance, "doesn't bother himself" about "the difficulty involved in obtaining certainty regarding the phenomenal aspect of the existence of Socrates." Can we ever know who Socrates really was? This question would constitute a critical problem that "does not disturb Hegel in the least." He seems to do a leap-frog over the questions concerning Socrates' existence which would be raised by a comparison of the texts of Plato, Xenophon, and Aristophanes, just as they would be raised in Plato alone by the confrontation of those dialogues more properly "Socratic" with the others—a distinction to which Hegel alludes, moreover, but only "in passing." Now according to the needs of the demonstration, Hegel picks and chooses indifferently among the texts. To tell the truth, "such *trifles* are wholly unknown to him." Even the critical work of someone like Schleiermacher cannot match up to the *elevated* aims of Hegelianism: "All such investigations are wasted energy on Hegel, and when the phenomena are presented on parade he is in too much haste and too aware of his role as commanding general in world history to have time for anything more than the regal glance he sweeps over them."

Hegel, then, gets right to the point and neglects what Kierkegaard is content to call *details* or *trifles*—though not without having what is "repressed" by his regal glance and military bearing come back in his text as "isolated remarks" or "observations" made in passing. So much so that we could look for the symptoms of what remains refractory to the System in Hegel's own writings, in the remarks strewn about here and there, in the whole package of accessories that comes along with the Hegelian text. Kierkegaard took advantage of this opportunity, moreover, in his thesis: " 'Many dialogues [Hegel had pointed out "in passing"] contain merely negative dialectic, and this is the Socratic conversation.' These particular statements are in complete agreement with what I have advanced in the first part of this essay."

Anticipating just a bit, let's say that the thesis is ironic, at least in one sense, since it treats Hegel with irony. And if it does "treat" him in this way, this is perhaps because irony represents a means of criticizing or resisting the "System" in a non-contradictory, thus in principle, in a non-dialectizable way—perhaps one of the only means of "contesting" speculative dialectics without immediately becoming part of it. By not stepping onto the field of its oppositions, irony exasperates dialectical thought: it displaces without opposing, it contests without contradicting. As a result, dialectics cannot figure out what to do with irony; neither how to get hold of it nor how to get rid of it. The reductive gestures made by dialectics bear this out, just as, from another perspective, it is borne out by a certain *tone*, a certain *pathos* which accompanies the Hegelian discourse as soon as it broaches the question of irony. And this did not escape Kierkegaard's reading, either; a reading that is less trusting and respectful than it might sometimes appear in its attempt to slip past a Danish university wholly won over to Hegelianism. Hegel never mentions irony without a certain exasperation, especially when it involves its modern representatives. Furthermore, he has been so blinded by his hatred of the Romantics and their (informed or uninformed) appropriation of irony for themselves, that he cannot even allude to irony without immediately launching into a diatribe against Schlegel. (Such is the case right in the middle of his *Lecture* on Socrates.) Hegel does not like irony. Before returning to the tone he assumes when speaking of it, though, we ought to recall what efforts were expended to dismiss it philosophically, in his *Lectures on the History of Philosophy*, as well as in paragraph 140 of *The Philosophy of Right*, where we read: "Irony is only a manner of conducting oneself with others in conversation." It has nothing to do with the Idea itself. In the same way in the *Lectures*: "Irony is a particular way of getting along with others . . . what [Socrates] wished to effect thereby was to make others express themselves." Here it is nothing but a pedagogical tool that makes use of a ruse, and it has nothing to do with speculation, nor with dialectics.

However, Hegel admits at the same time that Socrates knew nothing, which seems to contradict the thesis of a ruse. What is even more surprising is that this "conversational nuance" will be joined later on in the *Lectures* by two other meanings that are apparently incompatible with each other as well as with this earlier meaning. At times, irony has the effect of *disengaging* the *abstract* Idea from its empirical determinations—at others, (a most unexpected reversal) it allows abstract representations to become *explicit* and *developed* by making them *concrete*. "The irony of Socrates has this great quality of showing how to make abstract Ideas concrete and how to effect their development . . . it is a matter of developing what was mere representation, and for this reason, something abstract." Here, then, irony accomplishes the task of modern speculation, and this by *starting out* from the abstract in order to make it determinate. That Hegel ends up "by confusing everything," is clear enough, and Kierkegaard is happy enough to point this out. We might even go so far as to notice at least a certain perplexity on the part of Hegel. So much for Socrates.

How do things stand with romantic irony? Hegel makes a violent and merciless attack on it, *but* he takes care in so doing not to aim at irony itself; the only thing at issue here is that movement which, along with Schlegel or Solger, has arbitrary pretensions to irony. "The arbitrary name 'irony' is of little or no importance," Hegel adds in a note consecrated to Solger and attached to paragraph 140 of *The Philosophy of Right*. Likewise, the *History of Philosophy* disputes the right of the Romantics to have any pretensions to irony: "In recent times, too, much has been said about Socratic irony." (Hegel goes on to characterize all dialectic by its capacity to allow any given thing to accomplish its own self-dissolution.) However, "men have tried to make this irony of Socrates into something quite different, for they extended it to a universal principle." This "something," which comes from Fichtean philosophy by way of Schlegel, is nothing other than "a trifling with everything": "to this subjectivity nothing is serious any more." Let us recall that the Socratic moment represented the prelude to "a *more strenuous* effort after knowledge." Actually, what the Romantics call irony is only a matter of hypocrisy, of subjective caprice, of vanity. All the supposed profundity of their inmost being is merely the profundity of an emptiness—"as may be seen from the ancient comedies of Aristophanes." We should remember *The Clouds* in this context. But didn't Hegel himself show us how profoundly Aristophanes had understood and recorded Socratic negativity? The truth cannot be so simple, since "from this irony of our times, the irony of Socrates is far removed."

In those pages of the Introduction of the *Aesthetics* that are devoted to irony, the "romantic" use of the word is not challenged. The Schlegel brothers are introduced there as critics whose philosophical baggage is on the meager side. As the inheritors of Fichtean philosophy, they conceive irony as an exaltation of the infinite freedom of the Self, posited as the principle of all cognition. This Self of the living individual is lord and master of everything; everything, every determination, every content loses itself in its liberty. Left to the caprice of the Self, the world is reduced to the appearances it receives from that Self. Armed with this principle, the ironic artist adopts the point of view of a Self "which posits and destroys everything," wholly at its own pleasure. Once all bonds have been snapped, there is nothing left to "take seriously." How close the results of such a point of view come to those of the Socratic method of questioning, as it is delineated in its negative aspect by Hegel himself, remains to be seen. Concrete values are repudiated; neither justice, nor morality, nor truth is taken seriously anymore. But you don't just give up taking things seriously with impunity. The Self is not able not to aspire to truth and objectivity. Hegel is exuberant and now feigns pity; the ironist inevitably pays for his levity—he suffers. Unable to tear himself out of his isolation, the unfortunate ironist cannot help falling prey to "a yearning which we have also seen proceeding from Fichtean philosophy." The repudiation of objectivity is unhealthy—the argument is not without its merit— there is something debilitating about it. Dissatisfaction, the feeling of his own emptiness, plunge the beautiful soul into a *morbid* state full of nostalgia. *Beautiful soul* is to be understood ironically here, for Hegel adds immediately afterwards, "A *truly* beautiful soul acts and is actual." It should be remarked in passing that irony must be distinguished from the comical, since "the comical must be restricted to showing that what it destroys is itself something inherently null, a false and contradictory phenomenon, a whim, e.g., an oddity, a particular caprice in comparison with a mighty passion, or even a *supposedly* tenable principle and firm maxim." How can we classify the *genre* of Aristophanes' *Clouds*? A large number of highly scornful epithets completes the analysis of the ironist: "null in character and contemptible," "weakness and lack of character," "impotence," "vanity," "wishy-washy," "moral inferiority," "worthless yearning character," "bad useless people," etc.

Solger is granted a special indulgence. He died prematurely and thus did not have the chance to go beyond the dialectical moment of the Idea represented by infinite absolute negativity. This he surely would have done, had he but lived.

Did Hegel ever talk about irony?

Two hypotheses:

1) Hegel "overlooked" irony, blinded as he was by his contempt for Schlegel. Such is Kierkegaard's opinion in the matter, though he is just

Hegelian enough to accept Hegel's scorn for the Romantics as his own. "In one-sidedly focusing on post-Fichtean irony, Hegel has overlooked the truth of irony." In the meantime, the question of "style" surfaces: "I shall first attempt to illuminate . . . a weakness from which Hegel's entire conception of the concept of irony seems to suffer. Hegel always discusses irony in a most contemptuous fashion, indeed irony is an abomination of his sight. Now concurrent with the appearance of Hegel occurred Schlegel's most brilliant period." Furthermore, "The fact that Hegel lets the form of irony that is closest to him *get under his skin* has naturally distorted his conception of the concept. And if the reader seldom gets a discussion, Schlegel, on the other hand, always gets a drubbing. But this does not mean that Hegel was wrong regarding the Schlegels. . . . This does mean, on the other hand, that Hegel has *overlooked the truth of irony*." And finally, "As soon as Hegel pronounces the word 'irony' he immediately thinks of Schlegel and Tieck, and his style instantly takes on the features of a certain indignation."

2) Second hypothesis: the fact that Schlegel and Tieck have pretensions to irony is not simply fortuitous. The Romantics repeat in their own way a moment in subjectivity's exaltation, a moment of absolute freedom in which subjectivity "posits nothing" and "leaves nothing standing." Kierkegaard uses both expressions with reference to Socrates *as well as* to the Romantics. In the Romantics we find once again the haughty bearing, the elusiveness, the wariness, the vanity, the consciousness that maintains its distance from all empirical actuality, the sensuous enjoyment, the withdrawal into itself, the exemption from established morality, and all that negativity which is associated with Socrates. But especially this: wherever it is to be found, irony is the mark of displacement. If these Romantics have something in common with Socrates (and Kierkegaard), it is a mode of discourse that is *indirect* (allusive or poetic, for instance). And it is perhaps that which cannot help "getting under Hegel's skin." This form of discourse that, positing nothing, represents a negativity that is not manifest, that is not dialectically sublatable. (Socrates is never overtly negative, that is why he is infinitely negative.) Socrates sneaks off and lays no claim to having anything more to say about his own questions. Irony, or the ironist, is always missing from its place, and it is this gap (*cet écart*) with which Hegelian phenomenology can do nothing. "So then, Socrates is not allowed to stand there (*à l'écart*) like a *Ding an sich*, but must come forth whether he likes it or not." Whence the Hegelian need for a "positive" Socrates. One way of reappropriating—in order better to be rid of it—this sort of operation that both displaces and is displaced would be to assign it a permanent place, to make it a "moment" that is both dispensable and dispensed with once and for all: let's say by doing justice to it (Socrates *will*

have been necessary), while depriving it of any future relevance (irony can no longer be possible). "Finally, irony here met its master in Hegel." Whereas the first form of irony [Socrates] was not combated but *pacified* by doing *justice* to subjectivity, the second form of irony [the Romantics] was both combated and *annihilated*, for since it was unjustified, doing it *justice* could only mean sublating it."

All the same, without deciding on a definition for irony, Hegel denounces the lack of *earnestness*, provisional or definitive, of everything that is in any way connected with it. Socrates was *not yet* able to be earnest, that is, to gain access to speculative philosophy. He can be excused for having waited on the doorstep of philosophy, for that was his place. But that modern thinkers should allow themselves, in a regressive fashion, to adopt the point of view of subjectivity, to affirm its infinite freedom in defiance of all earnestness, that borders on scandal.

Kierkegaard could not have been expected to take the side of the "Romantics." Rather, he goes the Hegelian critique one better, in earnest it would seem, and reproaches the Schlegels for having wanted to "create a world of their own," for having wanted to deny all historical reality— thereby transforming the historical character of myth in the twinkling of an eye—finally and above all, for having wanted to free themselves from all morality and virtue. He could not read *Lucinde* without becoming indignant, and just like Hegel, he mixes both moral and aesthetic complaints together in the same critique and refuses to grant the novel any ironic value whatsoever. If Schlegel's text borders on impudence, it is not only because it signals the supression of objective values: "*Lucinde* has a most doctrinaire character." It *supresses* all virtue in order to end up in sensuality. The sensuous enjoyment of irony is not like this; rather it fulfills itself only in despair, and then turns religious.

The thesis won't be able to end without a certain ambiguity. For irony has at least two fates: either it is expunged, overcome at last (Hegel as its master), or else it turns into madness. It is engulfed by philosophy or religion.

Apparently, it is philosophy that carries the day: the conclusion of the thesis is Hegelian, or just about. But in a sort of digression, the chapter entitled "For Orientation" seems to indicate quite a different outcome, by means of which the ironist already has been able to make off, or do away with himself. This curious aside (*aparté*), which is not taken into account by the conclusion, will prevent the thesis from coming to a smooth stop.

But let's start at the end: irony mastered in conclusion. For the conclusion necessarily puts an end to irony, by exclusion, forclusion (foreclosure), or inclusion. If conclusion there be, then irony has to appear there in the end.

The truth *of* irony has to show up there, has to be recognized there. In so doing, it has at last found its place, by assuming the aspect of a *moment*. Everything turns out all right in the end. Though not without Kierkegaard's having subverted the notion of *moment* along the way by making a stage or moment of *personal existence* out of it. It is a moment of consciousness, but it is now a matter of individual consciousness, and it is indispensable—as moment—to every "human life." "Irony is like the negative way, not the truth but the way. Everyone who has a result merely as such does not possess it, for he has not the way." For the benefit of those unconditional partisans of the "system," who are in a hurry to have the results, Kierkegaard points out that there is no way of getting around irony: "There is an *impatience* that would reap *before* it has sown. By all means let irony chasten it."

Since irony names the moment of a necessary detachment, going beyond it entails recuperation, reconciliation, reappropriation. *For example*, an author discovers his identity by seeing in each of his works "a moment in his own development."

Insofar as he is productive, "the writer" will always have been an ironist, he will always have maintained an "ironic relation" with each of his productions. Considered in itself, every work is fragmentary, partial, finite; an author's irony is his awareness of this finitude. As if detached and absent, he "lets the objective prevail" in his work. Kierkegaard had already detailed this conception in the preceding chapter, which was consecrated to Solger. For Solger, God's existence has been turned into irony: "God posits himself constantly over into nothingness, takes himself back again, then posits himself over once more, etc." But as "philosophical spokesman for romanticism and romantic irony . . . it is in art and poetry that Solger seems to find the 'highest' actuality that becomes visible through the negation of finite actuality."

Such is not the case, remarks Kierkegaard, from the point of view of the Romantics themselves: "[Romantic poetry] strives essentially to bring to consciousness the fact that the given actuality is the imperfect, while the higher actuality only allows itself to be envisaged in the infinite approximation of presentiment and intimation (*Ahnung*): so it seems necessary once more to relate oneself ironically to every particular production inasmuch as each individual product is but an approximation." Like all finite actuality, the work requires ironic reserve. A reserve that is wholly provisional here, for the higher actuality *becomes* what it is: "this *higher actuality*, which is to become visible in poetry, *is nevertheless not in poetry*, but constantly becoming." The Romantics wouldn't have been able to understand this actuality of the work as a *moment*: "For the romanticist the particular poetic production is either a darling with which he is wholly infatuated and which he is unable to explain how it has been possible for him to call to life, or it is an object which awakens disgust. Both alternatives are naturally untrue. The truth is that the particular poetic production is simply a moment."

There is a dream of sublation, then, in this conclusion. In it the ironic distance of the poet regarding his "production" would finally be blotted out. Once irony has been subdued, it makes room for identity, in any case the identity of the author who is then reconciled with himself in the dialectical reappropriation of his works. Such is the advent of the work's truth in the totality of its meaning: an end to the gaps, the disguises, the asides, the ruses—to hell with irony! It will have been *mastered*, in other words, reduced to a mere moment, like all detachment (division, remoteness, withdrawal, suspension, separation, negation). The subjective is reunited with the objective, the inside measures up to the outside.

But where? Obviously not in the work, which remains always—*aparté*. It would be necessary to stop writing. Speak, maybe—but Kierkegaard will always give up on it, saying instead how impossible it would be. What "Point of View [of my Work as an Author]" would bring to light the ultimate coincidence?

If this conclusion is not able to bring the thesis to a definitive close, this is not because we know that Kierkegaard will later accuse himself of having been a "mad Hegelian" at the time that he wrote the dissertation. Rather it is because the text, as we have seen, remains constantly ambiguous, zig-zagging continuously, continuously reserved or signaling abruptly in a different direction, toward "something other." It is time, then, to take hold of the text short of its ending.

The lone chapter entitled, "For Orientation," marks a change in point of view. It is a question there of the various uses of irony in the current sense of the term, in other words, in the sense of a *stylistic figure* in which (as the dictionaries still tell us) one says "the opposite of what is meant." The irony so described is only an inferior kind. But already present here is the decisive possibility of play, gap, inadequation which Kierkegaard will identify as the possibility of a certain sensuous enjoyment.

By means of this stylistic figure known as "irony," the speaking subject affords himself the possibility of breaking free of the bonds that, when he is expressing "his thought" adequately, tie him to it and thus to himself. Should the ironist have accomplices who are in on the joke, however, the figure cancels itself out immediately. The irony which is savored in isolation is of another kind, and otherwise provocative. For instance, the ironist outdoes an absurdity, or, on the contrary, does not seem to know what appears to be the most common knowledge, feigning candor and giving himself out to be sillier

than he actually is. This is still deception, but of a secret kind: pure provocation. The ironist conceals himself so that another will come out of
concealment.

Finally, irony is also a simple matter of *pulling a fast one*. It is not a
question of "cheating" with a view toward realizing any particular gain from
it, for it is hardly misleading. Or else we could use the word cheat in the sense
that we say that someone temporarily "cheats death," or an author "cheats"
his reader of an expectation, a hope, etc. As such, it is a means of escape,
thanks to a subterfuge, from a given audience avid of information, dying of
curiosity; a kind of slipping off, thanks to a diversion, from the diverse forms
of supervision and power that insist that everyone declare his position and
then stick to it. Irony is less a true provocation or challenge, then, than it is a
means of resistance. If it pulls a fast one, or *changes* the tempo (donner *le
change*), it is not out of any concern for "contradiction," it is for the fun of it,
and in order to retain control (off on the side) over the play of substitutions.

If irony "makes its appearance through a relation of opposition,"
though, this is not in order to affirm this relation, but in order to liberate itself
from it. The ironist confuses the opponents and does not take the contradiction between them seriously. True and false; serious and laughable; as far as
he is concerned, they are all on the same team. Irony actually is involved with
opposition, but less in the form of opposition than of complicity. The ironist
is thus able to perceive in nature herself an unconscious irony; for instance,
in the way she "strangely conjoins mirth with lament, joy with sorrow." But
this is merely a perspective *on* nature, for nature herself is without malice.

Every manifestation that is not simply what it is, but that always appears
to be accompanied at the same time by its opposite, is related to irony: like
nature's voice in the music of Ceylon that "sings frightfully merry minuets in
tones of a deep, wailing, heartrending voice."

Sometimes as point of view, sometimes as style, what is always at stake
in irony is the subjective freedom that liberates itself from apparently contradictory finite determinations and established values. It is well-known that no
institution is above making occasional use of irony's dangerous point of view
so as to neutralize it better. All that is needed here is to regulate closely those
times at which irony is allowed. So it was during the Middle Ages when the
Church instituted, or at least tolerated, the Feast of the Ass, a feast during
which the "Ass's Prose" was sung after the animal itself had been led into the
church.

Irony, then, prefers duplicity to contradiction. It is at home in *discord*,
and almost all those words beginning with "dis" could serve to characterize
it. Inadequation: that is the only rule. The ironic style, always *allusive*, works

like a "play on words." It has always already extracted or distracted, diverted or perverted the meaning of its discourse, of its own discourse.

This means that irony is highly diverting. It is not without a certain interest to note here that words that indicate a turning aside, or a separation, for example "distraction," or "diversion," are words that also have connotations of amusement and pleasure. The ironist distracts (himself from) the thing (itself), diverts (himself) by turning (himself) aside, by making light of everything. But this game is amusing not because there is "distraction" (in the sense of *dis-tractio*, separation) or opposition in it, but rather because the oppositions in it all turn out to be the same thing. In this game, what seems to get away always ends up by coming back. Compromise or substitution; that's where the player finds his distraction.

But that is also where his madness lies. In play, the ironic consciousness flees from the anxiety of its alienation, though this is an infinite flight in which, by means of a generalized diversion or displacement, it finds a merely negative freedom. The other solution, the earnest one, would consist in preserving its equality with itself in alienation, in order to achieve—in knowledge—the mastered difference of consciousness. Irony's subject "is constantly in retreat"; he maintains a negative independence with respect to everything. This infinite skittering (*dérobade infinie*) is one way of not stopping at any particular moment, and yet it neither reconciles nor unites them all in anything but a playful manner. The ambiguity of ironic expression would thus be more closely related to the symptomatic formation of a compromise than to a dialectical synthesis. It is not the Hegelian who is "mad," but the ironist: "This is what might be called irony's attempt to mediate the discrete moments, not in a higher unity but in a higher madness."

Once irony finally turns "against the whole of existence," once everything has become nothingness before irony, then it approaches religious devotion, it takes on the *appearance* of piety—something that also affirms that "all is vanity": "[Irony] thereby expresses the same proposition as the pious attitude." There is no way to tell them apart; but this is in appearance only, since piety obliterates even itself in order to offer itself up to religious devotion, while the ironist has not yet learned to see his own vanity. All the same, are we so far removed here from the Socratic irony, which sweeps itself away into death? Isn't faith another name for death, the ultimate form of obliteration? Irony might thus represent the point of view nearest the religious point of view; it would be the prelude, not so much to speculation, as to religiousness. One more step and ironic scepticism opens on to religious humor.

Did Kierkegaard take this step? When did he do it? How are we to get our bearings here if the ironist, like the man of faith, always travels *incognito?* Nothing sets them apart from others, nothing sets them apart from one another, either.

Ordinarily, we only get to know pseudo-ironists, the ones who let you in on everything—but do we really know just how far? The weakness of the Romantics, from the point of view of irony, was to have laid claim to it. If the ironist flees from (positive) determinations, it is not so that he will get pigeonholed as an ironist. He must, then, look serious and refrain from offering an apology for irony. Irony is thus always possible; it does not attract attention to itself. Shouldn't a real ironist, moreover, go out of his way to repudiate irony and to make known in a loud voice just how little he thinks of it? Hegel himself could very well have been the real "master of irony." His entire philosophy could have been written as a diversion, in order to pull a fast one on us. Nor would it be any less likely that, having made us accomplices to his irony, such an ironist would suddenly, without warning, start speaking in earnest.

Someone else then might write a thesis *on* irony, treat it in all seriousness as though it were a concept, describe its mechanisms and develop its critique, its apology, or its historical significance with an entirely scientific objectivity. Should this doctor of philosophy later produce a work in which there gleamed the slightest hint of irony, we might be inclined to regard his meaning with suspicion, to be wary of whatever he might say in a fictitious mode or under pseudonyms. We would always be ready to give irony its due.

HENNING FENGER

Kierkegaard as a Falsifier of History

A book, you know, has the remarkable
property that it can be interpreted
any way you please.

W̲e all commit falsifications of history—consciously or unconsciously.
Unconsciously, if we misremember or ourselves believe what we write down.
Eight out of ten letters dated January plus a certain year are in fact from the
next year. Kierkegaard often quotes incorrectly. The many misquotations
from the repertoire of the Royal Theater can be blamed, perhaps, on the
actors, but even when Kierkegaard has the text on his bookshelf he seldom
bothers to verify quotations. His legendary memory is not precise about
details. The first dislocations of memory in the *Papers* occur, indeed, in I.B.6,
where he twice speaks of a "long passage of time," although it is quite well
known that not even a month had passed between the appearance of
Kierkegaard's polemic article "To Mr. Orla Lehmann" in *Flyveposten* of
April 10, 1836, and the book dealer's delivery of *Humoristiske Intelligensblade* on May 4. If II.A.20 is correctly dated to 1837, then it means that his
preoccupation with the motif of the master thief already lay "several years in
the past," that is, in 1835.

The conscious falsifications of the journal are more difficult to date.
Kierkegaard wrote in random notebooks—from the front and from the
back—and on loose sheets of paper. Unlike many other people, he often
reread what he had written down, put it in systematic order, and made comments on it in the margin, from the standpoint of later reading or later insight.
Are his attempts to erase the traces of his youthful passion of 1837–38 for

From *Kierkegaard, The Myths and Their Origin: Studies in the Kierkegaard Pages
and Letters,* translated by George C. Schoolfield. © 1980 by Yale University Press.

Bolette Rørdam from the period of his engagement (1840–41) or from a later time, when Regine was to be made into one of world literature's great beloveds at all costs? The answer rests in the Assistens cemetery.

Of course, it is most reasonable to think that Kierkegaard began to arrange his facts only after the breaking-off of the engagement in October 1841 and the subsequent leap into a poet's existence. He played the role of the irresistible seducer even in the presence of his best friend, Emil Boesen. The report of December 14, 1841, concerning the Viennese singer Mademoiselle Schulze, who "has such a striking resemblance to a certain young girl, so deceptive that it genuinely affected me to see her in Elvira, of all roles," is just as touchingly naive as are its continuation and its postulate: "When my wild mood comes over me, then I'm almost tempted to approach her, and not exactly with the 'most honest intentions'. . . . It could be a little diversion, when I'm tired of speculation. . . . She lives near me. Well, let's leave it at that." Why not?

With the publication of *Either/Or* in February 1843, Kierkegaard definitively established himself as an aesthetician in at least three meanings of the word: (a) as a scholarly analyst of the categories of the beautiful, (b) as a prose-poet in the most varied genres, and (c) as a nihilistic Epicurean. From then on we have rather little cause to depend upon his word; his contemporaries, at any event, took him seriously neither as an ethicist nor as a theologian.

KIERKEGAARD'S SNARES FOR HISTORICAL RESEARCH

It would be quite unfair to assert that Kierkegaard's contemporaries believed that he did not tell the truth, or could not. He simply put out snares for his contemporaries and, in the process, for posterity's historical researchers as well. His Socratic irony, his system of Chinese boxes, with editors and pseudonyms, and his indirect form of communication were confusing—then as now. How can we capture Kierkegaard in a statement which corresponds to the facts, or nail him to a standpoint for which he is willing to vouch?

His contemporaries had facts at their disposal which posterity can establish only by means of textual criticism. When Kierkegaard, on June 12, 1842, published an article in *Fædrelandet*, "Public Confession," and in it asked "the good people who are interested in me never to regard me as the author of something which does not bear my name," no one in Copenhagen's journalistic world regarded the statement as anything but a joke. To be sure, he had taken great pains with the publication of *Either/Or*, including the copy made by a hand not his own, the negotiations with publisher and printer, the planning of his publicity campaign for the book, and so forth. But it was precisely on this account that the editor of *Berlingske Tidende*, M. L. Nathanson . . . , P. V. Christensen . . . , his friend H. P. Holst, during whose tenure as editor of *Ny Portefeuille* he published his article "Literary Quicksilver" (February 12, 1843), and his new friend and assistant, J. F. Giødwad, the editor of *Fædrelandet*, knew perfectly well what was going on. Many other members of the literary inner circle, for example the Heiberg coterie—Hertz, Hans Christian Andersen, and P. L. Møller—and Goldschmidt, Israel Levin, and the circle around the *Corsair*, were likewise in on the secret.

It becomes perfectly clear from H. P. Barfod's first volume of the *Posthumous Papers* (1869) that Kierkegaard meant to give *Either/Or* a running start in at least four publications of the day— *Forposten, Den Frisindede, Fædrelandet*, and *Berlingske Tidende*: there are letters, unmailed, to Giødwad and Nathanson, the editors of the last two. Kierkegaard's desire to assure himself that his name would be connected with that of Victor Eremita, the editor of *Either/Or*, was scarcely for financial reasons but rather resulted from an altogether pardonable author's pride. He wished to be regarded as the originator of the great work—a wholly superfluous wish, since no one else has ever been seriously suspected of having done the deed. The case was diametrically opposed, for example, to that of *Hverdagshistorierne (The Everyday Stories)*, the authorship of which was ascribed to Heiberg, P. V. Jacobsen, Poul Møller, and many others—but not, of course, to Fru Gyllembourg, who did write them.

With *Either/Or* Kierkegaard participated in the favorite literary game of the day, playing puss-in-the-corner with anonymity—see Heiberg and "Forf. til 'En Hverdagshistorie' " ("The Author of 'An Everyday Story' "), alias Fru Gyllembourg, see Saint-Aubain and Carl Bernhard, see Hertz and "Forfatteren til 'Gjengangerbreve' " (The Author of 'Ghost Letters' "), see Overskou and "Forfatteren til 'Østergade og Vestergade' " ("The Author of 'Østergade and Vestergade' "). The examples are legion. In the 1840s, when Heiberg, Andersen, and Hertz were suddenly exposed to stiff head winds, they also had to conceal both their countenances and their names.

In his capacity as editor, Victor Eremita appeared in *Fædrelandet* on March 5, 1843, with the very ironic "Statement of Gratitude to Professor Heiberg." In the same place, on February 27, he had printed the little essay "Who Is the Author of *Either/Or*?" under the pseudonym "A. F. . . . . ."—a contribution in a conversational vein which, employing both external and internal criteria, makes fun of all the various possibilities concerning the book's authorship, calling attention en passant to the cost of publishing such a large volume.

In the meantime—that is, on March 1, 1843—Heiberg had published a little article in *Intelligensblade*, "Litterær Vintersæd" ("Literary Winter Crop"), where he chats for seven pages about the books published after New Year's—Winther's *Digtninger* (*Poetic Works*), Holst's *Ude og Hjemme* (*Abroad and at Home*), Thiele's *Folkesagn* (*Popular Legends*), mentioned only by name, and *Either/Or*, which—in four pages—is fobbed off with what today would be called a preliminary discussion. There was no question of Heiberg's writing a genuine review of the book's 800 pages—he had had little more than a week at his disposal. He gets around the problem carefully and deliberately by indicating what an imaginary reader, "one," can think about the book after a first hasty skimming. Heiberg's article, reprinted in the last chapter (omitted here) of the Danish edition of this book, is not as bad as Kierkegaard research would like to make it out to be, even though it clearly shows that Heiberg paid no mind to "The Diary of the Seducer" or to the essay about Scribe's *The First Love*. Heiberg was genuinely impressed by the work's second part, which he praises to the skies. However, three facts are decisive for Kierkegaard studies:

In the first place, "Copenhagen's cultural world" had expected an extensive review from Heiberg's hand, treating the book's basic elements. That is apparent from Signe Læssøe's letter of April 7, 1843, to Hans Christian Andersen.

Second, in his thank-you article to Heiberg of March 5, Kierkegaard is so ironic and sarcastic that he cannot for a moment have doubted that he was burning his bridges behind him, as far as the Heiberg circle was concerned. Thereby, in a single leap, Kierkegaard put himself in the camp of the young hotspurs—such as P. L. Møller, Goldschmidt, Carstensen, Brøchner, and Molbech junior—who had long been nipping at the heels of the very Heiberg whom Kierkegaard had particularly wished to please with *Either/Or*. After the "Winter Crop" article, Kierkegaard's *Papers* swarm with sallies against Heiberg, not all equally witty. The sluices had been opened.

In the third place, it becomes obvious that only now, for the first time, does the idea of connecting the aesthetic authorship with a religious one— that is, with the publication of a series of edifying discourses dedicated to the deceased hosier—arise in Kierkegaard's mind. That he was anxious to connect his name as the author of *Either/Or* with the religious production emerges from the article "A Little Explanation," in *Fædrelandet* of May 16, 1843, where he takes pains to point out that "the sermon which concludes a recently published work" is not identical with his sermon in the pastoral seminar of January 12, 1841. The article is signed S. Kierkegaard. *Two Edifying Discourses* also appeared on May 16, 1843. The chronological facts do not support Kierkegaard's later interpretations of the authorship as having been planned from the start in accordance with religious categories. Rather, the facts contradict these interpretations.

Kierkegaard also assiduously veiled the story of the origin of *Either/Or* by means of his countless commentaries and explanations. In IV.B.59 (which appears to be an article, ready for the printer, with the title "Postscript to *Either/Or* of Victor Eremita") there is the statement, "For five years I concealed the manuscript which in *Either/Or* I permitted myself to present to the reading public." This note of March 1844 leads us back to the beginning of 1839 and naturally is intended to be taken only as literary joke on Victor Eremita's part. But should his many efforts to get us to believe that the work was written in eleven months also be regarded as a legitimate kind of joking? In one copy of *Either/Or* there is the following notation (IV.A.215):

> Some people think that *Either/Or* is a collection of occasional papers which I have had lying in my desk. Bravo! As a matter of fact, it is the very opposite. The only thing this work lacks is a narrative, which I began but then decided to omit just as Aladdin decided to leave one window out. It would have been called "unhappy love." It would form a contrasting picture to the Seducer.

Papers IV.A.221 is also of the same sort: "If, upon publishing *Either/ Or*, I had not decided not to use anything old, I'd have found aphorisms, while going through my papers, which could have been put to splendid use." This memorandum of March 15, 1843, is illuminated by an aphorism, found on "a little piece of paper." In *The Point of View for My Work as an Author* Kierkegaard screws up his courage and carries his argument through to the end: "When I began *Either/Or* (of which, speaking *in parenthesi*, there literally existed only about a page, that is, a couple of diapsalmata, while the whole book was written in eleven months, and the second part first), I was *potentialiter* as deeply influenced by the religious element as I have ever been" (*SV*, XIII:526). Now, is one supposed to believe Kierkegaard's latter assertion about his religious seizure when one can prove that his former statement on the genesis of *Either/Or* is—shall we be kind and call it inexact?

Before offering our documentation, we can fairly ask, What does it actually mean—to *write* something? Anyone who is familiar with literary work knows that a thought, a sentence, a paragraph, a chapter, a treatise, or a whole book goes through every imaginable stage from the initial written sketch to the final proof. Kierkegaard is correct only if, by the phrase "was written," he is referring to his own ultimate version, before the secretary—

"my little secretary Hr. Christensen" (alias Peter Vilhelm Christensen, born 1819, who became a candidate in theology in 1842 and died in 1863 while pastor in Tønning)—prepared the fair copy of the manuscript. But that the manuscript was prepared in eleven months before the composition of the preface in November 1842 cannot be correct either—among other reasons, because P. V. Christensen could not have started on the fair copy (necessary to conceal Kierkegaard's own handwriting) until March at the very earliest and must have needed a very considerable time to copy a manuscript of such gigantic proportions.

Amusingly enough, P. A. Heiberg, Kierkegaard's faithful squire, is one of those who have demonstrated most clearly the incorrectness of the information Kierkegaard provides.

P. A. HEIBERG'S ACCOUNT OF THE GENESIS OF *EITHER/OR*

In 1910, the year before the publication of the third volume of the *Papers* (treating the period from June 2, 1840, when Kierkegaard submitted his examination request to the theological faculty, until November 20, 1842, when he finished the preface to *Either/Or*), P. A. Heiberg issued a 36-page pamphlet called *Nogle Bidrag til Enten-Eller's Tilblivelseshistorie (Some Contributions to the Story of the Genesis of* Either/Or). Heiberg bases his work in particular on the Berlin letters to Emil Boesen. His analysis of the manuscript and the works preparatory to it is reproduced in the third volume of the *Papers*, first in the chronology and finally in the imposing appendix where Heiberg distinguishes among sketch, versions (preliminary and final), and the printer's manuscript, and also adduces a special column for his own commentaries. By its thoroughness and its penetrating knowledge of Kierkegaard's literary effects, this impressive work commands our respect.

Heiberg's initial conclusions are that "the Equilibrium between the Aesthetic and the Ethical in the Formation of the Personality" was completed in Berlin circa December 7, 1841; that "The First Love" was written in the same city in December 1841 and January 1842; that the manuscript of "The Antique Tragic's Reflection in the Modern Tragic" was concluded in Berlin on January 30, 1842; and that "The Diary of the Seducer" was finished in Copenhagen on April 14. "The Direct Erotic Stages" was finished at the same place on June 12, 1842 (the day after the great cascade of words against the Danish Hegelians—"Public Confession"—had appeared in *Fædrelandet*), while "Shadow Sketch" is from July 25, 1842, more or less contemporaneous with the much briefer "The Unhappiest Man."

What is left of the mammoth book? Save for the preface of November 1842 and the many diapsalmata, there are "The Rotation of Crops," scarcely 20 pages long, among A.'s papers, and among B.'s, "The Aesthetic Validity of Marriage," 137 pages in length. There is also the sermon "Ultimatum," which B. sends to A. under the pretext of having received it from his friend, a pastor (*haud illaudabilis!*) on the Jutland heath, who "means to present it next year and is sure that he will get every peasant to understand it." It is the famous sermon concerning "The Edification Which Lies in the Thought That against God We Are Always Wrong."

Certain loose ends remained for Heiberg, who—fair is fair—does not unqualifiedly support the eleven-month theory. On page 6 he offers the information that Kierkegaard himself refers to "The Rotation of Crops" as a "polemic which, as far as essentials are concerned, I have finished in the red book at home," and on page 7 he points out that, "for the sermon concerning the edification which lies in the thought that against God we are always wrong," there exists a first sketch from Kierkegaard's seminary time, 1840–41. At the same time, Heiberg calls attention to the connection between B.'s first large treatise, "The Aesthetic Validity of Marriage," and a manuscript, signed by B., "An attempt to Save Marriage Aesthetically." The manuscript, which is older than B.'s opus written in Berlin, "Concerning the Equilibrium, etc.," must consequently have been written (in its definitive form?) in Copenhagen before the Berlin trip, which Kierkegaard undertook on October 25, 1841.

It emerges from the original Berlin letters—much more strongly, even, than in P. A. Heiberg's work—that *Either/Or* is a project sketched and begun in Copenhagen and to no small extent discussed with Emil Boesen, Kierkegaard's literary confidant—no doubt his only one. It is not clear when Giødwad enters the picture in earnest; many factors point to the period around 1840–41.

On December 14, 1841, Kierkegaard wrote to Emil Boesen: "I'm writing as though it were a matter of life and death. By this time I've written fourteen printed sheets. Thereby I have completed a part of a treatise which, *volente deo*, I shall submit to you. I have written nothing during the last week, I'm lying fallow and collecting myself, but I notice already that something's stirring within me." The treatise was not necessarily completed around December 7, but the most important part of "The Equilibrium between the Aesthetic and the Ethical, etc." must naturally have been done. The request for Heiberg's translation of Scribe's *The First Love* does not exclude the possibility that Kierkegaard had an earlier treatise at hand—compare P. A. Heiberg's observation (p.10) that "the first two acts of the manuscript of 'The First Love' are not as even, smooth, and free of corrections as is the rest of the manuscript."

On January 1, 1842: "You asked what I'm working on. Answer: It would take too much time to tell you now—just this much: it is the further work on *Either/Or.*" Thus *Either/Or* was already begun in Copenhagen, and Boesen knew what Kierkegaard was talking about. Compare Kierkegaard's letter of January 16, 1842:

> I'm working hard. My body can't stand it. So that you can see that I'm my old self, I'll tell you that I've been writing again, a large part of a contribution—*Either/Or;* it hasn't gone very rapidly, but that results from its not being a question of expository writing but rather pure poetic production, something which quite specially requires one to be in the proper mood.

This contrast between "expository writing" and "pure poetic production" explains Kierkegaard's problem as he was working on *Either/Or.* He had various manuscripts with "developments," that is, with aesthetic studies in the Heibergian-Hegelian spirit, but now he wished to transform them or to use them for pure poetic production—very often in order to be able to include his father and Regine in the "scientific" analyses of the various aesthetic categories.

On February 6 to Boesen: "*Either/Or* is quite a splendid title after all; it's piquant and has a speculative meaning at one and the same time." He feels that he absolutely must come to Copenhagen with the manuscript. "Either I'll get through with *Either/Or* this spring or I never shall." And, on February 27, "I'm coming to Copenhagen to complete *Either/Or.* This is my pet thought, and I live in it." An elementary explanation for this ill-timed departure from Berlin was given to Boesen as early as January 16, 1842: "For the rest, I wish I had my papers with me; for I miss them too."

Thus, P. A. Heiberg may well be right, after all: Emil Boesen had been "accustomed to see my works come into being," and the "rolls" which Kierkegaard mentions are manuscripts, folded in the middle and rolled up, so that they could be put into a pocket. Kierkegaard was not a man to use briefcases, and Heiberg's conclusion appears to stand to reason: "that, *before the departure for Berlin*, 'pieces of work' existed, which S. K. took with him to Boesen, in the form of *manuscript rolls*, protruding, for example, from his coattail pocket, in order to read aloud from them to him."

Most likely it was B.'s first treatise on "The Aesthetic Validity of Marriage" which Heiberg, on the basis of the mention of "Magister Kierkegaard," dates between the thesis defense of September 29 and the departure for Berlin of October 25, 1841. Quite apart from the fact that the handsome and freshly acquired academic degree can be stuck in anywhere after September 29, there is something touching in this dating by Heiberg: we are asked to believe that Kierkegaard wrote about the way one saves marriage aesthetically during the last two months of his engagement, months of falseness and double-dealing (documented by means of the original letters to Regine). *Nota bene*, how "one" saves marriage—not how *he* would, for he had long ago decided not to stick his foot into that trap.

THE ESSAY ON *THE FIRST LOVE*

Heiberg touches upon something of essential importance when, he mentions that Boesen doubtless had heard of (or seen) "a work," such as the one about *The First Love*, coming into existence. "I recall that you once sent me a little critique of Scribe's *The First Love*; it was written with an almost desperate enthusiasm"—lines which can be found again, word for word, in the preparatory manuscript to "The Aesthetic Validity of Marriage." Moreover, the essay and the treatise are "written on paper of an identical kind and size." At this point I shall not discuss the hypothesis which lies close at hand—that *Either/Or*'s B. is written with Emil Boesen in mind, that is, as Kierkegaard would have written if he had been able to wield the pen for Boesen; but there are undeniably various elements in the Berlin letters which support such an assumption.

At any event, the sketch for "The First Love" is an old item, perhaps the oldest of the layers in *Either/Or*. One can hardly give too much weight to the ironic introductory remarks. "This article should decidedly have been printed in a journal which Frederik Unsmann had decided to publish at decided times. Alas, what are all the decisions of man?" This remark cannot possibly refer to Heiberg's *Flyveposten*, whose interim editions had no certain dates of publication at all; and the treatise simply did not suit Heiberg's "speculative journal," *Perseus*. Can it refer to P. F. Barfod and P. L. Møller's *Nordisk Ugeskrift*, nos. 1–26, of 1837? In such a case, one has an explanation for an acquaintanceship between Kierkegaard and P. L. Møller as early as the 1830s. Or can it refer to *Søndagsbladet*, which H. P. Holst edited from January through March 1835?

Just the same, it is baffling—not to say suspicious-looking—that Kierkegaard writes, "Now on the other hand, since I have seen it produced again and again, on other stages too [he must refer to Berlin], only now do I grow genuinely thankful toward our stage artists," those for whose sake he would like to take a foreigner to the theater in order to show him our stage. But who precisely is it that Kierkegaard would like to show to that guest of his?

P. J. Frydendahl, born in 1766, died on February 20, 1836, after having trod the boards for the last time on October 2, 1835, in Holberg's *Barselstue (Lying-In Room)*; he had acted the role of iron-founder Dervière in Scribe's play for the last time on March 5, 1835. The play was removed from the repertoire for almost a year, after which C. Foersom took up Frydendahl's old part of February 24, 1836. At the same time the part of the many Rinville was passed along from Gottlob Stage to W. Holst, whom Kierkegaard does not bring up in any connection. In addition, Fru Heiberg is mentioned as Emmeline, but she played that role for the last time on December 18, 1837, and then the piece was allowed to rest until January 3, 1839, when Henriette Andersen took over Emmeline's part, with Fru Heiberg substituting for her on only one occasion, November 2, 1839. Only the indefatigable Phister, whom Kierkegaard also praises to the skies, continued to play Charles until May 29, 1849, when the play was removed from the repertoire for five seasons. Kierkegaard's concluding apotheosis in *Either/Or*, in February 1843, refers in other words to the play's total of twenty-five performances, up to and including that of March 5, 1835.

After that date, the play—starting with its revival on February 24, 1836—was performed a total of twenty-nine times, with a wholly new cast (save for Phister), up to November 1842, when the preface to *Either/Or* was finished. One does not require great mental powers to guess that, in Berlin, Kierkegaard did some embroidery upon an old treatise, an *Urform* of "The First Love." And one does not need to bring a great stylistic sense of language to bear, either, in order to conjecture that the original treatise was almost identical with the essay's introduction and that it closed with a quotation, by Paul Møller, from his "splendid review of *The Extremes:* herewith the introduction is at an end." Since this review is mentioned in I.C. 70 under the date "February 1836," and since Poul Møller's review—which is a mighty piece of homage to the grand old lady of the house of Heiberg, Fru Gyllembourg—appeared in the *Maanedsskrift for Litteratur*'s February issue of 1836, one does not need textual-critical genius to see that it was the revival of the play on February 25, 1836, with Foersom replacing the lately deceased Frydendahl, which provided the impetus for Kierkegaard's first article—compare *The Crisis and a Crisis in the Life of an Actress* (1848), again a case where a revival—of *Romeo and Juliet*—enticed Kierkegaard into writing. Whatever performances of *The First Love* he had seen since 1835, partly in Copenhagen with another Danish cast and later on with a French troupe of actors, partly in Berlin—all these performances could not dim the first and unforgettable impression, something which recalls the excitement he felt when he saw *Don Juan* for the first time at the Royal Theater.

The same stylistic deposits from the 1830s can be perceived in the treatise about "The Direct Erotic Stages or the Musical-Erotic," where, after the first enamored and witty pages in the "Insignificant Introductions," one hears Kierkegaard shift gears—that is, he takes out the old treatise: dry, creaking, overornamented, and aesthetically scientific:

> That which this investigation has taken as its primary task is to show the meaning of the musical-erotic, and toward that end once again to point out the various stages which, as they have that in common, that they are all directly erotic, at the same time agree in the fact that they are all essentially musical.

Here reference is made to Heinrich Steffen's *Caricaturen des Heiligsten*, vols. I–II (1819), which Kierkegaard's book dealer had delivered to him on January 13, 1836—a book whose thoughts on music still absorb him on October 9, 1836 (I.A. 260). In addition, attention should be paid to the *Irische Elfenmärchen* of the Brothers Grimm (1826), which occupied him in September and October 1837 (II.A.135 and 169), thus at a time when he long since had been making extensive sketches, following Heiberg's aesthetic scheme (I.C. 125), about the three Mozartean figures: the page in *The Marriage of Figaro*, Papageno in *The Magic Flute*, and Don Juan. The two latter roles were done by Cetti, and it is the performance of *The Magic Flute* on January 26, 1837, which inspired the entry in his papers. It is reasonable to believe that in 1837 Kierkegaard was working on an aesthetic treatise for Heiberg's *Perseus* and that he was left with it on his hands (as he was with his Faust treatise, when Martensen got ahead of him) and with his review of Andersen's *Kun en Spillemand (Only a Musician)*. He got the "review" published as an independent book, but a great part of the remaining material found its way into *Either/Or*.

Whether one says, or does not say, that this book *was* written in 1841–42 will remain a matter of personal taste. We do not know for sure how much Kierkegaard had saved of the papers which he complained to Emil Boesen that he had left in Copenhagen. Many of the pages in "The Antique Tragic's Reflection in the Modern Tragic" bear conceptual and stylistic traces of older sketches and projects. What is new in *Either/Or*, before all else, is the personal element, the many recastings of the relationship to his father and to Regine. Any number of times, P. A. Heiberg employs a metaphor which seems to be particularly clumsy, coming from the pen of a researcher as far removed from the natural sciences as he was—the picture of the fertilized egg in its various stages of development. It must suffice simply to establish that *Either/ Or* is a résumé of ten years of contemplations, thoughts, ideas, drafts, sketches, and attempts at writing. It is precisely for this reason that it provides a gateway into the central aesthetic-philosophical oeuvre of 1843–46, the era of the great works.

CONCERNING THE CONCEPT OF IRONY IN SØREN KIERKEGAARD

Among the many land mines which Kierkegaard planted for scholarship, the ironic ones are by no means the least dangerous. There is a multitude of examples, some wittier than others, beginning with Kierkegaard's very school days. But it is useful to keep firmly in mind what the bizarre but by no means unironic Israel Levin (1810–83)—man of letters, philologist, editor, complainer, boozer, and misogynist (and a good deal more)—says in his dictated "Remarks concerning S. Kierkegaard 1858 and 1869." They have always been a thorn in the flesh of Kierkegaard fanatics, for, as Kierkegaard's secretary and, for a time, daily companion, Levin had an intimate knowledge of his protector, observing him with a malicious eye for painful details. (Levin exhibited this talent for ironic and self-ironic surrender of secrets in the strange diary which, using the third person, he kept concerning his curiously triangular honeymoon journey to Fanø in August and September 1865, an account known only in an excerpt in *Weekendavisen* of July 18, 1975.)

> Whoever wishes to treat S. K.'s life should take care not to get burned, full as it is of contrasts, difficult as it is to get to the bottom of his character. He often refers to twofold reflection; all his speech was more than sevenfold reflection. He struggled to achieve clarity concerning himself, but he was pursued by every possible mood and was himself such a person of moods that he often made untrue statements, persuading himself that he spoke the truth. . . . Generally, he lived in a world of imagination and empty reflections which seized upon everything and transformed it in every possible way, examining it from all sides and reflecting upon it. He never understood himself, in his intellectual activity he sought nourishment for his infinite yearning. The idea itself was enough for him, he "imagined himself into" every sort of existence. . . . That is why he sought release in reveries and poetic images, and, with his gift for language and his demonic imagination, the effect he achieved was astonishing. . . . His imagination

was so vital that it seemed he saw pictures before his very eyes. It was as though he lived in a world of the spirit, and with a remarkable impropriety and eccentricity he could depict the most frightful things in a degree of vividness which was terrifying. . . . Everything about him consisted of inward emotions. His talk about a wild bachelor's life, about youthful sins, and so on can refer only to "sinning in the thought."

Levin's remarks are reproduced here in excerpts from Steen Johansen's *Erindringer om Søren Kierkegaard (Recollections of Søren Kierkegaard,* 1955), a book which contains everything of Levin's preserved in the Kierkegaard archive, together with a smaller piece by Levin otherwise to be found only in P. A. Heiberg's *Bidrag til et psykologisk Billede af Søren Kierkegaard i hans Barndom og Ungdom (Contributions to a Psychological Portrait of Søren Kierkegaard in His Childhood and Youth,* 1895), perhaps *the* work which, despite its merits, was the first to shove Kierkegaard research down a sidetrack. Are several of Levin's remarks missing? Were they removed by P. A. Heiberg, in whose eyes Levin was the worst desecrator of his idol? And who corrected the financial statements?

Levin's assertion that it was impossible to figure Kierkegaard out agrees with the judgment of other contemporaries. They simply did not know what to make of him. One can sense their reaction in the thank-you letters from Danish poets to whom he had sent the second edition of *Either/Or* in 1849 with subtly differentiated dedications. H. C. Andersen, who was anything but naive, could not conceal his joy at having been given the book: "I was very much surprised, as you well can believe; I didn't at all think that you had friendly thoughts about me, and now I see that you do, after all. God bless you for it. Thank you! Thank you!" One would like to have seen Kierkegaard's face when he received this honest letter from the hunted animal par excellence of Danish literature, whom he himself, in *From the Papers of One Still Living,* had pursued eleven years earlier, with such unrefined means. Paludan-Müller and Hauch are much more cunning and reserved in their expressions of gratitude.

Certainly, Heiberg was the one who saw through Kierkegaard earliest of all and repaid him—not only with the same coin but with passivity and an unshakable, impeccable politeness. After his "Statement of Gratitude to Professor Heiberg" on March 5, 1843, Kierkegaard did *not* receive the great review he had hoped for; unlike H. P. Holst and Rasmus Nielsen, he did not get to play a role in *Intelligensblade;* and he was no longer invited to the Heiberg home, which from 1844 on was located once and for all in

Søkvæsthuset (that handsome classical building on Christianshavn, in which the Heiberg Society is now located). And, finally, he did not succeed—something which plainly irritated him much more than anything else—in getting involved in a polemic with Heiberg after having made a direct attack by means of his sprightly and malicious book, *Prefaces* (1844). In other words, like his honored enemy, P. L. Møller, he was put in his place by Heiberg as one of those writers with whom one simply does not get involved. Heiberg was fully aware of what he was doing as, properly and elegantly, he maintained a distance between Kierkegaard and himself. The master of irony, however, scarcely understood it—he did not realize that he could be outdone at his own game.

Kierkegaard replied with quite primitive forms of irony, partly by playing people off against one another, partly by doing deeds which were the very opposite of what he said. He had made this a practice since his school days. The episode which Brøchner reports concerning Kierkegaard's visit in Sæding, where he was handsomely entertained as the son of the parish's benefactor and finally was to be saluted with a speech of thanks by the parish clerk, ended with his pinching the manuscript of the clerk's speech before the eyes of the flabbergasted schoolchildren. The ironic joke is a piece of student's impudence, or, truth to tell, sheer crudity. His offer of 1840 (III.B.1) to H. C. Andersen to finance the printing of *En Comoedie i det Grønne (A Comedy in the Open)* was of course meant as irony; fortunately, it was not printed until after his death. Beyond question, it was an act of boundless tactlessness toward the impoverished author—Andersen—onto whom he had forced himself. His behavior is wittier when, the next year, he concludes *Concerning the Concept of Irony* with a reference to Martensen's extravagantly flattering review of Heiberg's *Nye Digte (New Poems)* in *Fædrelandet* of January 1841—a reference meant, he said, for the person who "would like to have material for reflection" (*SV*, XIII:393). The irony was not directed at Heiberg but at Martensen, and *he*, of course, could speak for himself.

After his open break with Heiberg, Kierkegaard made a system out of his ironic banter. He did not neglect a single opportunity to poke fun at Dr. Hjortespring and his Hegelian conversion on April Fool's Day, and he made countless jabs at those builders of systems whose works appeared in a "nitid" binding—"nitid" became the catch phrase for referring to Heiberg, just as "matchless" always alluded to Grundtvig. At the same time he praised Fru Gyllembourg to the skies in "A Literary Review" of 1846, just as, in 1848, he wrote with masterful brilliance about Fru Heiberg's performance as Juliet. The house of Heiberg thanked him with a terribly correct sort of courtesy and "warmth," but none of its members gave much attention to these

Kierkegaardian intrigues. The situation was not improved by the fact that, both in the *Postscript* and in private, Kierkegaard paid the humblest sort of respects to those deadly enemies of the Heibergs, the famous stage couple Anna and N. P. Nielsen.

All of Kierkegaard's somersaults, and his attempts to play off the members of the Heiberg family against one another and against their clerical friends, Mynster, Paulli, Tryde, and Martensen, failed miserably, with the result that he was the one to be caught in irony's spotlight. For when the master of irony fell prey to the *Corsair*, with his trouser legs of unequal length, one finds him complaining in his diaries about the fact that "distinguished and respected people" did not come to his defense against the literary cads who wrote for the *Corsair*, and against the rabble which now, ironically enough, had suddenly become ironic.

KIERKEGAARD'S RATIONALIZATIONS-AFTER-THE-FACT AND HIS USE OF PSEUDONYMS

The importance of the episode with the *Corsair*—a turning point in Kierkegaard's life—cannot be exaggerated. He himself scarcely understood that it turned his relationship to the past upside down. He preferred to live backward, as it were, and to write either about those who were dead, like Poul Møller or his father, or about those who at any event were in no position to reply to him, such as Regine, who had too much tact to make a retort. He had "memorialized" Poul Møller by means of his literary assassination of Andersen in 1838, and by the dedication to *The Concept of Dread* in 1844, richly ornamented with "lion's feet and solderings," as the coppersmith says about the samovar in Hostrup's comedy. He had mythologized his father in *De omnibus dubitandum est*, which however appeared only in the second volume of Barfod's edition in 1872; but, starting in 1843, he had erected the pedestal for the monument to his father with his series of *Edifying Discourses*. He had made Regine Olsen, soon to be a Schlegel, world famous in Copenhagen with his writings of 1843–45, in particular *Either/Or* and " 'Guilty?'/'Not Guilty?' " Now there appeared, with an interval of a few days, the *Postscript*—in which Kierkegaard finally admits the paternity of the pseudonymous writings—and P. L. Møller's yearbook *Gæa*, of which the chief essay, *A Visit in Sorø*, submits the same writings to a penetrating, well–informed, and critical treatment. An enormous literary production by a brilliant poet and thinker, Kierkegaard, is evaluated here by the most exciting critical power of the age. Just then, Heiberg had more than enough to do with battles on external and internal fronts; intellectually speaking, with his unshaken Hegelian-Goethean position, he was at a great remove from Kierkegaard.

At this moment it was only logical that Kierkegaard—who was busily calling down still more of the *Corsair*'s mockery upon his head—should turn toward the past. In any event, he succeeded with surprising speed in persuading himself that he was making a voluntary sacrifice in this case, and that the persecution conducted by the *Corsair* (with 4,000 copies, it was Copenhagen's largest paper) was the logical capstone of a spiritual development. Interpretations and rationalizations-after-the-fact came swarming forth, and industriously employing the Procrustean principle, Kierkegaard now discovered, everywhere, a guidance of his fate and literary activities by Providence itself. He did not have the foggiest notion that H. C. Andersen, whom he held in such little esteem, was simultaneously doing the same thing—in a more talented way—with his *Märchen meines Lebens* (1847), and then with *Mit Livs Eventyr*, 1855 *(The Fairy Tale of My Life)*: see Topsøe-Jensen's dissertation of 1940.

This more—or, indeed, less—voluntary stage of martyrdom, of which Kierkegaard made a religious virtue, caused him to ponder long and persistently about the past. The bygone world became the raw material with which he fed the enormous dialectic machine of his journals. In its turn, the machine ground the material finer and finer. A great deal of effort lay behind the production of the riddles which the future was not meant to be able to solve, and behind the interpretations which it was intended to accept. One is permitted to believe that a large mill often grinds out nothing at all, that molehills are made into mountains, and that mountains once again give birth to ridiculous mice; but, as a literary historian, one must entertain a deep and fundamental distrust of the numerous volumes of the journal after 1846. Unhappily, it is precisely from this arsenal that Kierkegaard research has fetched so much of its material; indeed, the editors of the *Papers* have even used information from this source—for example, reports about the phases of the story of the engagement—as criteria for establishing dates. See, for example, in the third volume the altogether grotesque arrangement of the entries from the journey to Jutland in the summer of 1840. While Andersen prepared his apotheosis like a true genius, Kierkegaard did not come off nearly as well. Of course, he managed to twist Kierkegaard research until it became dislocated, but the effort provided him with a retinue which he was not always terribly interested in acquiring: among the retinue's members were the ecclesiastical theologians.

THE PSEUDONYMS

It is an accepted tenet of Kierkegaard scholarship that scholars must be required to make up their minds about the pseudonyms, the pseudonyms' relations to one another, and their connection to Kierkegaard himself. Lamentably, I cannot take part in this sport, which has filled hundreds of pages in books about Kierkegaard all over the world. In my view the pseudonyms are roles, and Kierkegaard an author who was also an actor. He acted the parts of his pseudonyms even as he wrote them down, but obviously he was fonder of some than of others. One has to be a Kierkegaard surgeon in order to determine how much of Kierkegaard there is in the various pseudonyms, and when, and how long. There is no answer key for the great men of world drama. How much Shakespeare is there in Richard III, Hamlet, and Lear, how much Molière in Alceste and Argan, how much Ibsen in Brand and Dr. Stockmann? One wonders if the poet himself knew.

Who dares deny that Kierkegaard's relationship to the theater is lifelong, personal, passionate, existential? He spent most of his life's evenings in the Royal Theater, and he was more frequently in the theater than in the church. No one is the same in all circumstances, but Kierkegaard carried the normal process of self–adaptation to the extremes. He deliberately—and splendidly—acted roles in the presence of his fellow man, and he had difficulty in determining whether he was in the land of reality or of illusion. What are the autobiographical writings save a confession of a lifelong piece of playacting in the service of a higher cause? Has anyone in world literature done it better than he? If so, it was Chateaubriand and Byron, his predecessors and brothers in conspiracy.

From the very outset the journal teems with projects for plays, sketches for dramatic scenes and characters, and experiments with lines of dialogue. The opera Don Juan and the masterful performances in The First Love had the effect of a religious awakening upon the hosier's son, in whose home theater and dance were worldliness and vanity and sin. Remarkably, he appears not to have been moved at all by the art of the ballet, although he was a contemporary of Bournonville (mentioned by the journals only en passant) and of Denmark's great prima ballerina, Lucile Grahn, who is left in silence.

These theatrical interests must have impelled Kierkegaard to playact in his home at an early age. Here, theatrical performances were carried out in a different way, if one is to believe De omnibus dubitandum est, with its accounts of the practice sessions for defending a dissertation, where the father and the two sons often exchanged roles—that is, defended one another's standpoints. After Kierkegaard, upon his father's death, had "had to take up his father's roles" (Brøchner), he could no longer hold the old man off with empty chatter but was forced to take his theological examination.

If Hjalmar Helweg is correct with his theory about the outbreak of the manic-depressive psychosis in the middle of the 1830s, Kierkegaard also

playacted outside the home. At the literary cafés and in the student association he acted the role of the merry son of nature, who nonetheless brooded
over a melancholy black as night. It was one of the literary attitudes of
Romanticism—as were the doubter and the seducer. For many years Faust
and Don Juan were Kierkegaard's favorite figures of literature and drama.
When in the spring of 1838 his father confided those terrible youthful sins to
him, he was also drawn toward Ahasverus and Hamlet. "The truth of the
presentiment is verified, that is why Hamlet is so tragic" is what it says in
II.A.584, no doubt from 1837. Villads Christensen and Johannes Sløk in
particular have had an eye for Shakespeare's enormous importance for
Kierkegaard.

Hamlet's role was undeniably tailor-made for Kierkegaard. The curse
resting on the family, the father's sins of the flesh, the torments of turning
pale thought into action, the melancholy bordering on madness behind a
mask of wit—nothing was missing. Not even a Horatio-Boesen and an
Ophelia with the poetic family name of Olsen. She is the young, innocent
thing whose love the fate of his family keeps him from reciprocating. A father
fixation and a father's sin stood in his way. "But break my heart, for I must
hold my tongue."

Then, when he discovered what it was he had become involved in:
engagement, marriage, even—possibly—children and an official position, he
changed, panic-stricken, to villain's roles. Regine would be forced to make
the break which he was neither man nor gentleman enough to arrange in a
decent way. In the autumn of 1841, in Copenhagen, he acted the role of a
cynic in the best Scribe style, without thereby being able to convince the queen
of his heart, who was much too healthy and natural not to see through his
pretended indifference and his vague loftier considerations. Kierkegaard's
later attempt at "getting himself a bad reputation" with respect to his former
beloved—in the church, in the city, on the sidewalks, or by means of books,
letters, and wills—is amateur theater. The dramatist Kierkegaard was not
capable of finishing his play so that the curtain could go down. The actor of
the same name spoiled his exit, a sin our Lord is not likely to forgive.

THE DRAMATIC IRONY

The dissertation of 1841 dedicates a thorough analysis to "executive, or,
as it could also be called, dramatic irony" (SV XIII:329). It is not sufficient to
dissemble: the subject must enjoy this irony, which has only itself as a target.
Kierkegaard practiced it to excess and thereby acquired an outlet for his indefatigable urge to act. The scenery from his stage still stands on Graabrødre-

torv, in Magstræde, and on the ramparts beside The Citadel. It was here he established a rapport with his fellow actors (who were wholly strange to him, and quite unsuspecting) by means of that unforgettable sidelong glance of his. He staged the *Corsair* squabble himself through his numerous encounters on the street, reported by Goldschmidt, but he never dreamed that his mise en scène would force him to undertake a role he did not desire, as a religious Erasmus Montanus.

Either/Or can be regarded as the logical result of the playacting of his early years. Now he abandoned himself to literature. Now he spoke behind masks and with many tongues: Victor Eremita, the aesthete A., Johannes the Seducer, the likewise-dead and most unfortunate man, the grandiosely tiresome ethicist B.—through all these roles Kierkegaard (at a safe distance from real life) could give that brilliant role which was, for him, the role of roles, as the great genius in the market town of Copenhagen. Fair is fair: he *was* his role. It was a matchless, a blinding performance, which continues to make posterity catch its breath.

H. C. Andersen improvised and acted his fairy tales. Kierkegaard let the pseudonyms multiply. That allowed him the chance both to write and play and to act it. The pseudonyms sprang out of a poetic spirit with a passionate inclination toward leading astray, and doubling oneself, and concealment. With some justice, Brandes called him "a Protestant Jesuit, who was his own pope." Sadly enough, Kierkegaard's public was quite limited in the years 1843–45, when he gave that series of performances which is unique in world literature. He did not act for mighty Europe itself but for that little, choice inner circle of the Heibergians, of whose theatrical passion he himself was an all too willing sacrifice. When he did not feel satisfied with the applause he got for his performances up to and including the *Postscript*, he changed to other and somewhat more elderly roles—the Socratic peripatetic who instructed his sole disciple in the wisdom of life, the reverent author of edifying tracts, the preacher who seldom appeared in his pulpit, the favorite victim of the *Corsair*, the genius who was not understood and who chose not to cast his pearls before swine, the sinner doing atonement, the pious hermit—and many other roles, all of which are both true and acted.

At last, everything was reduced to a masterly coup, the role of the martyr who stormed the churches and shook a whole nation. Even unto four and five generations after his death. I understand those humanists who, like Brandes and Høffding, excused themselves from Kierkegaard's service after having been bloodied by his sword in their youth. They are perhaps not the least among his disciples. No one can accuse Kierkegaard of having ruined his last exit. It was worthy of a Shakespeare, a Pascal.

This writing of literature with his own life is Kierkegaard's true greatness. He is related in the spirit to such supreme dramatists as Shakespeare, Molière, and Strindberg, and—on a lower level— to Pirandello and Anouilh. It goes for them all that, if the world is but a stage, then this stage is truer, more authentic, than real life. Every individual can choose for himself, deciding whether he wants to play the hero or the fool or the commentator standing outside the action. Kierkegaard early distinguished between writing and letting oneself be written: "It is one thing to write oneself, another to let oneself be written. The Christian lets himself be written, and in this respect a simple Christian leads a far more poetic life than many an extremely gifted mind." In the treatise on "The Aesthetic Validity of Marriage," presumably written about the same time, there is a depiction of how the very peak of the aesthetic experience is reached when the actor becomes one with his role:

> Here I am arrived at the peak of the aesthetic. And in truth, he who has humility and courage enough to let himself be aesthetically transfigured, he who feels himself to be an actor in the play the deity is writing, where the poet and the prompter are not separate persons, where the individual, like the practiced actor who has become one with his character and his lines, is not disturbed by the prompter but feels that whatever is whispered to him is what he himself wishes to say, so that it almost becomes doubtful whether he puts words in the prompter's mouth or the prompter in his, he who in the deepest sense feels himself to write and to be written, who in the moment when he feels himself writing has the line's original pathos, and in the moment when he feels himself written has the erotic ear which captures every sound—he and only he has reached the peak of aesthetics.

Only someone for whom the boundary between illusion and reality has been erased can speak thus: an actor-poet, who writes his own role, composes the whole army of pseudonyms with which he has kept other people at a distance from his soul, his passions, his melancholy, his thorn in the flesh, his feeling of loneliness—in brief, everything which elicits that sympathy from which Kierkegaard very much wished to be excused. For, after all, it is not out of pride that Kierkegaard writes of a god who can afford him worthy professional company, acting with and against him, on the stage of life:

> But world history is the royal stage for God, where He—not accidentally but essentially—is the only observer, because He is the only one who can be that. The entrance to this theater does not

stand open for any spirit now existing. If he wishes to persuade himself that he is an observer there, then he merely forgets that he himself, after all, is to be an actor on the little stage, leaving it up to that royal observer and poet how *He* wishes to use him in the royal drama, the *Drama Dramatum*.

Here the actor and poet of genius speaks with the right his "extraordinary powers" gave him. Only a blockhead can be of the frivolous opinion that this is the truth concerning Kierkegaard as a personality, an aesthetician, and a believer. But even a crumb of "the truth" is worth being taken, of course, from the great master's banquet table.

MARK C. TAYLOR

Natural Selfhood and Ethical Selfhood in Kierkegaard

STAGES ON LIFE'S WAY

Writing in his Journal in 1846, Kierkegaard admits: "My contemporaries cannot grasp the design of my writing. *Either/Or* divided into four parts or six parts and published separately over six years would have been all right. But that each essay in *Either/Or* is a part of a whole, and then the whole of *Either/Or* a part of a whole: that, after all, think my bourgeois contemporaries, is enough to drive one daft." The passing of years has done little to clarify this sutuation. For many "disciples at second hand," the coherence of Kierkegaard's pseudonymous writings remains as obscure as the overall structure of Hegel's *Phenomenology*. The problem of discerning the unity in the multiplicity of Kierkegaard's writings is, in some ways, more difficult than discovering the thread that ties together Hegel's complex argument. Kierkegaard develops his phenomenology of spirit in a series of diverse works written over an extended period and published under different pseudonyms. Each pseudonymous author and character represents a distinctive form of life that seems to stand in no *necessary* relation to other points of view. Nevertheless, Kierkegaard insists that these widely contrasting works actually "constitute stages in the realization of an idea I had conceived."

The recognition of Kierkegaard's pedagogical purpose suggests an angle of vision from which the coherence of the pseudonymous writings becomes apparent. We have seen that Kierkegaard, like Hegel, attempts to provide a cure for spiritlessness by developing a therapeutic aesthetic education that will lead the reader from inauthentic to authentic selfhood. Kierkegaard's understanding of the nature of spirit requires him to employ an educational method that constantly respects the integrity of the individual. Like Hegel, Kierkegaard decides that spiritlessness can be overcome most effectively by

From *Journeys to Selfhood: Hegel and Kierkegaard.* © 1980 by the Regents of the University of California. University of California Press, 1980.

the depiction of alternative forms of life that provide the occasion for the reader's self-examination and self-judgment. The personae of the pseudony-mous writings form the cast of characters with which Kierkegaard stages his version of the journey to selfhood. Kierkegaard's pedagogy also begins with the modern experience of self-estrangement. According to Kierkegaard, how-ever, spiritlessness involves the dissipation of concrete human existence brought about by a relaxation of the spiritual tensions characteristic of authentic selfhood. From this perspective, Hegel's attempted cure seems to feed the disease. Through "the abrogation of the passionate disjunction of subjectivity and objectivity," speculative philosophy obscures the decisive opposition between self and other. "The systematic idea," Kierkegaard explains, "is the subject-object, the oneness of thought and being. Existence, on the other hand, is their separation. It does not by any means follow that existence is thoughtless; but it has brought about, and brings about, a sepa-ration [Spatierer] between subject and object, thought and being." As should be evident by now, Kierkegaard, like Hegel, does not limit the problem of the relation between subjectivity and objectivity to the narrow confines of epis-temology. This multifaceted issue has not only philosophical but also psycho-logical, social, cultural, and religious dimensions. Kierkegaard's fulfillment of his mission as a "reformer," whose "whole life is an epigram to make men aware," is impossible apart from the redefinition of the full range of opposites and the rearticulation of the qualitative distinctions lost in the spiritlessness of the age. Kierkegaard's radical cure attempts to overcome the dissipation of concrete existence by decisively distinguishing subjectivity and objectivity. In place of Hegel's rational mediation of internally related contraries, Kierkegaard proposes the qualitative discrimination of mutually exclusive opposites. From Kierkegaard's point of view, the movement from spiritless-ness to spirit involves an incremental differentation of self and other which culminates in spirit's awareness of itself as a unique coincidentia opposito-rum, constituted by the individual's passionate decision.

While important differences separate those alternative spiritual pilgrim-ages, the Kierkegaardian stages on life's way and the Hegelian stations of the way share significant similarities. For Kierkegaard, as for Hegel, the journey to selfhood passes through a natural, an ethical, and a religious stage. In his consideration of natural selfhood, Kierkegaard examines the progression from the condition of nondifferentiation between self and other to the situa-tion in which the subject is aware of itself as distinct from the natural and social totality within which it had been immersed. The ethical stage of exis-tence explores the self's effort to define itself through deliberate decisions that concretely embody universal moral principles in the life of the particular conscientious actor. Religious selfhood, expressed in what Kierkegaard calls religion A, universal religiosity, and religion B, Christianity, represents the full realization of spirit in which the temporal self, isolated from all other selves, freely defines its unique individuality. By developing a dialogue among themselves and with the reader, Kierkegaard's pseudonymous personae reveal the characteristics, the tensions, and the contradictions definitive of contrasting forms of life. The stages Kierkegaard identifies are dialectically related in such a way that each successive stage displaces its predecessor from a position of centrality, yet preserves prior determinants of experience in a relativized form. As opposed to Hegel's phenomenology of spirit, in which different moments are necessariliy related by immanent dialectical development Kierkegaard's stages of existence represent distinct forms of selfhood that can be realized only through the contingent resolution of the individual's free will. Kierkegaard stresses that "from the abstract point of view there is no decisive conflict between the standpoints, because abstraction precisely removes that in which the decision inheres: *the existing subject*. But in spite of this consideration, the immanent transition [of speculative philosophy] is a chimera, is imaginary, as if it were possible for one standpoint necessarily to determine itself into an other; for the category of transition is itself a breach of immanence, a *leap*." This leap, Kierkegaard insists, "is neither more or less than the most decisive protest against the inverse procedure of the Method."

NATURAL SELFHOOD

Kierkegaard probes the outstanding aspects of natural selfhood in his description of aesthetic existence. He defines the initial stage of the journey to selfhood by distinguishing two types of aestheticism: immediacy and reflection. The common feature of these aparently antithetical forms of experience is the absence of genuine decision. This lack of free resolution results either from unreflective immersion in sensuous inclination and social life or from dispassionate absorption in abstract reflection. Since Kierkegaard regards spirit as the synthesis of opposites created and sustained by the individual's free decision, aesthetic existence represents the most extreme form of spiritlessness. Apart from personal decision, the self remains dissipated— lost in indeterminacy and plagued by inauthenticity. For Kierkegaard, "the more consciousness, the more self; the more consciousness, the more will; and the more will, the more self."

Generally conceived, Kierkegaard's phenomenology of spirit charts the subject's movement from undifferentiated identification with its environment, through increasing differentiation from otherness, to complete individuation in which the self becomes a concrete individual, eternally responsible for itself. Kierkegaard explains that in contrast with Hegel, whose analysis "has the conflict between the *I* and the world as the first stage," his own interpretation of spirit begins with the situation in which the individual "has not separated himself from his surroundings ('me')." Despite this important difference, Kierkegaard follows Hegel in describing the most rudimentary form of natural consciousness as "immediacy." Moreover, Kierkegaard agrees with Hegel's contention that immediacy is "indeterminate" or "indefinite." In an ironic reversal of Hegel's position, however, Kierkegaard argues that such indeterminateness is not the result of the abstract isolation of atomistic particulars but is a function of the *lack* of concrete particularity created by the nondifferentiation of self and other. Kierkegaard maintains that in immediacy, the self "is in immediate connection with the other [*i uniddelbar Sammenhæng med det Andet*], and thus is within the compass of the temporal and worldly and has only the illusory appearance of possessing in it something eternal." The nondiferentiation of self and other typical of immediacy involves the subject's direct identification with its natural and social world. Unconscious of its unique individuality and personal responsibility, the self is ruled by natural desire and social custom. This condition "of not being conscious of oneself as spirit is despair, which is spiritless."

At the beginning of its sojourn, the self, by virtue of complete immersion in the sensuous "here and now," is "in immediate unity with its natural condition." In an essay entitled "The Immediate Stages of the Erotic," Kierkegaard develops a careful analysis of desire, by means of an imaginative interpretation of Mozart's *Figaro, The Magic Flute,* and *Don Juan.* Sounding quite Hegelian, Kierkegaard describes the three stages of sensual immediacy:

> The different stages taken together constitute the immediate stage, and from this we may perceive that the individual stages are rather a revelation of a predicate, so that all the predicates steer a course toward the wealth of the last stage, since this is the real stage. The other stages have no independent existence; for themselves, they are only representations [*Forestillingen*], and from this one may see their accidental character as over against the last stage.

The movement through the immediate states of the erotic is marked by the progressive differentiation of desire and its object. In the first moment of immediacy, there is virtually no distinction between subject and object. Carried along in a stream of sensuality, the self is "not a single individual" but is thoroughly indefinite—a ceaseless flux of indeterminate sensation. In this primal form of experience, the object of desire has not yet emerged. Desire and desired, subject and object, self and other, remain bound in undifferentiated oneness.

At the second stage of immediacy, desire, in the strict sense of the word, awakens. Kierkegaard points ot that "only when the object exists does the desire exist, only when the desire exists does the object exist; desire and its object are twins, neither of which is born a fraction of an instant before the other." The development of desire creates the original bifurcation of self and other. This weaning of subject from object begins the long labor that eventually gives birth to individual selfhood. The "movement of the sensuous, this earthquake, splits desire and its object infinitely asunder for the moment; but as the moving principle appears a moment separating, so it again reveals itself as wishing to unite the separated. The result of this separation is that desire is torn from its substantial repose within itself, and consequently the object no longer falls under the qualifications of substantiality, but disperses itself in a manifold." While this moment represents a dawning awareness of the difference between self and other, objectivity is still completely indefinite. The object of desire is not specific but is a manifold of sensible intuition. In the final form of immediacy, this manifold is consolidated into a concrete object. Here desire is fully present. Again echoing Hegel, Kierkegaard gives what is at once a brief summary of the relationship among the three stages of immediacy and a clear characterization of the third stage:

> The contradiction in the first stage lay in the fact that desire could acquire no object, but without having desired was in possession of its object, and therefore could not reach the point of desiring. In the second stage, the object appears in its mainfold, but since desire seeks its object in this manifold, it still has, in a deeper sense, no object; it is not yet posited as desire. In *Don Juan,* on the other hand, desire is absolutely determined as desire; it is, in an intensive and extensive sense, the immediate unity of the two preceding stages. The first stage desired the one ideally, the second stage desired the particular under the determination of the manifold; the third stage is a unity of these two. Desire has its absolute object in the particular, it desires the particular absolutely.

It is essential to recognize that even at the final stage of immediacy, the self has not arrived at consciousness. The distinction between subject and object is affective rather than cognitive. In addition to this, the self is not yet an autonomous individual who stands in relation to the particular object but is a restless embodiment of purely natural force. Although desire has been distinguished from its object, neither self-consciousness nor self-determination through free decision has developed. Kierkegaard suggests that the leading character in Mozart's *Don Juan* ideally represents the life of sensual immediacy. Don Juan is "the sensuous erotic genius" who is nothing less than "flesh incarnate, or the inspiration of the flesh by the spirit of the flesh." Kierkegaard underscores the lack of individuation in immediacy when he writes: "If I imagine a particular individual, if I see him [Don Juan] or hear him speak, then it becomes comic to imagine that he has seduced 1,003; for as soon as he is regarded as a particular individual, the accent falls in quite another place. When, on the contrary, he is interpreted in music, then I do not have a particular individual, but I have the power of nature." When sunk in sensual immediacy, selfhood is dissipated in the transient moods and multiple pleasures of the effervescent moment.

From Kierkegaard's perspective, such dissolute selfhood is not only typical of sensuous eroticism but characteristic of its apparent opposite—the decorous life of the complacent bourgeois citizen. While the sensuous erotic genius is a reflex of natural forces, the crowd-man is directly identified with the social matrix and is completely ruled by predetermined social custom. Though more refined than the pleasure-seeking dilettante, the crowd-man is no less immediate. He "finds it too venturesome a thing to be himself, far easier and safer to be like the others, to become an imitation, a number in the crowd." Such a person might gain the world, but "by being entirely finitized, by having become instead of a self, a number, just one more man, one more repetition of the everlasting *Einerlei*," he loses his own self. In this form of existence, the subject is dissipated in the objective life of society.

The spiritlessness of immediacy can be described in alternative terms. At the beginning of the first stage on life's way, the self is not creative synthesis of the opposites ingredient in authentic spirit. To the contrary, the subject is stuck in finitude, reality, necessity, and time, and is unaware of infinitude, ideality, possibility, and eternity. Hopelessly entangled in the natural-social environment, the self is a prisoner of its own facticity. The chains of immediacy can be broken only by the emergence of reflection.

In a manner reminiscent of Hegel's intepretation of the transition from the immediacy of sense-certainty to the mediacy of perception, Kierkegaard contends that "what annnuls immediacy is language." However, over against Hegel's emphasis on the propensity of language to sublate abstract particularity, Kierkegaard stresses the capacity of language to negate indeterminateness by articulating determinate distinctions. "Language," he argues, "involves reflexion, and cannot, therefore, express the immediate. Reflexion destroys the immediate, and hence it is impossible to express the musical in language; but this apparent poverty of language is precisely its wealth. The immediate is really the indeterminate, and thus language cannot apprehend it; but the fact that it is indeterminate is not its perfection, but an imperfection." Reflexion, as we have seen elsewhere, is the cognitive activity through which contraries are identified and opposites are defined. Kierkegaard maintains that "the determinations of reflexion are always *dichotomous*, e.g. ideality and reality, soul and body, God and world, . . . and so on." The discriminating discernment of reflexion negates the utter indefiniteness of immediacy by defining contrasts and differentiating opposites. When understood in this way, reflexion is the necessary presupposition of consciousness and self-consciousness. Consciousness entails the precise articulation of the difference between subject and object which is only vaguely felt in the last moment of immediacy. Through reflexion, the self further differentiates itself from its world. "Here there is, in fact, a certain degree of self-reflexion, and so a certain degree of observation of oneself. With this certain degree of self-reflexion begins the act of discrimination [*Udsondrings-Akt*] by which the self becomes aware of itself as something essentially different from the environment, from externalities and their effect upon it." For Kierkegaard, reflexion not only draws a distinction between person and world but also enables the self to distinguish itself from itself. Consciousness, turned back upon itself, becomes self-consciousness. When reflexion becomes self-reflexive, the subject cognitively differentiates its reality and ideality, necessity and possibility, and finitude and infinitude. No longer lost in the fleeting present, the wayfarer becomes aware of the past from which he has come and the future toward which he can proceed. Even though reflexion effectively draws distinctions, it is unable to synthesize differentiated opposites. In overcoming the spiritlessness of immediacy, reflexion creates the possibility of another form of inauthentic selfhood—reflective aesthetic existence.

Standing between the sensuality of immediacy and the decisiveness of ethical existence, the reflective aesthete is absorbed in the infinity of abstract reflection. As a self-conscious human being, the subject is no longer simply an extension of natural force and social custom. But since the person still has not become a self-determining agent, he is not yet a concrete individual. This stage on life's way repressnts an "imagination existence [*Phantasie-Existents*]," which, Kierkegaard explains, is "an existential possibility tending toward existence, and brought so close to it that you feel how every moment is wasted as long as it has not come to a decision." The reflective aesthete "keeps existence away by the most subtle of all deceptions, by thinking; he has thought everything possible, and yet he has not existed at all."

Within Kierkegaard's phenomenology of spirit, reflection is the dialec-

tical inversion of immediacy. Having distinguished himself from his surroundings and from given determinants in his own being, the reflective
aesthete "becomes intoxicated, as it were, by the infinity of possibles," and
seeks "to cancel all actuality and set in its place an actuality that is due to the
lack of infinitude and possibility, reflection is the despair of infinitude and
possibility due to the lack of finitude and necessity. These contasting forms
of experience are two variations of the same malaise, spiritlessness. Neither
the immediate nor the reflective aesthete achieves the genuine coincidence of
opposites definitive of authentic selfhood. Describing the shortcomings of
reflective aestheticism, Kierkegaard writes: "That the self looks so and so in
the possibility of itself is only half truth; for in the possibility of itself the self
is still far from itself, or only half itself. So the question is how the necessity
of the self determines it more precisely. . . . Instead of summoning back possibility into necessity one runs after possibility—and at last he cannot find
his way back to himself."

Kierkegaard elaborates his interpretation of the reflective form of aesthetic existence by developing a vignette of a "reflective seducer." In "The
Seducer's Diary," Kierkegaard presents a figure named Johannes, who is the
reflective counterpart of the sensuous erotic genius. In contrast with Don
Juan's sensual frenzy, which overpowers 1,003 women, Johannes devotes
himself to an imaginative romantic intrigue whose sole aim is the seduction
of a single maiden—Cordelia Wahl. What engages Johannes even more than
anticipated erotic satisfaction is the sheer pleasure created by the free play of
his imagination. Fascinated by the plurality of possibilities, Johannes
attempts to create interesting situations he can observe with detachment.
"Life for him is a drama, and what engrosses him is the ingenious unfolding
of this drama. He is himself a spectator, even when performing some act."
Preoccupied with reflection and unwilling to take definitive action, Johannes
remains an enigma to himself and others. By means of agile mind and quick
wit, he translates every decisive either-or into an equivocal both-and. The
ethical Judge Wilhelm explains to his young friend: "For the polemical result
which resounds in all your songs of triumph over existence has a strange
resemblance to the pet theory of the newer philosophy, that the principle of
contradiction is dissolved." Although Johannes has much to do with reality,
Kierkegaard insists that he does not belong to the real world. Drawn to possibility and away from actuality, Johannes avoids involvement in concrete
existence. In fact, he never really enters into an actual relationship with Cordelia, but manipulates her in such a way that she forms herself in his own
image. "What she must learn," Johannes admits in the privacy of his diary,
"is to go through all the movements of infinity, to sway, to lull herself in her

moods, to confuse poetry and actuality, truth and romance, to toss herself about in the infinite." By the end of his "psychological experiment," Johannes is convinced that "he has developed the many-tongued reflection within her, that he has developed her aesthetically so far that she no longer listens humbly to one voice, but is able to hear many voices at one time." Multiple voices, however, are cacophonous, and protaean possibilities perplexing. Deserted by her erstwhile lover, Cordelia is left "to struggle with the doubt as to whether the whole affair was not a figment of the imagination."

In the final analysis, the seducer is also seduced, not by confused Cordelia, but by his own confusing imagination. Increasingly detached from actuality, the reflective aesthete finally loses touch with the "mainland of reality" and drifts into the fantasy world of unreal possibility.

> Possibility then appears to the self ever greater and greater, more and more things become possible, because nothing becomes actual. At last it is as if everything were possible—but this is precisely when the abyss has swallowed up the self. . . . At the instant something appears possible, and then a new possibility makes its appearance, at last this phantasmagoria moves so rapidly that it is as if everything were possible—and this is precisely the last moment, when the individual becomes for himself a mirage [*Luftsyn*].

It becomes apparent that Kierkegaard's vignette of Johannes is really a "shadowgraph." "In such a dream of imagination, the individual is not an actual figure but is a shadow, or rather the actual figure is invisibly present and therefore is not content with casting one shadow, but the individual has a multiplicity of shadows, all of which resemble him and for the moment have an equal claim to be accounted himself." Reflection turns out to be just as spiritless as immediacy. Kierkegaard's sojourner overcomes the dissipated life of sensuality only to be anaesthetized by the ether of pure possibility. As Judge Wilhelm points out, the self of the aesthete, be he immediate or reflective, "is like a plot of ground in which all sorts of herbs are planted, all with the same claim to thrive; his self consists of his multiplicity, and he has no self that is higher than this."

Drawing on Hegel's interpretation of unhappy consciousness, Kierkegaard concludes his examination of the aesthetic stage by arguing that the reflective aesthete is really "the unhappiest man." When absent to and estranged from the present because of constant reflection on the past and speculation about the future, the self "lives as one already dead." Remembering that for which he ought to hope and hoping for that which he ought to remember, the unhappiest man "cannot become old, for he has never been young; he cannot become young, for he is already old. In one sense of the word, he cannot die, for he has not really lived; in another sense, he cannot live, for he is already dead." One of the *symparanekromenoi,* the unhappiest man finally confesses: "I lie stretched out, inactive; the only thing I see is emptiness, the only thing I move about is emptiness." The aesthetic stage on life's way ends in what Kierkegaard calls "melancholy [*Tungsind*]." The melancholy personis aware of the meaninglessness of his life but takes no steps to resolve the existential impasse into which he has fallen. Although this malaise is a symptom of the sickness unto death, Kierkegaard insists that it is not without therapeutic value. Melancholy is "the hysteria of spirit" which is a "presentiment of a metamorphosis." Kierkegaard is convinced that there comes a moment in the life of the self when "spirit would collect itself, as it were, out of this dissipation and explain itself to itself—the personality would become conscious of itself in its eternal validity." Reflection alone cannot effect this spiritual metamorphosis. Aesthetic dissolution can be overcome only through ethical resolution. The "way of reflection is unending, and can come to an end only if the individual arbitrarily breaks it off by bringing something else into play, a resolution of the will, but in so doing the individual brings himself under ethical determinations, and loses aesthetic interest."

ETHICAL SELFHOOD

In one of his lengthy epistles to Johannes, Judge Wilhelm writes: "But what is it to live aesthetically, and what is it to live ethically? What is the aesthetic in a man, and what is the ethical? To this I would reply: the aesthetic in a man is that by which he is immediately what he is; the ethical is that by which he becomes what he becomes." The becoming that is essential to ethical selfhood arises through the subject's free decision. In contrast with the aesthetic avoidance of decision as a result either of identification with sensuous inclination and social custom or of preoccupation with abstract reflection, self-conscious decision is the nerve of ethical existence. "The act of choosing," declares Kierkegaard's ethical persona, "is a proper and stringent expression of the ethical." Such deliberate decision is an essential moment in the process of individuation and marks a crucial stage of the journey to selfhood. The ethicist "has himself as a task." Unwilling merely to be swayed by passing mood or contingent circumstance and disillusioned with the "world of possibilities, glowing with imagination becoming himself. Expressing dismay over aesthetic dissipation, Judge Wilhelm queries, "Can you think of anything more frightful than that it might end with your nature being resolved into a multiplicity, that you really might become many, become, like those unhappy demonics, a legion, and you thus would have lost the inmost and holiest thing of all in a man, the unifying power of personality?" The ethicist attempts to quell aesthetic depair by means of resolute activity in which he "consolidates himself [*consolidere sig*]" or "collects himself [*samler sig*] out of dissipation." No longer a bundle of conflicting desires or an array of fantastic possibilities, the self becomes a concrete individual through its own free will. In ethical action, the subject gains a history that is unified by the coherence and consistency of purposeful striving. This personal history is the self's "revelation [*Aabenbarelse*]" of itself to itself and to others. Temporality, therefore, is the medium of the subject's self-expression. Released from unreflective immersion in the present and abstract reflection on the past and the future, the ethicist creatively joins past and future in "the true present, which is a unity of hope and recollection." The freely acting temporal subject negates the abject spiritlessness of aestheticism and points toward the authentic form of spirit realized in religious existence.

Judge Wilhelm maintains that his form of life is decisively different from the point of view of his young friend and from the philosophy whose embodiment he believes Johannes to represent—Hegelianism. The Judge carefully distinguishes his concrete either-or, in which contraries are contrasted, from the allegedly abstract aesthetic principle of both-and, in which opposites are mediated. While readily admitting that "there are situations in life where it would be ridiculous or a species of madness to apply an either-or," he insists that "there are also men whose souls are too dissolute to grasp what is implied in such a dilemma, whose personalities lack the energy to say with pathos, either-or." This is no minor point for Judge Wilhelm. Were he to admit the validity of what he understands to be the perspective of speculative philosophy, he believes, the foundation upon which his world rests would crumble. "If we concede mediation," he argues, "then there is no absolute choice, and if there is nothing of that sort, then there is no absolute either-or."

But one must always be wary of taking a pseudonym at his word, even a law-abiding character like the Judge. More often than not, they fail to comprehend completely what they are saying. When fully examined, Judge Wilhelm's form of life is remarkably similar to its apparent opposite—the shape of selfhood Hegel unfolds in his interpretation of spirit's progression from Sittlichkeit to the self-certain conscientious moral actor. Though the consistent emphasis on individual resolution is a distinctive feature of Kierkegaard's ethical analysis, the form of selfhood actualized by this self-conscious decision is extremely Hegelian. In light of this intentional parallel, Kierkegaard's insistence that the wayfarer must move beyond the ethical authenticity is not surprising. The Judge clearly recognizes that the realization of genuine selfhood requires the joining of contraries through free decision. But he lacks sufficient appreciation of the depth of the antitheses the self must synthesize, and consequently does not achieve the coincidence of opposites definitive of spirit.

The unique contours of ethical selfhood begin to emerge with a careful consideration of the Judge's understanding of choice. From the ethical viewpoint, choice or decision is not a simple phenomenon but is a complex activity comprising a plurality of interrelated factors. In the most comprehensive sense, ethical decision involves "the choice of oneself in one's eternal validity [at vælge sig selv i evige Gyldighed]." The Judge distinguishes this central ethical category from the aesthetic maxim concisely expressed by Socrates: "Know thyself." As we have noted, over against the aesthetic, which is that by which a person is immediately what he is, the ethical is that by which one becomes what he becomes. Paradoxically, however, the initial moment of self-formative becoming is the free choice of what one is. In the first instance, the self's choice of itself in its eternal validity is the decision to decide, the choice to choose. In Kierkegaardian anthropology, self-consciousness is a necessary but not sufficient condition of authentic selfhood. One must will to will. At this point, "it is not yet a question of the choice of something in particular, it is not a question of the reality of that which is chosen, but of the reality of the act of choice." Prior to the possibility of reaching specific decisions, the self must consciously recognize and freely appropriate itself as a self-determining being. Judge Wilhelm writes: "But what, then, is this self of mine? If I were required to define this, my first answer would be: It is the most abstract of all things, and yet at the same time it is the most concrete—it is freedom."

As soon as a person accepts responsibility for himself as a free agent, other dimensions of selfhood come into sharp focus. Most importantly, the subject clearly distinguishes what it is from what it ought to be by differentiating its givenness and its possibility, its reality and its ideality. The self that the ethicist wills to become "is not an abstract self which passes everywhere and hence is nowhere, but [is] a concrete self which stands in living reciprocal relation with these specific surroundings, these conditions of life, this natural order. This self which is the goal [Formaalet] is not merely a personal self, but a social, a civic self. He has, then, himself as a task for an activity in which, as this definite personality, he grasps the relations of life." The ethicist is competely aware of the natural and social determinants of being that immediately dominate aesthetic experience. Through prolonged self-scrutiny, he "becomes conscious of himself as this definite individual, with these talents

[*Gave*], these dispositions, these instincts, these passions, influenced by these definite surroundings, as this definite product of a definite environment. But being conscious of himself in this way, he assumes reponsibility for all this." The free act of self-choice effectively mediates aesthetic immediacy. The ethicist simultaneously annuls complete determination by, and appropriates (*ophæve*) his dependence upon, the given natural and social aspects of selfhood. Kierkegaard contends that "in choosing itself, the personality chooses itself ethically and excludes absolutely the aesthetic, but since he chooses himself and since he does not become another by choosing himself but becomes himself, the whole of the aesthetic comes back in its relativity."

Having accepted the finite limits of its facticity, the subject is in a position to assess realistically the possibilities it might realize or the ideality it might strive to actualize. "This self the individual knows," Kierkegaard stresses, "is at once the real self and the ideal self that the individual has outside himself as the picture in likeness to which he has to form himself and which, on the other hand, he nevertheless has in him since it is the self. Only within him has the individual the goal after which he has to strive, and yet he has this goal outside him, inasmuch as he strives after it." As the ambiguous "being which is nevertheless a non-being," the ideal self represents what the subject essentially is, yet actually is not. The ethicist expresses the dialectical relation of essence and existence by distinguishinig universality and particularity. In the opinion of Judge Wilhelm,

> only when the individual himself is the universal is it possible to realize the ethical. This is the secret of conscience, it is the secret that the individual life shares with itself, that it is at once an individual life and at the same time the universal, if not immediately as such, yet according to its possibility. He who regards life ethically sees the universal, and he who lives ethically expresses the universal in his life, he makes himself the universal man, not by divesting himself of his concretion, for then he becomes nothing, but by clothing himself with it and permeating it with the universal.

At Kierkegaard's ethical stage on life's way, as in Hegel's moral view of the world, the self both acknowledges the existential disparity between universal moral law and the particular acting subject, and initially insists upon the possibility of a harmonious reconciliation of these opposites. The self-confident actor attempts to bring about this integration of contraries by elevating his idiosyncratic particularity to universality. Convinced of the essentiality of universality, "the task the ethical individual sets himself is to transform himself into the universal individual [*almene Individ*]." The Judge speaks for all ethicists when he states: "The truly extraordinary [*ualminde-lige*] is the truly ordinary [*almindelige*] man. The more of the universally human an individual is able to realize in his life, the more extraordinary he is. The less of the universal he is able to take up in his life, the more imperfect he is. He is then an extraordinary man to be sure, but not in a good sense." The realization of the universally human, or the transformation of oneself into the universal individual, "is only possible if I already have this [univer-sality] in myself *kata dunamin*." In ethical action the individual freely actual-izes his latent possibilities by self-consciously enacting the universal moral law. Since this law not only transcends the conscientious subject as the telos toward which he moves but also is immanent in him as his own ideal or essen-tial self, the autonomous moral actor really "has his teleology in himself, has inner teleology, is himself his teleology. His self is thus the goal toward which he strives." Within the ethical framework, of course, such self-realization pre-supposes the cultivation of the social relations within which the individual stands. "In the movement toward himself, the individual cannot relate him-self negatively toward his surroundings, for if he were to do so, his self would be an abstraction and remain such. His self must be opened in relation to his entire concretion; but to this concretion belong also the factors which are designed for taking an active part in the world. So his movement, then, is from himself through the world, to himself." The precise naturae of this movement to one's self by way of relation to other can be clarified by analyzing the ethicist's interpretation of duty.

The universality the ethical agent seeks to actualize is not abstract and indefinite, but is present to the self in the form of its particular duty.

> Duty is the universal which is demanded of me; so if I am not the universal, I am unable to perform duty. On the other hand, my duty is the particular [*det Enkelte*], something for me alone, and yet it is duty and hence the universal. Here personality manifests itself in its highest validity. It is not lawless, neither does it make laws for itself, for the definition of duty holds good; but person-ality reveals itself as the unity of the universal and the particular.

As Judge Wilhelm unfolds his understanding of duty, it becomes appar-ent that his point of view represents a latter-day version of Luther's docrtine of early vocation which Kierkegaard believes typical of the "healthy-minded" this-worldliness of Christendom. The Judge identifies two primary domains of duty: *Liebe und Arbeit.*

As a dedicated civil servant, the Judge is persuaded that every person has a calling. "The ethical thesis that every man has a calling," he explains, "is the expression for the fact that there is a rational order of things in which every man, if he will, fills his place in such a way that he expresses at once the universally human and the individual." Not only does earthly vocation lend meaning to an otherwise meaningless life, it also plays and essential role in the individual's self-cultivation. Through free particapation in the object of social order, the subject attempts to sublate its particularity and to realize its potential universality. Implicitly drawing on Hegel's analysis of the master-slave dialectic, the Kierkegaardian ethicist contends that "it is precisely by working that man makes himself free, by working he becomes lord over nature, by working he shows that he is higher than nature." In the labor process, the ethicist alienates himself from himself in the act of self-objectification, and returns to himself by consciously recognizing and freely reappropriating self in other. Fulfillment of duty both generates the objective, universal social substance, and actualizes the individual subject. In this way, the movement of the ethical agent is, as Kierkegaard has noted, "from himself through the world, to himself." At the ethical stage of existence, relation to other is conceived as mediate self-relation.

The paradigm of ethical life is to be found in love and marriage. In a phrase that recalls Hegel's account of his *Phenomenology of Spirit,* the domesticated Judge Wilhelm defines marriage as the self's "most important voyage of discovery." The essential intersubjectivity of ethical selfhood is most concretely realized in marital love. The Judge describes his relation to his wife in thoroughly Hegelian terms: "What I am through her, that she is through me, and we are neither of us anything by ourselves, but only in union."When singing the praises of marriage, the usually sober and prosaic Judge waxes poetic. In one of his more lyrical effusions, he proclaims:

> Marriage is "the fullness of time." . . . Such is marriage. It is divine, for love is the miracle; it is of the world, for love is nature's profoundest myth. Love is the unfathomable bottom which is hidden in obscurity, but resolution is the victor which like Orpheus fetches love out to the light of day, for resolution is love's true form, its true transfiguration, hence marriage is holy and blessed by God. It is civic, for thereby the lovers belong to the state and the fatherland and the concerns of fellow citizens. It is poetic, ineffably poetic, as love is, but resolution is the conscientious translator who translates enthusiasm into reality, and this translator is so precise, oh, so precise! . . . Such is marriage.

As the "fullness of time," marriage is the harmonious integration of the contraries inherent in the self. It is the wedding of univerality and particularity, subject and society, infinitude and finitude, eternity and time, freedom and necessity, divinity and humanity. This harmony, of course, is not immediate but is mediated by the free resolution of consenting subjects. For the ethicist, marriage is a moral duty. Yet this is no onerous obligation, for it is the "precise translation," the "true transfiguration," of love.

In attempting to convince Johannes of "the aesthetic validity of marriage," Judge Wilhelm argues that love is a "unity of contradictions." "It is the unity of freedom and necessity. The individual feels drawn to the other individual by an irresistible power, but precisely in this is sensible of his freedom. It is a unity of the universal and the particular [*Særegne*];" "it is sensuous and yet spiritual; it is in the moment, is definitely in the present tense, and yet it has in it an eternity." At first, however, love is fortuitous, contingent, accidental—after all, one *falls* in love. The integration of contraries constitutive of immediate love is unstable and is always subject to disintegration. Love, the ethicist argues, is "an unreal *an sich*," whose explicit realization presupposes the dutiful resolve of the lovers. By transforming love into duty, lovers seek to arm love against the threat of dissolution. Duty, therefore,

> comes as an old friend, an intimate, a confidant, whom the lovers mutually recognize in the deepest secret of their love. And when he speaks, it is nothing new he has to say; and when he has spoken, the individuals humble themselves under it, but at the same time are uplifted just because they are assured that what he orders is what they themselves wish, and that his commanding is merely a more majestic, a more exalted, a divine way of expressing the fact that their wish can be realized.

According to Judge Wilhelm, the public marriage vow is the resolution through which immediate love is transfigured from abstract unreality into concrete actuality. In the face of Johannes's protest to the contrary, the Judge asserts and reasserts that marriage consummates rather than annihilates love. "And how I invert everything and say: the aesthetic does not lie in the immediate, but in the acquired—but marriage is precisely the immediacy that has mediacy in itself, the infinity that has finitude in itself, the eternal that has the temporal in itself." This is the aesthetic validity of the ethical, and the ethical validity of the aesthetic—a freely willed union in which self and other seem to form a unity-in-difference, both within and between themselves.

But the Judge does not stop here. Within the ethical Weltanschauung, marriage also has religious validity. We have seen that duty "is merely a more majestic, a more exalted, a *divine* way of expressing the fact that their [the lovers'] wish can be realized." Reveling in the harmony of terrestrial and celestial spheres, Judge Wilhelm exhorts his reader: "Harken and be amazed at the harmonious accord of these different spheres. It is the same thing, except that it is expressed aesthetically, religiously, and ethically." The ethical God is no strict and demanding moral legislator but is a humane, lenient father who asks only what his children wish. At the ethical stage of existence, the unity of desire and duty and the harmony of human and divine intention is so complete that any conflict between these spheres is unthinkable. For Judge Wilhelm, God does not "torment men with the most terrifying collisions—and hardly could a more frightful thing be conceived than that there might be a collision between love for God and love for the persons for whom love has been planted by Him in our hearts." The ethicist sees the aesthetic, ethical, and religious dimensions of experience as "three great allies." The belief in the harmonious accord of the different spheres of life leads the Kierkegaardian ethicist to agree with the Hegelian assessment of all forms of otherworldly spirituality as essentially "unhappy." The Judge explains: "marriage I regard as the highest *telos* of individual existence, it is so much the highest that the man who goes without it cancels with one stroke the whole of earthly life and retains only eternity and spiritual interests—which at first glance seem no slight thing, but in the long run is very exhausting and also in one way or another is the expression of an unhappy existence." If religious obligation were to conflict with ethical duty and personal desire, the equilibrium—[*Ligevægt*] for which the ethicist strives would be upset. Moreover, the entire temporal process would be reduced from an end in itself to a mere "time of probation [*Prøvetid*] in which again and again one is put to the test without anything really resulting from it, and without the individual getting further than he was at the beginning." The Judge believes that his profession and marriage protect him from such unhappiness. "When the ethical is rightly viewed," he maintains "it makes the individual infinitely secure in himself." Moral duty and religious obligation do not create insatiable yearning by turning the individual's eyes toward an ever transcendent telos. The ethical view of the world "affords peace, assurance, and security, for it constantly calls to us: *quod petis, hic est*—what you seek is here." Through *Liebe und Arbeit,* Judge Wilhelm establishes a "heartfelt sense of community" that overcomes the unsettling feeling of being "a stranger, and an exile [*en Fremmed og Udlænding*] in the world." Apparently released from the disease of homelessness, the ethicist feels completely at home in the world.

But what if this form of life is the domestication, not the realization, of spirit; what if the end of life is not secure, meaningful occupation and a *hyg-*

gelig family life; what if self is not fully actualized in community; if individuality is not best expressed in universality; what if eternity is not within time; if infinitude is not in finitude; what if desire and duty conflict; what if God *does* create dreadful collisions; if God demands renunciation, not consummation, of love; if God requires lover to forsake beloved; if God orders the sacrifice of a son, perhaps his own son, perhaps the son of another; what if . . . ; what if . . . ; what if . . . ? Frightful uncertainty, terrible insecurity— *horror religiosus*. Of this the ethicist knows nothing; but he suspects. And this gnawing suspicion slowly unravels the fabric of ethical life.

Within the context of Kierkegaard's overall dialectic of existence the ethical stage is "only a transitional sphere" between aesthetic and religious forms of life. Although ethical existence sublates important features of the indeterminateness and dissipation of aestheticism, moral selfhood finally negates itself in the struggle to affirm itself. Kierkegaard argues that "ethics points to ideality as a task and assumes that man is in possession of the conditions requisite for performing it. In this way, ethics develops a contradiction, precisely by making the difficulty and the impossibility clear." Unlike Hegel's conscientious subject whose actions disclose the inherent identity of opposites, Kierkegaard's ethicist gradually discovers the depth of the oppositions, the disparity of the differences, and the exclusivity of the contraries within the self. "The aesthetic sphere is that of immediacy," Kierkegaard explains, "the ethical is that of requirement, and this requirement is so finite that the individual always goes bankrupt." When ethical obligation is grasped with total seriousness, and ethically it can be taken in no other way, its fulfillment appears more and more impossible—ideality seems unrealizable, possibility unactualizable, infinitude unattainable, eternity transcendent. The more earnestly one struggles, the deeper the disparity becomes until at last the self acknowledges a persistent conflict between the opposites it ought to synthesize. The awareness of this failure to fulfill the ethical task brings with it a sense of the self's guilt. Kierkegaard's ethical stage does not culminate in beautiful souls contemplating their own divinity but in the guilty individual painfully conscious of his separation from and opposition to the absolute.

For the individual who apprehends himself as guilty, the naive self-confidence with which the ethical sojourn began appears humorous, "Humor," Kierkegaard maintains, "is the last stage of existential inwardness prior to faith." Kierkegaardian humor, however, is no Hegelian comedy. Unlike the comedian who is completely self-certain and regards his own subjectivity as absolute essence, the humorist, plagued by self-doubt, is convinced of his own inessentiality. "As the border of the religion of hidden inwardness, humor comprehends guilt consciousness as a totality." This recognition of guilt reveals the abiding contraditions of moral selfhood, and profoundly unsettles wayfarers who dwell at the ethical stage on life's way. Humor, therefore, is at once the limit of the ethical and the "boundary of the religious." This border forms the frontier of a wilderness that leads to Moriah, or perhaps even to Golgotha. To sojourn in this land of promise, the pilgrim must leave behind wife and family, mother and father, and journey alone.

LOUIS MACKEY

Once More with Feeling:
Kierkegaard's Repetition

There is only one real tragedy in a woman's life.
The fact that her past is always her lover, and
her future invariably her husband.

—OSCAR WILDE

The title of this book is *Repetition*. But his subject will be . . . woman. *Repetition?* About woman? Yes, in the only way it can be. By being about everything else under the sun. Woman is reality. This is not under the sun.

The book describes itself as "an essay in experimental psychology." In his epistle to the reader the author reveals that the subject of his experiment is a fiction and his adventure is a fabrication. The narrative metonymies of the text dissimulate a metaphoric identity of truth and fiction. Unsuccessfully. This too is not in the world.

The first part of the text, not entitled, is uninterrupted narration. Its typographical continuity suppresses an intricate scheme of divisions and relations. Brought to the surface, the scheme is as in the figure on the facing page.

A)1.   In the philosophical parenthesis that opens the book, Constantine Constantius reflects: recollection glances off the present moment into an idealized past, while hope turns away from the present toward an idealized future. The point would be to recuperate every present moment for the ideal and to install the ideal in every present moment, so that the actual becomes the repetition (re-presentation) of the ideal and the ideal becomes the repeti-

From *Kierkegaard and Literature: Irony, Repetition, and Criticism,* edited by Ronald Schleifer and Robert Markley. © 1984 by the University of Oklahoma Press.

tion (the meaning and truth) of the actual. In this way repetition would redeem what is lost in hope and recollection alike.

The Structure of Kierkegaard's *Repetition*, Part 1

	1. An opening philosophical parenthesis
	2. The story of the young man
A)	3. Transition: on "the interesting"
B)	4. A second philosophical parenthesis
	5. Constantine Constantius' trip to Berlin
C)	[In this account is the digression on the farce, which falls outside the story.]
	6. Conclusion: the apostrophe to transience and the invocation of death

In another sense recollection and repetition are the same movement turned in opposite directions. What is recollected is repeated backwards; what is repeated is recollected forwards. Retreating from the present that is, recollection is unhappy; advancing to meet the present that comes, repetition is happy. It has "the blessed certainty of the instant," which is the power of endurance. Repetition is "reality . . . and the seriousness of life." Without it one would be a tablet on which time writes at every instant a new inscription, or a mere memorial of the past: the present irrecoverably past or perpetually passing.

Recollection is to repetition as the ancient (that is, pagan) view of life is to the modern (the Christian). On the ancient view time is without direction and without order, so that one can only "escape backwards" (upwards?) into eternity; one tries "to find a pretext for stealing out of life, alleging . . . that he has forgotten something." An umbrella, perhaps? On the Christian view time is ordered and directed; eternity, to which one moves through time, lies ahead at the end of history. The ancient and the modern views of life offer alternative soteriologies. The former recommends redemption from time. The later proposes to redeem time itself: fruits, not flowers. Repetition is incarnation and resurrection.

A)4.   The discussion of repetition with which the book begins prefaces the story of the young man's unhappy love. In the brief passage that introduces his own failed attempt at repetition Constantine says that modern philosophy has not yet developed the category of repetition, but must do so: "Repetition is the new category which has to be brought to light. . . . The dialectic of repetition is easy; for what is repeated has been, otherwise it could not be repeated, but precisely the fact that it has been gives repetition the character of novelty." The novel is such only in relation to a past and a constant of change, else it were opaquely unique. Radical novelty is radically unintelligible and cannot even be comprehended under the rubric "novel":

> When the Greeks said that all knowledge is recollection they affirmed that all that is has been; when one says that life is a repetition one affirms that existence which has been now becomes. When one does not possess the categories of recollection or of repetition, the whole of life is resolved into a void and empty noise.

Temporality is intelligible only in relation to the eternal. Apart from recollection or repetition, which are the possible forms of this relation, existence in time is sound and fury, signifying nothing. "Repetition is the *interest* of metaphysics, and at the same time the interest upon which metaphysics founders." One asks, Who am I? in the sense of, Where did I come from? in order to know, What shall I do? The temporalizing of essence makes metaphysics interesting. But since metaphysics is properly disinterested it is also the rock on which metaphysics goes aground. Therefore "repetition is the solution contained in every ethical view." Everything merely temporal is discretely and unrepeatably "this now." Only the continuity provided by the eternal allows for the repetition necessary to moral decision and the development of character. But the eternal alone is also an uniterated "now," and only its distribution along the course of time yields repetition. Without the possibility of repetition the moral ideal remains a bondage from which there is no release, a problem without a solution. Repetition is, finally, "a *conditio sine qua non* of every dogmatic problem." On the other side of faith, "repetition will have the meaning of atonement" (*Sören Kierkegaard's Papirer*). From the standpoint of Christian doctrine, repetition means the restoration of fallen human nature to the image of God.

Apart from faith, "a religious movement by virtue of the absurd," "the finite spirit falls into despair." The first part of *Repetition*—at least the first part—is the despair of the finite spirit.

B)2.   A young man falls in love. He represents immediacy. Constantine Constantius tells his story. Constantine is reflection. Or language, which is the actuality of reflection. Falling in love is an immediate passion. But no sooner has he fallen than the young man begins to recollect his love as a thing past. His recollection takes the form of language. As falling in love is to the recollection of love, so the young man is to Constantine Constantius.

In the letter to the reader with which he concludes his book, however, Constantine confesses that he has imagined the young man. And Constantine himself is a pseudonym of Søren Kierkegaard. The plot(s) thicken(s). Constantine's immediacy is his concern to know whether repetition is possible. He creates the young man and his story as a "psychological experiment" to try the possibility of repetition. But there is also Søren Kierkegaard's immediacy, which impels him to inscribe this fiction and ascribe it to a figment. Kierkegaard's immediacy is his unhappy relationship to Regine Olsen. The book is, in its multiply indirect way, Kierkegaard's attempt to scout the possibility of repetition with Regine. The faulted repetition of the young man is, across all the intervening distances of reflection, Kierkegaard's own.

Like Kierkegaard himself, the young man cannot marry the girl. And so, saved not by the grace of God but by the magnanimity of woman, he becomes (take that word in the strongest possible sense) . . . a poet. The actuality of Søren Kierkegaard is his texts. He is a discourse. Everything—Kierkegaard, his fictions, and his fictions' fiction—is language.

In the first part of *Repetition* there is no repetition. No recuperation of immediacy on the other side of reflection. In the book as a whole (we shall have to ask if it is a whole) there are none but faulted repetitions. Unless we count Job. But we shall have to ask: in what sense is Job (*Job?*) in this book?

The young man's recollection of his love distances the girl. It also breaches his identity with himself. He is in love with the girl. Call that relation 1:

$$YM \underline{\quad\quad R1 \quad\quad} G.$$

He recollects his love for the girl. Call that relation 2:

$$(YM \underline{\quad R1 \quad} G) \underline{\quad R2 \quad} [YM].$$

He recalls his love by repeating again and again a stanza of Poul Möller's *The Aged Lover*. Call that anticipation of senility relation 3:

$$(YM \underline{\quad R1 \quad} G) \underline{\quad\quad R2 \quad\quad} [YM] \underline{\quad\quad R3 \quad\quad} (YM \text{ old}).$$

Reflection preserves the virginity of the girl by effecting the impotence of her lover.

The young man's recollection of his love for the girl, a recollection that follows directly upon his first falling in love, effaces his presence to her by thrusting it into the past. Being in love is transformed by reflection into the preterite having been in love. The same recollection thrusts the young man into the future and effaces his presence to himself. By reflection he becomes an old man who has lived his life and can recollect it only in the same impuissance of absolute seniority. The agent of this double effect is language: poetry.

In the event there is no presence at all. The young man and the girl are absent from each other and from their original relationship. The young man is distanced from himself. Only the girl abides intact in the self-presence of her immediacy; an immediate self-presence, however, which as such must remain a fruitless *an sich*. In the absence of a unity of immediacy and reflection there is no hope of repetition. The young man has lost his immediacy, the girl has not attained to reflection (she does not speak in this book), and their love can never enter upon the repetition of marriage.

The condition of woman's virginity is the impotence of her lover. Woman is reality, a reality not enlightened by the sun of reflection. Existence remains pristine because reflection is powerless to invade it. Being is forever too young; reflection is always already too old. Reality not illumined by consciousness remains in the dark. In the glare of reflection it cannot be seen. In the day as in the night all cows are invisible. There is neither marrying nor giving in marriage.

(This story, which is at first presented as a case history, is at the end re-presented as Constantine's recollection of his own creation. Constantine's visit to Berlin both repeats an earlier visit and parodies the young man's dilemma. Yet Constantine has imagined the young man, and all that he says and does is calculated to "throw light upon him.")

When the girl finally marries someone else (the young man reads about it in the paper), her loss of innocence restores the young man's potency . . . as a poet, not a husband. His repetition, which only doubles his reflective self-awareness, is not perfected. A Job would have married the girl, *quia absurdum,* but the young man can do nothing. Constantine says:

> He was in love, deeply and sincerely in love; that was evident, and yet at once, on one of the first days of his engagement, he was capable of recollecting his love. Substantially he was through with the whole relationship. Before he begins he has taken such a terrible stride that he has leapt over the whole of life. . . . Recollection has the great advantage that it begins with the loss, hence it is secure, for it has nothing to lose. . . . His mistake was incurable, and his mistake was this, that he stood at the end instead of at the beginning. But such a mistake is certainly a man's undoing.
>
> And yet I maintain the correctness of his mood as an erotic mood, and the man who in his experience of love has not experienced it thus precisely at the beginning, has never loved. Only he must have another mood alongside of this. . . . It must be true that

one's life is over at the first instant, but there must be vitality
enough to kill this death and transform it into life.

Yet there is no vitality at all. The lover can only recollect his love and spout
poetry. The girl can never become a woman. She is merely the occasion that
awakens his poetic gift. By making him a poet, turning him into language,
she signs her own death warrant. She is remanded to perpetual virginity, and
he is committed to a guilt he cannot expiate.

Of course, he has options. He could go ahead and marry the girl anyway.
But that would be a lie, since they are essentially unmarriageable. He could
tell her the truth; that she is only a semblance of the ideal, a figure of something more important than herself. But that would mortify her, and his pride
will not allow him that. Or he might arrange to make himself despicable in
her eyes. Following Constantine's plan, he might cause her to believe that he
is living in sin with a loose woman. Believing that, she would surely break off
the relationship herself. Thus retaining her own integrity, she would restore
his freedom. But he lacks strength for this option.

He remains, therefore, the melancholy knight of recollection. A Job
would have married the girl.

B)5.   Although it is prophesied on the first page of his book, Constantine Constantius's second trip to Berlin parodies the sad story of his young
friend. Having once experienced (i.e., recollecting) a half day of absolute con-
tentment, certain that he will never enjoy the same experience again, Constantine nonetheless becomes interested in the possibility of such a repetition.
As an experiment to test this possibility, he undertakes to repeat an earlier
sojourn in Berlin, of which he has the most pleasant memories. Hoping to
match his recollections of the first visit, he settles in the same apartment, fre-
quents the same cafes, attends the same theaters. But all the particulars have
altered, Berlin is not the same, and the experiment fails.

That is the parody. Or part of it. In the young man's case repetition
would have to occur at the level of spirit through the agency of freedom. For
him repetition would have meant the recovery by an alienated spirit of its lost
immediacy. But Constantine expects immediacy to confirm his recollections.
And that expectation spoils the whole thing. Constantine himself is clear
about this—more or less:

> I discovered that there is no such thing as repetition, and I had
> convinced myself of this by trying in every possible way to get it
> repeated. . . . Time and again I conceived the idea of repetition
> and grew enthusiastic about it—thereby becoming again a victim

of my zeal for principles. For I am thoroughly convinced that, if I had not taken that journey for the express purpose of assuring myself of the possibility of repetition, I should have diverted myself immensely on finding everything the same. What a pity that I cannot keep to the ordinary paths, that I will have principles, that I cannot go clad like other men, that I will walk in stiff boots! . . . How . . . can one get so foolish an idea as that of repetition, and, still more foolishly, erect it into a principle?

Constantine's parody, like any other worthy the name, exposes the weaknesses, the lines of stress, and the concealed hiatuses in the structure it "copies backwards." To make a principle of repetition, to try for it, is exactly what makes it impossible. Repetition must occur in the realm of the spirit: it is the recovery of nature by and for freedom. It does not just happen. But it may not be contrived. Shrewdness is of no use. The recovery of immediacy by and for reflection is not another immediacy (though it may be a *new* immediacy); neither is it a further reflection. Immediacy is gone as soon as it is there, and reflection is incurable.

Job might say: It takes a thunderstorm. But Constantine Constantius does not believe in thunderstorms.

And yet. Although Constantine's experience is a travesty, it is still a repetition. A parodic repetition. And it does incorporate several repetitions. Constantine's failure to achieve a repetition is repeated so often in Berlin that he finally becomes weary of repetition. But these *are* parodies, repetitions in reverse, in which life takes again (*tager igjen*) what it gives without giving a repetition (*Gjentagelse*).

Constantine's serious preoccupation is something he calls "the interesting." In principle unrepeatable, the interesting is a token of transience, which is a portent of death. Figures on the ground of nothingness.

C)3.   The interesting "does not lend itself to repetition." "A girl who does not crave the interesting believes in repetition. Honor to her who is such by nature [immediacy], honor to her who became such in time [by repetition]." But "a girl who craves the interesting becomes the trap in which she herself is caught." The interesting is something from which a wise girl can save a man, something that a foolish girl might elicit from him. The interesting is not defined, but Constantine's metaphor is sexual. And a metaphor, while it may be no argument, is no accident either. It is the metaphor of accident. What is it that women (the wrong kind) desire in a man, from which other women (the right kind) would redeem him? Seduction, from which a man (!) is saved by marriage. By the magnanimity of woman.

It is not accidental that the metaphor of accident dominates this transitional episode in the text. The interesting is the confinium between the actual and the ideal, conceived aesthetically as the occasion of surprise. A threshold. The same threshold, ethically conceived, is opportunity: the opportunity, earnestly desired by the resolute will, to actualize the moral ideal. Marriage, for example. For sure. Interest, as opposed to the interesting. Repetition is reality and the seriousness of life, the interest on which metaphysics founders, and the solvent of ethics. The interesting, a thing of no essential interest, is the interruption of the ideal by the anomalous actual. From which, once you succumb to it, there is no salvation but repetition: the sine qua non of dogmatics. For example?

Seduction cannot be repeated. The seducing male requires novelty and variety: a constant supply of original sexual occasions. He is obliged to run wild. For the feminine victim seduction is, simpliciter, the loss of innocence, *einmalig* and irreparable. A trap. Virtue is something that men must acquire but women can only lose. There is no repetition in seduction. You can only (be) seduce(d) once. Marriage is the renunciation of seduction. Seduction is either an interminable pursuit or a dead end. For the male, transience; for the female, death. The two are indistinct.

The feminist phalanx will advance on this argument. But it is only a metaphor. It is interesting (is it an accident?) that Constantine fills this interval of his story with the account of an occasion on which he refused a chance at seduction. He does that more than once.

C)6.   Transience and death. The first part of *Repetition* ends with that. Constantine apostrophizes the post horn ("that is my instrument"), which is a symbol of transience and the impossibility of repetition. On this instrument you can never play the same note twice. Or, what is worse, you cannot be sure of it.

Temporality is the rhetoric of death. Life, neither comic nor tragic, is interesting. But life does not captivate like death. Death has the superior eloquence: *peisithanatos*. By the transience of life it persuades all things to mortality. A conclusion of sorts. Of this, no repetition. This is the despair, and the hope, of the finite spirit.

HORS-TEXTE

The first half of *Repetition* ends with Constantine Constantius (and, we may presume, the young man) giving up on repetition. The whole of part one is calculated to enforce this defeat. But there is a part of the first part that falls outside its structure: at once outside and inside the trinity of binaries that organizes this region of the text. We have:

A)1 and A)4:   Recollection versus repetition
B)2 and B)5:   The stories of the young man and Constantine
                 Constantinus
C)3 and C)6:   Repetition (in the sense: redemption from "the inter-
                 esting") versus the triumph of transience and death

Embedded in B)5, in the structural center of the text, is the digression on the theater occasioned by Constantine's visit to the Königstäter in Berlin. This is no accident.

> Surely there is no young man with any imagination who has not at one time been captivated by the enchantment of the theater, and desired himself to be carried away into the midst of that fictitious [*kunstige*] reality in order to see and hear himself as an *alter ego* [*Doppeltgaenger*], to disperse himself among the innumerable possibilities which diverge from himself [*i sin al-mulige Forskjellighed fra sig selv*], and yet in such a way that every diversity is in turn a single self. Of course it is only at a very early age such a desire can express itself. Only the imagination is awake to its dream of personality, all the other faculties are still sound asleep. In such a dream of imagination the individual is not a real figure but a shadow, or rather the real figure is invisibly present and therefore is not content with casting one shadow, but the individual has a multiplicity of shadows, all of which resemble him and for the moment have an equal claim to be accounted himself.

Through the agency of that fictitious reality (the theater), the youth, all of whose egos are alter, is enabled to disperse himself among numberless possibilities. All these selves are imaginary, mere shadows; and equivalently, since his other powers are dormant, each of them is himself. Or would be, were it not for that invisible presence:

> Every possibility of the individual is therefore a sounding shadow. The cryptic individual no more believes in the great noisy feelings than he does in the crafty whisper of malice, no more in the blissful exaltation of joy than in the infinite sigh of sorrow; the individual only wants to hear and see with pathos, but, be it observed, to hear and see himself. However it is not really himself he wants

to hear. That is not practicable. At that instant the cock crows, and the figures of the twilight flee away, the voices of the night fall silent. If they continue, then we are in an entirely different domain, where all this goes on under the alarming observation of moral responsibility, then we are at the demoniacal. In order not to get an impression of his real self, the cryptic individual requires that the environment be as light and ephemeral as the figures, as the frothy effervescence of the words which sound without echo. Such an environment is the stage, which for this reason precisely is appropriate to the shadow-play of the cryptic individual.

The play provides a show of possibilities for the *cryptic* one: the person who is still hidden within himself, buried in the crypt of his immediacy. Until the cock crows (for the third time?), announcing the dawn of moral responsibility, such a man can only imagine his being, still secreted from himself, as a procession of evanescent passions. Because he requires an ephemeral environment, figures of foam, and words without resonance, a man like this desires the serious theater: it is all the reality he has; the stage is "not merely for pleasure."

But the mature person turns to farce:

Although in the individual life this moment vanishes, yet it is reproduced in a riper age when the soul has seriously collected itself. Yes, although art is perhaps not serious enough for the individual then, he may perhaps have pleasure in turning back occasionally to that first state and rehearsing it [repeating it, not practicing it] in sentiment. [Once more with feeling: *i en Stemning.*] He wishes now to be affected comically, and to be himself in a comically productive relation to the theatrical performance. Therefore, though neither tragedy nor comedy can please him, precisely because of their perfection, he turns to the farce.

Second time as farce. All the characters and situations of farce are types: abstract generalities represented in fortuitously concrete particulars. (Constantine is having a bit of fun at Schiller's expense. Naïve is to sentimental as serious theater is to farce. Naïveté diffuses its reality in the imaginary; or rather, since it has no reality as yet, it *is* the imaginary. Sentimentality recovers the reality it has never lost, farcically, in the instantiation of the imaginary by the accidental.)

After the ideal comes in the very next place the accidental. A wit has said that one might divide mankind into officers, serving-maids, and chimney-sweeps. To my mind this remark is not only witty but profound, and it would require a great speculative talent to devise a better classification. When a classification does not ideally exhaust its object, a haphazard classification is altogether preferable, because it sets imagination in motion. A tolerably true classification is not able to satisfy the understanding, it is nothing for the imagination, and hence it is to be totally rejected, even though for everyday use it enjoys much honor for the reason that people are in part very stupid and in part have very little imagination. When at the theatre one would have a representation of a man, one must either require a concrete form corresponding absolutely to the ideal, or else the fortuitous. . . . In the case of farce, the subordinate actors produce their effect by means of that abstract category "in general" and attain this by a fortuitous concretion. With this one has got no further than to reality. Nor should one seek to go further; but the spectator is reconciled comically by seeing this fortuitous concretion claiming to be the ideal, which it does by treading into the fictitious world [*Kunst-Verden*] of the stage.

The superiority of the farce (for mature persons) consists in this: in the farce the accidental secures reality, or the effect of reality, for the essential. Comically, the ideal generality achieves fortuitous concretion. Like Beckmann's ability to "come walking" (literally *at komme gaaende*, "to come going"), by which he creates an environment for himself.

Farce therefore is the comical repetition. You do not even have to follow it closely and carefully; you can watch it as casually as it presents itself. In the farce the ideal and the actual are reconciled in laughter, a laughter produced as much by the capricious attention of the observer as by the wholly gratuitous events on the stage.

Of course: this farcical repetition has its serious side. The girl in the box opposite Constantine's, maybe also the lady at the inn, surely the farm girl whose idyllic ambience concludes the digression on the theater; all of them are women whom Constantine scrupulously refuses to seduce. The tender gravity of these scenes is a necessary supplement of (is it also finally superior to?) the raucous laughter of the Königstäter's gallery. The farcical repetition, "blissful" as it is, is an experience of exuberance, but is for that reason unsettling. It needs to be put to rest by the reality (or is it the dream?) of innocence and by the promise (or is it the illusion?) of true love. "Happy girl! If ever a man should win your love, would that you might make him as happy by doing everything for him as you have made me by doing nothing for me."

The digression on the farce tells what the first part of *Repetition* shows. As in the farce, so in the first part of this book, the only viable meaning of repetition (is it unsettling or pacifying?) is the chance conjunction of the abstract ideal and the unmotivated actual. Freedom and nature accidentally made one. An uncertain and unstable recuperation that begs, sentimentally, for the reality it comically dissimulates.

Like life itself, the farce is neither tragic nor comic but ambiguously shuttles back and forth in the space between. Interesting. It may even be of interest.

A whore-text? Maybe a pretext. . . .

The first part of *Repetition* is untitled. Part two, repeating the title of the book, calls itself "Repetition." A repetition within the work of the work as a whole. (What does that do to its integrity?) And the accomplishment at last of that project which in the first part was abandoned in despair. Now it begins in earnest. Again. (What does that do to the accomplishment?)

The architecture of part one was intricate and insidiously concealed. By contrast, the divisions of part two are simple, symmetrical, and plainly marked:

A) Constantine Constantius: introductory essay
B) The young man: letters to Constantine Constantius (August 15– February 17; these letters include the discourse on *Job*.)
C) Constantine Constantius: second essay
D) The young man: letter to Constantine Constantius (May 31)
E) Constantine Constantius: letter to "N. N., this book's real reader," dated at Copenhagen, August 1843

A) Constantine's introductory essay, written some time after his return from Berlin, assesses the young man's condition in the wake of his unfortunate engagement. "There is nothing left for him," Constantine says, "but to make a religious movement." The realization of his love being impossible— it "cannot be declined in accordance with the case forms of the regular declensions"—it can come about, if at all, only "by virtue of the absurd." He is melancholy by nature. And his nature is androgynous.

In the first part of this book Constantine Constantius is the androgyne. He is moved to feminine devotion by the melancholy beauty and the passionate intensity of his young friend. But he is masculine-manipulative at the same time, in relation to the youth and all the other subjects of his psychological experimentation. Part two of *Repetition* (the "repetition") begins with a reversal of roles.

Like a woman the young man requires positive assurance of the legitimacy of his confidante: some token of trustworthiness. But like a man he wants a negative guarantee: he would as soon unburden himself to a madman or a tree. The sexual ambiguity of the young man puts Constantine in an equally ambiguous position. He is both being and nonbeing, at the whim of his friend. Constantine, whom formerly he regarded as queer, he now describes (Constantine alludes proleptically to the young man's letter of August 15) as mentally deranged. Constantine does not resent this attribution. It almost flatters him. As he says, "Now he knows my most intimate secret." Eventually, Constantine conjectures, the young man will kill him with his confidence. The position of an observer is dangerous.

The girl, when her fiancé disappears, is at first unaffected and only gradually slumbers "gently into a dreamy obscurity as to what has occurred and what it might mean." Another ambiguity. Both physically and spiritually the young man has vanished to a place unknown, leaving behind him a girl adrift, a confidant in a contradictory situation bordering on madness and death, and . . . uncertainty. A story that begins abruptly, ends indecisively, and bears ambiguous meanings, or none at all.

The youth himself is in a state of ambivalence. Really, but he imagines himself still in love with the girl, an imagining thrown up by his melancholy and his androgynous sympathy. He is, more than all else, captivated by the regret that he may have done the girl a terrible wrong. May have. This too is not certain. Is his guilt real or, like his love, only imagined?

At the outset of part two the positions of the personae are perfectly indeterminate, and the future of the narrative is obscure. Three undecided people in an undecidable relationship. Equivocation on all hands has settled into indifference. But: a troubled indifference. It may be the quiet just before the storm.

The young man wants to "come back." His problem has narrowed itself to a point:

> Indubitably it is not possession in the strictest sense which concerns him, or the content which develops from this situation; what concerns him is return, conceived in a purely formal sense. Though she were to die the day after, it would not any more disturb him, he would not feel the loss, for his nature would be at

rest. The discord into which he has been thrown by contact with her would be resolved [*forsonet*] by the fact that he had actually returned to her. So again the girl is not a reality but a reflection of the movements within him and their exciting cause. The girl has a prodigious meaning, he actually will never be able to forget her, but what gives her meaning is not herself but her relation to him. She is as it were the boundary of his being. But such a relation is not erotic. Religiously speaking, one might say that it was as it God himself employed the girl to capture him; and yet the girl herself is not a reality but is like the artificial flies one sleaves upon hooks.

What concerns the young man is return in a purely formal sense. The girl is not the obscure object of desire but only a reflection of the movements within himself. And their efficient cause. She has momentous significance, not erotically but as the limit of his being. She is, like the characters and situations in a farce, the fortuitous intrusion of transcendence into the circuit of reflection. But her effect is not comic. Her reality slants the indifference and disturbs the ambiguity of the dialectic. Something stirring in the depths that ever so slightly ruffles the surface.

She is like the bait on a fishhook with which God proposes to capture the young man for himself. The cross of Christ is a fishhook and Christ himself the bait with which God catches the devil.

What baffles the young man is neither more nor less than repetition: return in the purely formal sense. And repetition is always transcendence: the eruption of the other into the circuit of the same. No other way to the reconciliation of the alienated. Therefore the young man gets no help from Constantine Constantius or from the philosophers ancient or modern. Immanence (here: reflection) is of no use. His problem is religious, and no man can solve it. So he turns to Job.

Job too was bait. The stake, ostensibly, in a wager between God and Satan. But in fact: the bait with which God caught his unruly son.

Constantine will not deny the reality of repetition. How could he? But he cannot manage a religious movement. And his desire—that he might induce the girl to persuade the young man that she is married so as to disengage him from his melancholy conviction that he loves her—is offset (ambivalence again) by his misgiving—that the bait might be tempted to play God, that the girl might decide to capture the youth for herself by appealing to his melancholy. In that case, Constantine fears, the matter will come to a bad end—for the girl. The young man's revenge on existence, for making him guilty when he was innocent, would become the revenge of existence on the girl, for wanting to exploit his guilt.

Suppose that Job, or Christ, had decided to catch the Devil himself.

Constantine's assessment of the situation ends as part two begins, uneasily poised between the absurd possibility of repetition and the dreadful possibility of irrecoverable loss.

B) *August 15.* We have already had, in Constantine Constantius's opening essay, a review of this letter. The original first appears as the revisitation of a revision. It repeats, from the young man's point of view, what has already been repeated from Constantine's perspective. The indeterminateness and ambiguity of the situation, reported dispassionately in Constantine's essay, are here pathetically suffered. Constantine's madness, which concerns himself only analytically, is here confronted with fervent horror. The repetition of the repetition is the origin of the beginning.

The young man (he has never been named) has lost his own name and acquired a false name. He desires no name. Not his own, which (still unnamed) belongs to the girl (whose name he never utters), and not a glorious name if it is not his own. Throughout this correspondence he signs himself "your devoted nameless friend," "your nameless friend," "devotedly yours," and sometimes "   ."

In his self-imposed exile (he is in Stockholm but gives no address) the young man exhausts himself in aimless and fruitless activities. "The man who believes in existence," he says, is as well insured as the man who, to hide his feelings when he prays, holds before his face a hat without a crown. But life evokes no feelings and existence is void of meaning: it smells of nothing. The nihilism is bleak and total: Constantine, the girl, and the young man, are all brought to nothing, like clouds that tumble down into the womb of earth and there make their grave.

That, depressingly enough, is the state of affairs at the beginning of the second part of the story. The decisive event reported in the letter of August 15 is the young man's loss of his name. The loss of his name, a name that he has never had, expands to become the loss of name-in-general: the loss of the function of the name. Identities evaporate on every hand: impending madness, inexponible grief, the distraction of unaccountable guilt. Impotently ambivalent, language collapses in the confusion of tongues. Words, words, words.

THE JOB LETTERS

Beginning with the letter of *September 19,* a new language and a new

text are woven into the language of this text: a text and a language called *Job*.
A different discourse altogether. Job contends with God and makes his complaint before Him. A loud complaint that echoes in heaven and evokes, in
response, the voice of the thunderstorm. The language of Job breaks through
the bounds of immanence and forces a word from beyond. As Job is to his
comforters, so the young man is to the "miserable shrewdness" of Constantine Constantius. As Job is to God, so the young man is to . . . ? The movement of transgression begins. Transcendence hangs in the air like the calm
before a storm.

In the letter of *October 11* the speech of Job is contrasted with human
language, a wretched invention that says one thing and means another, the
miserable jargon of a clique, a collection of poems, proverbs, and pithy say-
ings gleaned from the classics and from *Balle's Lesson Book*. Human language has no words for the young man; it cannot without contradicting itself
tell the truth about his condition. At this moment, however, the young man
is already beginning to speak of himself in the language of *Job*. Even as he
complains of the inadequacy of human speech, he inscribes his predicament
in this new and (from a human point of view) paradoxical system of signs.
The canonical text, breaking into the discourse of man, restructures and
rewrites it. But to describe himself in the language of Job is not to make himself intelligible to men. The young man and his problem remain (from a
human point of view) nameless.

The transcendent, which here takes the form of the sacred Scripture,
bursts irrationally into the normal and (from the human point of view) nor-
mative conversation of the world. Where did Job come from? He appears
abruptly and without explanation at the beginning of the letter of September
19: "Job! Job! O! Job!" His eruption into the correspondence at this point
has the effect of deforming all its words and deranging all its significations,
from henceforth.

"Existence," the young man writes, "is surely a debate." Between God
and man? Man is rationality is language. The other than man is the irrational,
the language man cannot speak. God?

In the letter of *November 15* the young man says that he sleeps (not with
the girl but) with the words of Job under his pillow. He makes transcripts
of them in characters of all sorts on sheets of all sizes. But he will not (though
in these letters he repeatedly does) quote them. That would be to appropriate
them. Even as he makes them his own, the young man knows they do not
apply. Except as therapy. The words of Job, transcribed, are a divine poultice,
laid like the healing hand of God upon his sick heart.

Job is stationed at the confines of poetry. In the same breath: he stands at the limits of faith.

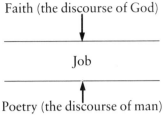

Faith (the discourse of God)

Job

Poetry (the discourse of man)

As the language of God, Job cannot be quoted. His speech is inappropriate and may not be appropriated. But if Job is "a poetical figure, if there never was any man who talked like this, then I make his words mine and assume the responsibility." The real Job may not be represented in the discourse of man. Job as *figura dictionis* goes without remainder into the letters of the young man, himself at most a poet and at last a poetic figure.

Between faith and poetry there is only silence. A silence broken by Job's anguished cries. "This I understand, these words I make my own. The same instant I sense the contradiction, and then I smile at myself as one smiles at a little child who has put on his father's clothes." Were anyone but Job to say what he says, the effect would be humorous. And still the mere reading of these words produces dread.

Job and the girl are beginning to converge. She too is a boundary of the young man's being, as if dropped there by God to captivate him. Nothing in herself, she is, like a fishing lure, artifice to the angler and reality to the fish. At the limit that divides being from nonbeing. The boundary situation is the scene of this text and the place at which repetition is (not conceivable, but) by virtue of the absurd possible.

The interesting is also at the borderline. The confinium between life and death. Repetition is the interest of metaphysics, but where the possibility of repetition beckons, the threat of seduction looms. There is more than one way to be surprised.

The next three letters are preoccupied with categories of the boundary. *December 14.* Job is in the right. But his rectitude transgresses the limits of human jurisprudence. Every interpretation of his case misunderstands it. He and God understand one another, but this understanding cannot be rendered in human language. The passion of freedom within him "is not stifled or tranquilized by a false expression." Beyond the jurisdiction of man, he takes leave of his friends, certain that God can explain everything, if only one can get Him to speak.

Job is subjected to a trial of probation. But this is a thing unspeakable, a phenomenon that escapes every science. Job is made the exception, in whom ethical and religious categories (the human and the divine) collide. Both sacrifice and phoenix, he burns and blooms in the fire of purification. "The border conflicts incident to faith are fought out in him." He is "the whole weighty plea presented on man's behalf in the great suit between God and man." Therefore "probation" is not expressed in the discourse of immanence. "Neither aesthetic, nor ethical, nor dogmatic, it is entirely transcendent." To be on trial as Job is on trial is to stand in contradiction to the divine: Job is the plea of man spoken against the judgment of God. Of a single man. Job's trial is *his* thing. It exceeds explanation "at second hand." Not the sublation of time into eternity, which would "erase . . . reality as a whole," Job's probation is the confrontation and reconciliation of time and eternity in time. A repetition. Dealt into this game by the wager in heaven, advised by an expert to "curse God and die," the chosen one plays out his hand. He cannot win. Barring a change in the weather.

January 13. Job gets his repetition. At the precise moment when it is perfectly clear that all is lost, the storm breaks:

> Job is blessed and has received everything *double*. This is what is called a *repetition*. How much good a thunderstorm does after all! How blessed it must be after all to be reproved of God! . . . Who could have conceived this conclusion? And yet no other conclusion is conceivable—and neither is this. When everything has come to a standstill, when thought is brought to a halt, when speech becomes mute, when explanation turns homeward in despair—then there must be a thunderstorm. Who can understand this? And yet who can discover anything else?
>
> Did Job lose his case? Yes, eternally; for he can appeal to no higher court than that which judged him. Did Job win his case? Yes, eternally, because he lost his case *before God*.
>
> So then there is a repetition. When does it make its appearance? That is not easy to say in any human language. When did it appear for Job? When all conceivable human certainty and likelihood had found it impossible.

And so (*February 17*) the young man awaits *his* thunderstorm: the repetition that will restore his potency and make him a husband.

Job is acquitted . . . by the *Donnerwort* that condemns him. Had he won his case against God, he would have demonstrated conclusively that life cannot be endured. The swift logic of a woman. It is a parlous thing (the education of Eve) to win your case against God. Happily Job loses and so, absurdly, wins.

When human language has exhausted its powers and broken against the boundary of transcendence, then God may speak. When the discourse of man has talked itself out, then the voice from the whirlwind may ask its devastating and redeeming questions.

C)	Constantine is not impressed. He thinks the young man badly confused. Against all logic he expects a thunderstorm to make him a husband. But, although he thinks himself fortunate that he did not "follow your admirable clever plan," he would still be well advised to get rid of the girl. That is the way of a man with a maid, or the way of reflection confronted with an awkward and inconvenient reality. The youth suffers from an "untimely melancholy magnanimity" that only a poet's brain could nurture. Let him take a religious view of his predicament and misread nervous apoplexy as divine intervention. He would have done better to exhaust his human shrewdness. Or Constantine's, since the young man himself seems to have none.

As usual, Constantine is right, in his way. Human shrewdness must be carried at least to the breaking point, and the young man may, too, previously have cast himself as an erotic Job. How does one know when he has reached the limit?

The young man is a disappointment to his mentor (his poet). He has not respected the ideal possibilities inherent in his situation. No help may be expected from the girl. Women (so Constantine) are incapable of the ideal, though they routinely use it as a ruse with which to dupe poets. The unhappy lover has not employed the idea as a regulative principle in the conduct of this affair. Even he admits that his flight to Stockholm, a particularity infinitely remote from the ideal, was a bungling and mediocre move. In these circumstances there is little chance of a thunderstorm.

Into the young man's overheated and long-winded pathos, his frantic invocation of Job, and his fascination with thunderstorms, Constantine's Olympian detachment, his algebraic summary of the ideal options, and his curt dismissal of the whole performance as a mass of confusion and misprision come like a blast of cold analytical air. The place needed airing. Repetition is possible, by virtue of the absurd, only after the exhaustion of human possibility. But to use up the humanly possible means not only to carry oneself in passion to the point at which, all passion spent and all the discourse of passion voided, one is exposed to the whirlwind. It also requires the dialecti-cal reduction of this passionate evacuation to ludicrous misconception and bungling malfeasance. The romantic agony is incomplete without the ironic deflation.

Both Constantine and the young man are textual fictions produced by Constantine Constantius (it is not as clear about Job).

D)   Reality (not Søren Kierkegaard) surprises both of them. Without consulting her lover or his confidant or (presumably) the ideal possibilities, the girl finds a husband:

> She is married—to whom I do not know, for when I read it in the paper it was as though I had a stroke of apoplexy, and I lost the notice and have not had patience to make a closer inspection. I am again myself, here I have the repetition, I understand everything, and existence seems to me more beautiful than ever. It came as a thunderstorm, too, though I owe it to her magnanimity that it happened.

When his beloved marries someone else, the young man loses no time in ful-filling Constantine's predictions. He calls it a thunderstorm, though he admits it felt a bit like apoplexy. And he attributes his release to feminine magnanimity.

But he gets his repetition. "I am again myself. . . . The discord in my nature is resolved, I am again unified. . . . Did I not get myself again, precisely in such a way that I must doubly feel its significance? . . . The magic spell which bewitched me so that I could not return to myself has now been bro-ken. . . . I am born to myself."

"I belong to the idea." The self to which he is restored is not his imme-diacy. *That* he could only have recovered in marriage by virtue of the absurd. A religious movement. He is instead restored by virtue of the magnanimity of woman, to the idea. He is (re)born as a poet—to "the flight of thought, . . . the service of the idea"—when the girl (woman is reality) takes herself out of the way. Ilithia unfolds her hands (!), and a man is born again. But he returns not to his primal state, that first fine rapture of first love, but to his subsequent recollection of love. A recollection that has made him happy at last by making him miserable at first. He is released not to the sobriety of the actual but to the inebriation of the ideal.

His repetition, therefore, is ever so slightly faulted, his return ever so slightly abbreviated, and his rebirth ever so slightly aborted. It is difficult not to sense an undertone of cynicism, ever so slight, in his panegyric to the magnanimity of woman.

Like the letter of *November 15*, which wonders whether Job is a real man or a poetical figure, this one has no closure. Like all of them, it bears no signature.

E)   Constantine Constantius's concluding letter is addressed to "Mr. N. N., this book's real reader." The real reader of this book is masculine. He is also "a fictitious figure [*en poetisk Person*]." N. N., who is "not a plurality but only one," is something of an ideal reader, who reads the book, as opposed to the host of unreal readers (carefully listed and identified by Constantine) who read in(to) the book only their own anxieties, prejudices, desires, professional psychoses, and privileged doctrines.

Constantine writes like Clement of Alexandria, so that the heretics will not be able to understand him. But the real reader will perceive, through the "inverted development" of the thought, what the book is about: the dialectical struggle whereby the exception breaks with the universal and is justified not by getting around it but by going through it. Like Jacob/Israel wrestling with the angel. Like Job contending with God. Like the one sinner who repents, over against the ninety and nine just persons who need no repentance. Or like the poet emerging victorious from his conflict with existence.

The poet, as a justified exception to the universal, is a stage on the way to that superior exception, the religious man. The universal, that which is required of every man (the word *Almene* also means, "common, general, public"), is a coherence of freedom and nature confected by duty. Marriage, for example. And in principle: the marriage of Kant's practical freedom and Hegel's ethical substance. Constantine's young man is justified when existence itself (reality is woman) absolves him from his guilt: that he has defaulted his obligation to being by recollecting it rather than wedding it. In the nick of time the girl withdraws her accusing presence and releases the poet into his exceptional absence. The debt is canceled, and the account is cleared.

His liberation ab extra is quasi-religious. But only "as if." He is never more than latently religious. For the young man repetition is not "reality and . . . the seriousness of life." It is just "his own consciousness raised to the second power." To make him a religious exception, the shock would have to come from higher up. From God, who can do what no ordinary woman, no matter how self-effacing her magnanimity, can even aspire to. Man is reflection, and woman is reality. But only that reality which is (defined as) alienated by language. Both male and female lie this side of the boundary of immanence. They are conceivable, and only conceivable, together, as the othered and the othering. Within this domain the Hegelian logic plays its nasty little game in neverending closure. God is reality in an altogether different sense: the transcendent, the wholly Other, which language can neither distance nor appropriate, because He is always already infinitely far off and infinitesimally proximate.

The young man's problem is solved and his repetition achieved within the circuit of the same. As the shifting sexual identities in this story indicate, the difference between male and female structures an immanent dialectic, of which man and woman are the terms always posited and ever again sublated. The ideal and the actual are two mirrors reflecting each other to infinity.

Job, however, is addressed by the Other. His transgression is precipitated and his protest silenced by the divine prerogative, which neuters the dialectic of man and woman as it moots the argument between Job and his comforters. The unspeakable transcendent takes Job through the universal and beyond it: the universal (marriage), from which the poet is conveniently exempted by the amiable dispensation of existence, becomes in the religious instance the universal (justice), from which Job is terribly redeemed by the connivance of God and Satan.

There remains the difference of infinity between religion and a poetry which has the presentiment of religion. This text, which is poetry of a sort, can incorporate the religious only by excluding it. The sacred gloss, appropriated by the young man to describe his own perplexity, is written in the margins of *Repetition*. Intruding ambiguously into Constantine's fiction, *Job* proposes an unaskable question.

Constantine's fiction. Who is Constantine Constantius? A ventriloquist's dummy. A psychologically necessary presupposition. A serviceable spirit who serves by repeatedly becoming someone else. His name is a mockery . . . of the name. Who is the real author of this book? Who concludes by offering his real reader (who?) the barest hint of a possibility of reconciliation (a repetition?) after all the bewildering transformations through which the book has led him? Whose name goes in the blank marked "N. N."? The blank marked "C. C."? There is a blank marked "Søren Kierkegaard." There is also . . . a mark.

But this is serious business. In part two of *Repetition*, called "Repetition," the repetition vainly sought in part one is finally achieved. After a fashion. The story of the young man repeats, in its own way, the story of Job, which repeats, in its own way, the story of the young man. At the end of it all the "real reader" is offered a chance at his own repetition. (*Forsoning*. In theological terms, atonement.) He is invited to "be reconciled" to the text that has brought him to this pass.

A young man in Stockholm (no address given) is failing to contact a girl in Copenhagen who has recently changed her name. He's lost his own. Job on his ash heap is shouting at the wind. His words are blown back in his throat. Someone has just finished reading an illegible script. A repetition of sorts. This is getting us nowhere. Where were we?

Some birds can be taken only from the rear. Here is a little salt for the tail:

> The idea of the book is the idea of a totality, finite or infinite, of the signifier; this totality of the signifier cannot be a totality, unless a totality constituted by the signified preexists it, supervises its inscriptions and its signs, and is independent of it in its ideality. The idea of the book, which always refers to a natural totality, is profoundly alien to the sense of writing. . . . If I distinguish the text from the book, I shall say that the destruction of the book . . . denudes the surface of the text. That necessary violence responds to a violence that was no less necessary.
>
> (Jacques Derrida, *Of Grammatology*)

Bound securely between its covers, *Repetition* appears to be a book. A finite totality of signifiers, organized by a superintendent meaning that assigns to beginning, middle, and end their rightful places in a system closed upon-within itself. We expect it to contain, or be contained by, all it expresses.

Yet it begins with a digression remarking the contrast between the Eleatics' absurd denial of motion and Diogenes' equally absurd denial of that denial. It ends with an open letter to the reader, Mr. N. N., that asks him to be reconciled to the errant ways of the narrative. To continue (for how long?) the dialectic of repetition which the book begins to enact. Or perhaps to achieve for himself (how?) the repetition which Constantine's experimental psychology has shown to be impossible. An invitation to an indefinitely postponed atonement. The middle of the book is a blank: a silence and a silent passage of time between the death with which part one concludes and the "repetition" with which part two begins.

The putative totality of the signifiers called *Repetition* is exceeded by the digression on the farce. It is breached and invaded by the canonical discourse of *Job*. It is the work of a protean author, a shape-shifter ironically named "constant," and it is addressed to a real-ideal reader who is only a blank without a name. If *Repetition* is a book, it is a book of which there is no definitive edition. A book that does violence to itself as book.

There is reason to think that this "book" is (in the technical sense and *avant la lettre*) a text: writing in which the violence done to writing by the book is countered by the violence inherent in the nature of writing itself. A necessary violence. The book attempts a conquest of being through the consolidation of meaning. But if the guardian of the integrity of being is the impotence of language, then it is expedient that *Repetition* (which says as much) perform the solicitation of this conquest and the dissemination of this meaning. A repetition. Of sorts.

In the body of the narrative there are two proper names, both of which stand (in) for absences. Somewhere in Stockholm the young man takes refuge from the scene of his engagement. Paul Martin Möller, deceased for five years when *Repetition* was published, provides a (pre)text for recollection. Remotions in time and space. The letter to the reader is situated and dated, but in the course of the letter Constantine's identity is dissolved at last and for good. "Copenhagen, August 1843" marks the place and the moment at which *Repetition* was finished by its "real" author, whose absence from his text is absolute.

It is only where the text transgresses the story, Constantine's *aparté* on the farce, that it is suddenly punctuated by names that function as indices of presence: the Royal Theater in Copenhagen ("not merely for pleasure"), the Königstäter in Berlin, the actors Beckmann and Grobecker. Reality enters the text only at that place where the text is beyond itself: being is always the excess of the text. And perhaps at that place where the text is interrupted ab extra. The *Job* letters. Perhaps. For who knows whether Job is a human being or a trope? Job? or *Job?* That is only, but always, a maybe. We might check up on the Königstäter and its troupe. There is no way to verify Job. The being that is the excess of the text might be pursued. The being that invades the text—for that we would require a thunderstorm. Whose voice would we hear? And how would we know?

In the hierarchy of life-styles by Johannes Climacus, humor is the proximate confinium of faith. In the Aristotelian sense, its place.

One of the excesses of this text (his name appeared on the Stationer's Register) was a subject of Christian VIII named Søren Kierkegaard. A writer on religious subjects. Through the pseudonym Johannes Climacus he professes an interest in Christianity, proclaimed throughout history as the incarnation, in history, of the Word of God, and demanding a decision, also in history, for or against the miraculous Presence. So historical is the reality of Christianity that history itself, since the Incarnation, has had no reality but Christianity. Yet Climacus, for all his concern with the concrete historical actuality of Christianity, is exclusively preoccupied with the abstract dialectic of rationality and radical alterity: not the historical reality but the absurd historicity of Christianity is the sole *topos* of his meditations. He even goes so far as to suggest that we could dispense with the New Testament and the whole of Christian history if only the contemporaries of Jesus had left "this little advertisement, this *nota bene* on a page of universal history": " 'We have believed that in such and such a year God appeared among us in the humble figure of a servant, that he lived and taught in our community, and finally died.' " Those few words, alleging the bare fact of incarnation, would have been enough to provide the opportunity for faith and the occasion of offense.

This is a contradiction only if we forget that the historical incarnation, the Christ who is also Jesus, is, like the characters and situations in farce, a fortuitous concretion. On the one hand, history is beside the point. What matters are the "dialectic movements." But on the other hand, to be a Christian is to be contemporary with the historical Christ and to appropriate the history of Christianity. The Christian is not one who has correctly worked out the logic of incarnation. He is one who lives a perfectly determinate kind of life: *imitatio Christi*. Although the concretion is fortuitous (how could it be otherwise when the category to be incarnated is the Absolutely Other?), yet it *is the* concretion of the Absolutely Other and therefore the Absolutely Other itself. This particular actor, who just happens to work at the Königstäter, *is* the miles gloriosus. Likewise the gratuitousness of the incarnation of the Word in the man Jesus, like the second birth of every new Christian, is no accident. Although it is an absolute surprise.

Is it an accident that in *Repetition* the young man and the girl are never made concrete, not even fortuitously? He is described, but description is abstraction, and he remains for all of it a category: the young man. The girl is not even described. She is never more but never less than the alienated term of an allusion *ins Ferne*.

Reality is, in relation to every movement of reason, the unmotivated. An other which the dialectic can never generate and so never consume. The irrational. Woman is reality. Like the Christ absurdly incarnate in Jesus, that impossible possibility whose reality we call the God-man, woman can save us all. From the interesting. From ourselves. We are all men. The women too. All of us bear, inside out or outside in, the signifier of our lack. This is not under the sun.

This is absurd. Of course. Nevertheless, in *The Point of View for My Work as an Author*, Kierkegaard says that his life has been a love affair with God, who is metonymically identified with Regine, and rejected bride, and Michael Pederson, the dead father. God, his true lover, is also the mother he never had, replacing and effacing the biological mother, whom his father had possessed without right, to his lifelong despair. This too is absurd. But the sexual identities in his life, as in his texts, will not respect the limits of gender.

In the possibility opened by the death of the father, God gives himself as mother and bride to the prodigal who returns from harlotry to his true home. A repetition of sorts ("he came to himself"), in which Kierkegaard returns to that origin from which he never departed. How far is the grace of God from the magnanimity of woman?

In the book, as the forced containment of the irregularity of writing, phallogocentrism asserts its possession of the signifier and essays the appropriation of being. (Anne Lund, so rudely forced.) But if the book is an attempted rape of reality, then the original violence of writing responds to the violence of the book with a gesture of castration that liberates the transcendent. In *Repetition* the signs neuter themselves. The verses of Paul Möller, by which the young man quotes himself into senility. His copybook, containing citations from the classics and the catechism, and his transcripts of the biblical text; his removal from Copenhagen to Stockholm; and his letters themselves, addressed to "my silent confidant" and left unsigned: signifiers of something missing. Occupying the place of an absence and exposing its impotence, *Repetition* renounces dominion and imperium. The mastery of being by the book is unmasked as sterile self-manipulation; the hymen remains intact.

From Philostratus the Elder, Kierkegaard took a motto for *Repetition*: "On wild trees the flowers are fragrant, on cultivated trees wild the fruits." The conjunctions (wild-flowers, cultivated fruits) are paradoxical. These words, Kierkegaard remarks (*Papirer*), could stand as an epigram over the relationship between paganism and Christianity. Paganism, in all its declensions a religion that centers in fertility and procreation, only flowers. Christianity, which has decentered sexuality to the point of glorifying perpetual chastity . . . bears fruit. Untamed nature expends itself in show. Artifice gives birth. (A virgin birth?) In both cases it is a question of fragrance, and therefore of perception at a distance.

It is paradoxical, and beyond paradox surprising, to be told that Christian fruits smell like pagan flowers. But Christianity repeats paganism as the fruit repeats the flower. And a repetition is always something of a surprise. To be taken again (*gjentages*) is to be overtaken (surprised): taken over, without warning, perhaps unawares. Seized or captured by that which is always there before you because it runs faster (*overraske, überrasche*). Faster even than irony, of which surprise is in a sense the opposite. Irony knows everything, and more than everything. It has used up reality and explored possibility and found them wanting. Irony is beyond surprising. Insofar as every text takes itself out of the race by turning on itself in a cipher of emasculation, every text is ultimately troped as irony. Therefore repetition is never inscribed in the text. Especially a text entitled with a double irony, *Repetition*.

And yet: irony is a necessary condition of repetition. Only the unsurprisable is absolutely surprised. The ash heap comes before the thunderstorm. "No authentic human life is possible without irony," and every authentic human life is a function of repetition, "a history wherein consciousness successively outlives itself, though in such a way that happiness consists not in forgetting all this but becomes present in it" (Kierkegaard, *Irony*). Repetition cannot be written. *Repetition* is a way of writing this.

The Crucifixion was an event in history, as the Creed testifies. He was crucified under Pontius Pilate: a time and a place and an undistinguished agent of the imperial Roman government (now forever marked with a distinction he might have wished to decline, from which his wife tried to save him). After 1900 years the human race managed, in Nietzsche, to comprehend the Crucifixion. This is in the world. But the Resurrection took place in accordance with the Scriptures. An event beyond history, of which history knows nothing but an empty tomb. The signifier of absence. Tolkien has said that Christianity is the fairy tale that came true. The man-god, the historical Jesus who died and the eternal Christ who was reborn in him, is the metonymy that became metaphor. This is not in the world, though the Resurrection (of which the Crucifixion is the impossible possibility) is the repetition that contains the world. Creates it anew and for the first time by restoring to it that beginning from which it never departed.

But the Crucifixion comes first. Being cannot be forced by the signifier. Like truth, she keeps her legs crossed. The violence of language turns on itself. The catechrestic seizure of being by the sign yields only the indefinite deferral of presence and the dispersal of the sign itself in sterile dissemination. Alluring fruit and miserable pittance, which do not satisfy. Fragrant flowers of evil.

Maybe. These may be dragonseed. It is necessary to pass by the dragon. The impotence of language preserves inviolate the alterity of being. And thereby—perhaps—opens the way for repetition. But the hook must be baited. Irony is the penance of language, by which it acknowledges its original fault: the incapacity to let be. And a kind of reparation. A refusal to foreclose the possibility that reality may, in the extremity of language, bestow itself. The manna that satisfies with benediction. Beyond irony there is the possibility—*just* the possibility, which can neither be activated nor shut off, but only allowed to remain in its absolute dehors—that being may, gratuitously, give itself. Being is inconceivably conceivable as gift. A graceful and gracious self-giving of which the restoration of Job is a singularly thunderous instance. Of which the magnanimity of woman (the self-withholding of being) is an ironic inversion.

Or is it? In the first draft of *Repetition* the young man kills himself in febrile imitation of Werther. When Kierkegaard learned that Regine had married Fritz (from whom she had been temporarily distracted by Søren), he rewrote the ending. The magnanimity of woman saved, among other things, this text. Among other things, Søren Kierkegaard? Perhaps: a fortuitous concretion of the young man, Søren in *Repetition* repeats his love affair, and his faulted self-recovery, with feeling. Not quite autobiography, since the life follows and repeats the fiction. The end of the story and the beginning of the history were written by Regine. Regine is the grace of *Repetition*. What saved Regine?

Pogo says, very sensibly, that bait never wins. But the girl achieved a repetition. She found another man and began a new life. Who was he and what did she do for him? "She is married—to whom I do not know. . . . I read it in the paper. . . . I lost the notice and have not had the patience to make a closer inspection." His signifier is effaced in the very mention. But he got the girl. The unsurpassable is surpassed. The "movement" by which the girl finds a man and enters upon her marriage is made by virtue of the absurd; it is unmotivated by her "ideal" relationship to the young man. This bait died and was resurrected: she had the vitality to kill her death and transform it into life. What was for her lover a matter of life or death became for her a matter of life and death. The past her lover, the future her husband. Is that a tragedy? Perhaps it is a farce. More than interesting, it is the interest of this text.

Being, which can never be taken at the origin but only repeated, is grace. The beloved and fruitful wife of whom one never tires.

In Hebrew she is the maternal grandmother of our Savior.

KEVIN NEWMARK

Between Hegel and Kierkegaard:
The Space of Translation

What goes on between Hegel and Kierkegaard invites a reading that is pre-
dominantly historical in nature. Within a succession of German idealists that
would have to include Kant, Fichte, Schelling, and Hegel, Kierkegaard represents a dramatic change of course or disruption. The fact that at the same
time an essentially *linguistic* displacement is at work here—i.e., the *translation* of the German tradition in and by the Danish idiom—is apt to appear as
a mere geographical contingency, an accident, within the larger historical
context of conceptual questions at issue. All the same, nothing should immediately preclude the possibility that the relationship between the Danish
translation and the historical transition is more complicated than that of a
simple opposition between geography and history, or between time and
space. By accepting at face value the significance of the historical over the
geographical (which in this case is also the linguistic), we are already giving
in to Hegel's well-known dialectical *Aufhebung* of space *by* time and hardly
allowing Kierkegaard to have his own say in the matter.

Indeed, it cannot be simply accidental that Kierkegaard's critique of
Aufhebung—the central Hegelian concept of *mediation* that produces the
dialectical movement from space to time to Thought—is advanced as easily
by means of purely linguistic effects as by way of the historical exigencies of
philosophical debate. Thus, the Danish word Kierkegaard uses to translate
Aufhebung (Ophaevelse) not only captures the truly Hegelian ambivalence
between annulment and elevation, it also brings to mind the common idio-

From *Genre* (Special Issue: The World as Text: Nonliterary Genres) 16, no. 4 (Winter
1983). © 1983 by the University of Oklahoma.

matic expression, *at gjøre mange Ophaevelser over*, to make a fuss over, to
do a song and dance about something that really isn't worth it. (As in the
expression, "at gjøre Ophaevelser over Udgifterne," which means to grumble
about, to make an unnecessary fuss, or to cavil over the expense of something.) On a loose diary entry of 1838, Kierkegaard spells out the implicit
criticism that is always present in his translation of Hegel: "The Hegelians
come up with many sublations (*foranstalte mange Ophaevelser*) of the concept which are just not worth taking the trouble to fuss over (*at gjøre mange
Ophaevelser over*)."

Kierkegaard's translation, then, not only repeats the speculative movement present in Hegel's text, it exceeds it by matching the seriousness of
mediation (*Aufhebung*) with the frivolous chatter of fussing about (*Ophaevelser*). By cleverly linking Hegel's *Aufhebung*—one of the most important
concepts in Philosophy—to the Danish expression *at gjøre Ophaevelser
over*—much ado about nothing—Kierkegaard is actually sublating the very
concept of sublation. Kierkegaard's translation *is* "Aufhebung" inasmuch as
it unites a positive determination with its opposite negative content, mediating the earnest discourse of thought (*Aufhebung*) with the meaningless twad-
dle of chit-chat (*Ophaevelser*). But this time the *Aufhebung* of *Ophaevelser*
puts into question the value of continuing the speculative process. For once
philosophy has been mediated into a simple matter of song and dance, what
is the ultimate difference between thought and any old vaudeville act?

The incidental question of translation thus turns out to be a radical challenge to speculative thought itself. The gravity of this question, moreover, is
by no means attenuated by its appearance in the somewhat disreputable guise
of a pun, tucked away in a dusty corner of Kierkegaard's journals. For it is
difficult to imagine a text further removed from the levity of this kind of gratuitous word play than *Fear and Trembling*, and yet that text, too, is the
product of a meditation on the unsettling dynamics of translation. "Fear and
trembling," or to use the Danish name Kierkegaard actually gave to his book
on Abraham's faith, *Frygt og Baeven*, is more than just a translation of Saint
Paul's letter: "Slaves, be obedient to those who are your masters, with fear
and trembling work toward your salvation." *Fear and Trembling* is in fact
the story *of* translation. What is at stake in the book is the possibility of
understanding the story of Abraham's faith, but this possibility is undermined by making it dependent on the inevitability of a translation: "That
man was not an exegetical scholar. He did not know Hebrew; if he had
known Hebrew, he perhaps would easily have understood the story of Abraham." In order to enter into the story of Abraham, to follow Abraham and

his faith along the road to Mt. Moriah, the reader is forced to go by way of a detour around a translation.

The spatial figure of the road, or detour, along which the reader of the translation must travel, merges very quickly with the temporal figure of a march through history which is represented by God's promise to Abraham. It is precisely the promise of receiving from God a son, Isaac, that allows Abraham to conceive of a "future" for himself and all his descendants. The Promised Land, then, is far less a circumscribed *area* than it is an infinite prolongation of *time* that passes through Abraham and his progeny. But what constitutes the "problem" in Abraham's story—and what undoubtedly accounts for the reader's continued difficulty in "understanding" the translation he reads over and over again—is the fact that Abraham is asked to *sacrifice* Isaac, to give up not only his son, but in addition to renounce the one possibility of securing a future in the unfolding movement of history. This is why the narrator of *Fear and Trembling* cries out in frustration: "All the glorious remembrance of his posterity, the promise in Abraham's seed . . . what meaning would it have if Isaac should be sacrificed?" Without Isaac, there is no future for Abraham, no space in which God's promise to Abraham can acquire any meaning. Isaac thus represents not only the future as such, but also the future as the hermeneutic possibility of *meaning*, the temporal site in which Abraham's life, that is, his relationship to God, can find its ultimate significance.

The route to Mt. Moriah becomes in this way an unthinkable threat; the radical loss of meaning, the obliteration of Abraham's future and the impossibility of making any sense out of God's promise to Abraham. But thanks to his faith, Abraham withstands this threat and gets Isaac back again. Back again? Through his faith, Abraham had gotten Isaac for the *first* time. The stumbling block in *Fear and Trembling* is precisely this second form of faith. Why was it not sufficient to have had the original faith which believed in spite of all appearances to the contrary that Sarah would be capable of providing Abraham with a future in the form of a son? What happens to God's original promise when it is allowed to be repeated in a derivative manner on Mt. Moriah?

In this regard, it is worth recalling that the story line of *Fear and Trembling* is itself doubled: not only is there an attempt by an allegorical *reader* to understand the translated text of Genesis ("once upon a time there was a man who read the story of Abraham"); the main body of the text is an attempt by an *author* to reply to the philosophical text of Hegel's reading of Abraham's faith. Hegel's own treatment of Abraham is "wrong," and the argument of

Johannes de Silentio, the pseudonymous author of *Fear and Trembling*, is at least in part a timely polemic aimed at setting Hegel and his followers "right":

> I for my part have applied considerable time to understanding Hegelian philosophy and believe that I have understood it fairly well; I am sufficiently brash to think that when I cannot understand particular passages (*Steder*) despite all my pains, he himself may not have been entirely clear.

What Hegel has been "unclear" about in his treatment of Abraham is how in the world the singularity of Abraham's faith could ever become mediated (*aufgehoben*) in the universal dialectic of speculative philosophy.

Johannes de Silentio takes Abraham to be a special case, a privileged instance of resistance to Hegel's seemingly irresistible dialectic mediations. For Hegel, Abraham represents a preliminary moment in the necessary passage (*Übergang*) from Nature to Spirit, or from Adam to Christ. As such, Abraham is both a breaking point (*eine Trennung*) and an origin (*der Stammvater einer Nation*). For de Silentio, on the other hand, Abraham's singularity remains exceptional; the experience of faith *cannot* be re-integrated into the Hegelian dialectic. *Fear and Trembling* is at one and the same time a critique of Hegel's dialectical reading of Abraham and a demonstration of the way in which Abraham escapes that reading.

Ironically enough, though, it is precisely this impossibility of making Abraham into a dialectical passage (*ein Übergang*) which assumes almost at once emblematic value for all those textual passages (*die Stellen*) where Hegel is not quite clear, where the smooth dialectic of speculative thought splutters and stalls in a state of paralysis. In a curious reversal that is nothing if not Hegelian, the same quality that makes Abraham absolutely *heterogeneous* to Hegel's dialectic of history (the fact that Abraham's singularity cannot be *mediated* into any kind of universal category) is what also makes him a perfect *representative* for history's eventual critique of Hegel's idealism (the insistence on the importance of the individual's concrete experience at the continuing expense of abstract forms). Hegel's reading of Abraham—which Kierkegaard did his utmost to combat and debunk—becomes itself an irresistible model for a "modernist" reading of Kierkegaard. From France in the 1930s to America in the 1980s, that is to say from critics as superficially far apart as Jean Wahl and Paul Bové, Kierkegaard is read simultaneously as the site of a rupture with Hegel (*eine Trennung*), and as the origin of twentieth-century philosophies of lived-experience, or action (*der Stammvater einer Nation*).

The appeal of such a schema is as deep-rooted as it is apparent. History, in the form of a twentieth century which is "beyond" Hegel, is recuperated at the same time that a fundamental space is opened up for the activity of the individual subject whose "singularity" exceeds the reductive nature of Hegel's universals. And from the point of view of a "criticism" of Hegel, this dialectical pattern of conflict and resolution is entirely in keeping with the spirit of de Silentio's writing. But what of the author's double here, the *reader* whose own story is only coincidentally related to a critique of Hegel, and whose only aim is to decipher the (translated) story of Abraham?

> Once upon a time there was a man who as a child had heard that beautiful story of how God tempted Abraham and of how Abraham withstood the temptation, kept the faith, and contrary to expectation, got a son a second time. . . . The older he became the more often his thought turned to that story. . . . and yet he could understand the story less and less. Finally he forgot everything else because of it; his soul had but one wish, to see Abraham.

Is it possible to assimilate this fairy-tale (once upon a time) to the dialectical exchange between de Silentio and Hegel? Can we be sure that we understand Kierkegaard and our own story about his place in modernity before attempting to read the story of this one reader and his efforts to understand Abraham?

What complicates any consideration of these questions, however, is the peculiar status which *Fear and Trembling* assigns to the category of the understanding. In fact, the understanding is that which *cannot* be included in the story of Abraham and the unexpected retrieval of his son Isaac. Faith is not a form of knowledge, it is an "incomprehensible" act that presents an insurmountable obstacle to the dynamics of cognition, and in particular to the cumulative process of understanding most conveniently attributed to Hegel. Since there is no *sense* in God's having demanded from Abraham the sacrifice of that which He had already promised to Abraham as the very possibility of sense, we are forced to recognize the impossibility of ever comprehending Abraham's behavior. From the standpoint of the understanding, Abraham's behavior is a scandal, and it can amount to no more than having wanted to *murder* Isaac. But in the moment of faith, Abraham's relationship to his sole heir can be reduced neither to a willingness to murder his son, nor to a desire to preserve him. This logically repugnant space is called "faith," and it resists all attempts to understand it.

Thus, when Hegel tells the story of Abraham's faith within the context of a universal history of reason, he is actually admitting to not having wholly "understood" it. By making Abraham into just another stage in the process of absolute knowledge, Hegel not only misunderstands the status of his faith, he also betrays the radicality of the individuality which this faith imposes on Abraham. For the product of thought—which is also the form of knowledge—is the *universal*, or the abstract in general. The activity of speculative thought, inasmuch as it tends toward universality, is necessarily opposed to all that is particular, contingent, and individual. The task of each and every individual, of the particular "I," consists in constantly expressing itself in the universal generality of thought. In order to achieve this self-expression, the individual mediates itself through language, and in so doing gives up the contingency of its own particularity.

But Johannes de Silentio points out that this is precisely what Abraham *cannot* do. De Silentio tells us quite clearly that Abraham is *par excellence* the figure of silence. Abraham retains his individuality by remaining mute in the face of all dialectical solicitations to express himself in the language of the understanding. His faith is the absolutely particular which declines every mediation in the universal. De Silentio has every right to cite Hegel: "As soon as I open my mouth, I express the universal"; but Hegel has no business whatsoever telling the story of a faith Abraham himself could never bring himself to disclose. Abraham's trial, which is by the same token the test of the individual, necessarily includes a vow of silence. The man of faith falls silent, though, not so much as the result of any pre-meditated desire to escape mediation in the universal, but rather on account of already finding himself in a situation where he has nothing to say. Abraham is not merely tight-lipped, he is actually struck dumb by the fact of his faith.

Consider de Silentio's elaborate description of this debilitating impairment:

> Abraham remains silent—but he *cannot* speak. . . . Even though I go on talking night and day without interruption, if I cannot make myself understood when I speak, then I am not speaking. This is the case with Abraham. He can say everything, but one thing he cannot say, and if he cannot say that—that is, say it in such a way that another understands it—then he is not speaking.

This one thing that Abraham could never speak up about is just the fact of not being in a position of mediation *with* the universal. Abraham wouldn't quite know how to say that the possibility of intelligibility—namely the promise of posterity in his son Isaac—is predicated on a violent sacrifice of this same possibility. It is this interruption of meaning that remains inaccessible to the language of universal mediation. In order to express itself within the confines of language, the instance of faith would have to be mediated in the very discourse of reason which it disrupts. Abraham cannot make comprehensible ("say in such a way that another understands it") how it could be that he is in a place where nothing is yet available to the understanding of speculative reason. Hence the figure of an endless peroration; an infinite chain of words that never becomes "speech," since it remains impotent to "conclude" its particularity in the medium of the understanding. An act of faith, then, is a type of nonsense, something out of which speculative thought can make no sense since its endless string of syllables never amounts to saying anything at all.

It is for this reason that the polemic thrust of *Fear and Trembling* is so plainly applicable to the Hegelians, who take for granted the possibility of mediating the "unmediated" position of faith in the continuous process of dialectical thought. "In our own age no one is satisfied with faith, but goes further." For the Hegelians, Abraham's faith would constitute a preliminary apprenticeship that paves the way for, and finds its ultimate validity in, the speculative activity of a master workshop. The entire argument of *Fear and Trembling* is mobilized as a vigorous denial of such a move "beyond" Abraham: "Faith is the highest passion in a person. There are perhaps many in every generation who do not even reach it, but no one gets further."

If there is no longer any question of "going beyond" faith in order to attain a speculative position of reason from which to "understand" it, what then is the status of the *future* which God has promised as the reward for faith? Where can we find the legacy of Abraham's faith? The articulation of the category of the Individual undoubtedly represents Kierkegaard's most sustained attempt at dealing with these questions. And once the universal generality of the understanding has been challenged by the paradox of an entirely particular instance of Abrahamic faith, Johannes de Silentio proposes three "Problems" for consideration by his readers: the unique and irreducible status of the Individual with respect to the General; the absolute obligation of the Individual towards an Absolute that is not merely the General; and the dilemma of the Individual who cannot express intelligibly in the language of the General his relationship to the Absolute.

The representative of this Individual in *Fear and Trembling* must be the solitary and mute figure ("once upon a time there was a man") who flickers across the opening page of de Silentio's "Exordium" before disappearing altogether from the more or less philosophical tract that ensues. In order to situate more closely the status of this Individual, it will be necessary to leave the pseudonymous text of *Fear and Trembling* for a moment, and to examine a text in which the question of Kierkegaard's Individual comes to the fore. "Two Notes about the Individual" was not published during Kierkegaard's lifetime, but it is a text which was more than likely destined to serve as a companion piece to the major autobiographical statement, *The Point of View for My Work as an Author*. Speaking in his own name now, Kierkegaard insists,

> With the category "the Individual" I marked the beginning of the literary production bearing my name, and that was repeated in a sort of stereotyped formula. So with the Individual it is not a question of something I have recently invented, but rather my first.

In this text, the unique proper name of the author, Søren Kierkegaard, endeavors to coincide in a definitive manner with all his previous writings.

But this "direct communication," or "report to history" by the individual Søren Kierkegaard is at the same time a confirmation of the fundamental category of the Individual, which has itself become a kind of "signature" for the writings. Who is doing the signing here? Kierkegaard seems to be saying that he signed these texts with another name, that of the Individual (*med den Categorie "den Enkelte" maerkede jeg min Begynden*) but he also signed the same texts with his own name (*min navngivne Produktivitet*). No wonder Kierkegaard's autobiographical confirmation of the Individual must be described as the "repetition of a stereotyped formula," since the original mark of the Individual appears in a text which was already signed. In the beginning was the mark of the Individual, doubled in the same text by the beginning of the individual, Kierkegaard's own signature. Signature of the signature, beginning of the beginning, the individual finds himself marked out from the start as a category that divides itself into *two* identities.

Being pseudonymous in this fashion is not choosing to hide behind a number of clever disguises in order to better articulate one's point of view. The indirectness of this discourse is rather an admission of not being able to limit identity to one particular locus, or voice. Signing itself *again,* Kierkegaard's endorsement of the Individual consigns itself to a rather curious repetition that ends up looking like a bewildering counter-signature, a *resignation,* just when we were led to expect its most authentic engagement. There can be little doubt, though, that it is just such a resignation of the Individual that Kierkegaard's autobiography narrates when it finally concedes, "I have nothing further to say, but in conclusion I will let another speak, my poet, who when he comes, will assign me a place." What place can be assigned to an Individual who resigns himself in favor of another at the very moment he speaks in his own voice?

An indication of this place is given earlier in the text, when Kierkegaard considers the troubling question of an unbridgeable gap between his "aesthetic" and his "religious" writings:

> It might seem that a simple assurance by the author himself would
> be in this respect sufficient; for he ought to know best what's
> what. I place, however, little store in assurances when it comes to
> matters of literary production. . . . If I could not, in the capacity
> of a third party, as reader, establish by the writings that things are
> as I say. . . then it would never occur to me to claim the advantage
> in what I would thus consider a lost cause.

When it comes to literary matters, the assurances of the subjective voice of the author, of the authoritative "I," are no longer relevant. Only in the form of a rather nondescript "third person," as opposed to the eminently recognizable "first person," as *reader* rather than *author*, can the Individual's point of view be salvaged from an otherwise lost cause. This is because the first person subject, the "I" of authority, is a philosophical category easily assimilable to the dialectical processes Kierkegaard is so anxious to disrupt. In fact, speculative thought is itself given in the form of subjectivity, albeit in an abstract Subject which expresses itself as the self-positing and self-recognizing "I" of the understanding.

Inasmuch as Kierkegaard's Individual resists the specular discourse of dialectical thought, it resigns itself to a position outside the limits of first-person subjectivity. The third person singular of a noun patterned on a binary relationship from which it is by definition excluded (*en Trediemand, ein Dritter*), designates less a kind of disinterested objectivity than it marks a radical separation from all that is familiar. In the specular dialogue between Johannes de Silentio and Hegel which takes place in *Fear and Trembling* the third-party figure of the reader has absolutely nothing to say:

> Wo sich zwei vertragen,
> da hat der dritte nichts zu sagen.

This fundamental silence is what makes him ultimately "invisible"—because the singularity of his faith excludes him from the dialectical exchanges between the first and second persons of philosophical debate, it remains impossible to "locate" him, even if the specular subject were to attempt to search him out over a period of years.

How then are we to make any contact whatsoever with the Individual all alone in his faith? The Knight of faith may be entombed within an absolute vow of silence, but the representative which he leaves us here on earth is by the same token entrusted with the power to *recall* the truth of his individual-

ity. Even though it remains impossible to "see" Abraham, to communicate
with him in the fulness of his presence, we can nonetheless commemorate his
faith through an act of memory. If the individual has an obligation to resign
himself to a third-party anonymity, it is always an obligation that also entails
leaving something behind, bequeathing the last word to another: "I have
nothing further to say, but in conclusion I will let another speak, my poet,
who when he comes will assign me a place."

The Individual's truth—which for Kierkegaard is always his faith—is
made available to us in the form of a remembrance by the poet. In *Fear and
Trembling*, Johannes de Silentio had already suggested the same idea:

> Just as God created man and woman, so he created the hero and
> the poet, or orator. . . . [The poet or orator] is recollection's
> genius. He can do nothing but bring to mind what has been done.

As Abraham's sole representative on earth, the poet is the other side of the
coin of faith. In relation to Abraham's complete silence, the poet incarnates
the possibility of pure voice, or speech; or to put it in terms that will become
crucial for one of Kierkegaard's most influential readers (Heidegger), in relation to the concealment of Abraham, the poet represents the possibility of
disclosure. Alongside the *being* of Abraham's faith stands the *story* in which
the poet recalls Abraham's heroism. At this point it becomes very tempting
to identify Kierkegaard's (or de Silentio's) own eloquence as the site of an
aesthetic category that could eventually occupy the space left open by
Kierkegaard's radical critique of (speculative) philosophy.

A close reading of *Fear and Trembling*, though, shows that de Silentio
refuses to grant the "poet" the requisite dimension of "style," or "subjectivity" that would be the natural corollary of such a category of aesthetics, or
literature. The poet is neither man nor woman, rather the relationship of the
poet to Abraham is *like that* of man to woman, that is to say, complementary.
But since Abraham himself is the figure for that which escapes the communal
bonds of social relationships, his own "complement" is bound to exhibit a
corresponding lack of definition, or identity. Just as Abraham is a "third
party" excluded from the dialectical polarity of male and female, so too is the
poet a third party in their specular mediations. Just as Abraham becomes
anonymous through his silence, the poet becomes anonymous through the
ubiquity of his voice. As things turn out, the poet is unavailable for subsequent recuperation by way of aesthetic categories because he is *indiscrimi-
nately* available; thus the poet's "song" can be neither beautiful, nor
personal:

> Venerable father Abraham! Thousands of years have run their

course since those days, but you have need of no belated lover to snatch your memory from the power of oblivion, for any language (*ethvert Tungemaal:* any, each, every, tongue, or language) calls you to mind.

From the moment there is language (*Tungemaal*), there is a reminder of Abraham's faith. But how can this be so? What is it that each and every tongue can tell us about Abraham's faith?

In order to appreciate de Silentio's paradoxical linking of Abraham's particularity with the universal phenomenon of language—the man of silence with the means of expression—we must once again call to mind Kierkegaard's ongoing critique of Hegel. For Hegel, Abraham was merely one instance of the transition (*Ubergang*) from Nature to Spirit. On the more refined level of conceptuality, the anthropological movement of faith—the articulation from the immediacy of Abraham's present to the mediated significance of Isaac's future—is replaced by the speculative passage from sensory perception to philosophical thought. What corresponds, in this progression from perception to thought, to the moment of faith, is precisely the institution of language; a radical sacrifice or break (*eine Trennung*) with the immediacy of the objective world that comprises at the same time the promise of a meaningful future (der Stamm einer Nation).

What every tongue reminds us, then, is that its own promise of future meaning is predicated on the original sacrifice of a natural relationship to the world. All language necessarily recalls Abraham's story insofar as it repeats a severance of generic ties; no longer immediately related to the world by the certitude of representation, or resemblance, every tongue celebrates its semiotic independence from the slavish constraints of sensory perception. Prior to mediating the particularity of the Subject's "I" in the generality of speculative thought; that is, before becoming a dialogic affair between Self and Other, language must "re-enact" Abraham's sacrifice of his son Isaac by allowing the third-party "poet," the tongue that is neither man nor woman, to *separate* itself from all that is closest to it. What de Silentio calls the poet or orator is thus merely the non-specular, third-party figure which remains outside the family of man, or the discourse of dialectical thought. The fact that there can be no language without this separation, no future of meaning without Abraham's senseless break with his family ties, is at the same time the power of all language to "assign" Abraham a place by forever recalling his heroic sacrifice, and thus "saving" him from total oblivion.

Every tongue brings to mind Abraham's story; not so much because it is literally able to speak the name "Abraham" in everything it says, but rather because each time it assigns itself a future of meaning it necessarily does so in the name of a radical break with the world of immediate perception that recalls Abraham's sacrifice of Isaac. Thus "Abraham" is not only the proper name for the original act of faith, it is also a figural name which is re-enacted with every linguistic denomination. And since the original faith remains majestically silent, we have access to Abraham *only* through the deferred names of linguistic recollection. What we bring to mind whenever we remember names is the story of Abraham's faith. But this story is precisely the promise of our future meaning. Language always commemorates the original promise of a future; it therefore remembers what is supposed to bestow on it a future. Consequently, the future is *recollected* instead of awaited; the future actually lies in a past that is forever remembered as a promise that was made once upon a time.

It is for this reason that Abraham and his faith can never become fully present as a first, an original occurrence. Obliged to manifest itself as the remains of a name, in the form of a recollection, the story of Abraham's faith is never allowed to enter consciousness as anything other than what has already been heard, already committed to a memory that preserves it in another form. We never read the story of Abraham in the original; since it is available to us only second, or third hand—through the intermediary of the poet, or the orator, who "inherits" the task of recalling it from an already "third" party—Abraham's story is *always* an adaptation, a copy, or translation of an original that is mute by definition. It is no wonder, then, that the third party in de Silentio's dialogue with Hegel, the reader, is not described as meeting Abraham for the first time; he appears only in his repeated attempts to *return* to a story whose translation makes it less and less possible for him to understand.

By placing *Fear and Trembling* under the allegorical sign of the anonymous reader—"once upon a time there was a man who read the story of Abraham over and over again"—Kierkegaard displaces the *historical* polemic between Johannes de Silentio and the Danish Hegelians toward a *linguistic* region whose temporality is undefinable past, and whose locus is that of translation. Such a displacement seems to erect an insurmountable barrier—not only between Hegel's dialectic and Abraham's faith, but also between de Silentio's critique of Hegel and a modernist recuperation of Kierkegaard's third person, or faceless Individual. For what stands in the way of the reader's *progress*, what keeps him secluded within the unapproachable *Es war einmal* of an absolute priority, or pastness, is his inability to mobilize the forward-moving dialectic of the understanding, and this incapacity is due entirely to the peculiarities of translation; were an individual not compelled to read Abraham in translation, "he perhaps would easily [understand] the story."

In this respect, translation becomes a convenient term for the kind of resistance which Kierkegaard offers the entire Hegelian system of dialectical thought. Still, we may well ask ourselves whether this is truly the end of the story. Does Kierkegaard, in other words, actually represent a reliable alternative to Hegel. For by coining a name for the locus of their difference, we immediately risk re-entering the dialectical circuit from which that discrepancy seemed to remove us. Translation thus *becomes* "Aufhebung" just as inevitably as the movement from Hegel to Kierkegaard is re-appropriated by categories of historical consciousness:

> By faith [he] was *translated* into heaven so that he should not see death; and he was not found because God had translated him. (Heb. 11:5)

Translation is the admission of both an impossible *reading*—if Abraham could be "read" in the first place he would not have to be translated; he could be "found" in the original—and a necessarily defective *writing*—translations exist only to the extent that they preserve the original impossibility from oblivion; they inscribe the place where the original can no longer be "found." Kierkegaard's reader in *Fear and Trembling*—the authentic representative of Abraham's faith—is there only insofar as he is inscribed (translated) and thereby subsumed (*aufgehoben*) by the writer de Silentio. From the somewhat broader scope of our initial question, then, we might further note that it is by way of elaborating such curious translations that Kierkegaard eventually comes closest to his own (impossible) reading of Hegel. And like it or not, when we refuse to acknowledge the pertinence of this reading, when we insist instead on inscribing the movement from Hegel to Kierkegaard within a unilaterally historical model—whether that take the form of political, theological, or even aesthetic determinations—then we are only bearing witness yet again to our own inability to read it.

Chronology

1813   Søren Aabye Kierkegaard is born on May 5 in Copenhagen, Denmark to Michael Pederson Kierkegaard, a retired merchant, and to Ane Lund Kierkegaard, who had first entered the Kierkegaard household as a maid to Michael Kierkegaard's first wife. He is the youngest of seven children. At the age of nine, he begins school at the Borgerdydskole in Copenhagen.

1830   Søren Kierkegaard graduates from the Borgerdydskole and enrolls in the University of Copenhagen.

1834–36   Kierkegaard publishes his first articles in the *Flying Post*.

1837   Kierkegaard starts work at the Borgerdydskole. He meets Regine Olsen for the first time while visiting mutual friends in Frederiksberg.

1838   Father dies on August 9 at the age of 82, and Kierkegaard inherits a substantial sum of money. On September 4, he publishes *From the Papers of One Still Living*.

1840   Søren Kierkegaard passes his examinations for a degree in theology in July, receiving the grade of "laudabilis," and leaves for a three-week pilgrimage to his father's birthplace in Jutland. On September 8, he proposes to Regine Olsen, who accepts him two days later. In November, he enrolls at the Royal Pastoral Seminary.

1841   Kierkegaard preaches his first sermon in January. During the summer, he finishes his dissertation for the Master of Arts, *The*

Concept of Irony. His public dissertation defense on September 29 is well-attended. Shortly after that, he breaks his engagement with Regine Olsen and leaves for Berlin.

1842   Kierkegaard audits Schelling's lectures in Berlin. In March, he returns to Copenhagen and begins work on *Either/Or.*

1843   *Either/Or* is published in February. Kierkegaard publishes *Two Edifying Discourses* in May, and makes a second visit to Berlin. In October, *Repetition, Fear and Trembling,* and *Three Edifying Discourses* are published. *Four Edifying Discourses* appears in December.

1844   Kierkegaard publishes *Two Edifying Discourses* in March, and *Four Edifying Discourses* in August. In June, he publishes *Three Edifying Discourses,* the *Philosophical Fragments, The Concept of Dread,* and *Prefaces.* In October, he moves out of his apartment and into his family's house.

1845   In April, Kierkegaard publishes *Stages on Life's Way* and *Three Discourses on Imagined Occasions.* In December, Paul Møller, a professor at the University of Copenhagen, attacks "Guilty/Not Guilty" in the journal *Gaea.* Kierkegaard retaliates with a piece in *Faedrelandet,* to which Møller will respond in the same journal.

1846   The satirical journal *Corsair* begins to lampoon Kierkegaard in early January; its attacks continue for about six months. Kierkegaard publishes a response in *Fædrelandet* on January 10. That spring, he publishes the *Concluding Unscientific Postscript* and *A Literary Review.* In July, he begins to read the books of Magister Adler and to write *The Book on Adler.*

1847   Kierkegaard publishes *Edifying Discourses in Various Spirits* and *The Works of Love.* In November, Regine Olsen marries Friedrich Schlegel, the man with whom she had broken when Kierkegaard proposed to her. In late December, Kierkegaard, now in some financial difficulty, sells the family home.

1848   Kierkegaard publishes *Christian Discourses* and the two-part article, "The Crisis and a Crisis in an Actress's Life." He also writes *The Point of View for My Work as an Author,* which will be published posthumously.

1849   Kierkegaard publishes the second edition of *Either/Or*, *Two Minor Ethico-Religious Treatises*, and *The Sickness unto Death*.

1850   Kierkegaard publishes *Training in Christianity* and *An Edifying Discourse*.

1851   In August, Kierkegaard publishes *Point of View for My Work as an Author* and *Two Discourses at Communion on Fridays*. He publishes *For Self-Examination* a month later, and begins writing *Judge for Yourself*.

1852   *Judge for Yourself* is completed; it will be published posthumously. Kierkegaard moves into a cheaper apartment.

1853   Toward the end of the year, Kierkegaard makes the last entry in his journal.

1854   In February, Kierkegaard writes an article attacking Hans Martensen, a candidate for bishop, and the established church. He does not publish it until several months after Martensen is actually named bishop.

1855   Kierkegaard publishes *This Must Be Said, So Let It Now Be Said*; *Christ's Judgment on Official Christianity*; and *The Unchangeableness of God*. From January to May, Kierkegaard attacks the established church in a series of articles published in *Fædrelandet*. In May, he begins publishing his own polemical broadside, *Øjeblikket* [*The Instant*], which runs for nine numbers. On October 2, he collapses in the street, having just withdrawn the last of his inheritance from the bank. Kierkegaard is taken to the hospital and dies there in early November, probably of a lung infection.

Contributors

HAROLD BLOOM, Sterling Professor of the Humanities at Yale University, is the author of *The Anxiety of Influence*, *Poetry and Repression*, and many other volumes of literary criticism. His forthcoming study, *Freud: Transference and Authority*, attempts a full-scale reading of all of Freud's major writings. A MacArthur Prize Fellow, he is general editor of five series of literary criticism published by Chelsea House. During 1987–88, he served as Charles Eliot Norton Professor of Poetry at Harvard University.

GEORG LUKÁCS was among the most distinguished—and controversial—Marxist thinkers of the twentieth century. His works include the early, Hegelian *Theory of the Novel*, the seminal theoretical work *History and Class Consciousness*, and book-length studies of Hegel, Thomas Mann, Goethe, and Alexandr Solzhenitsyn.

THEODOR W. ADORNO was the major philosopher of the Frankfurt School. He was equally at home in the fields of philosophy, culture critique, sociology, and music theory. His works include *Negative Dialectics*, *Aesthetic Theory*, the aphoristic *Minima Moralia*, and studies of Hölderlin, Schoenberg, and Kierkegaard. He also contributed to the collective volume *The Authoritarian Personality*, and wrote *Dialectic of Enlightenment* with Max Horkheimer.

KARL JASPERS was the most systematic of contemporary existentialist philosophers. He was trained as a physician, and published several works on psychopathology before he turned from psychology to philosophy. His works available in English include *Man in the Modern Age*, *Reason and Existenz*, *Truth and Symbol*, and *Myth and Christianity*.

PAUL RICOEUR is a professor at the University of Chicago Divinity School and at the Université de Paris (Nanterre). His works available in English include *Freud and Philosophy* and *The Conflict of Interpretations.*

STANLEY CAVELL is Professor of Philosophy at Harvard University. His essay on Kierkegaard in this volume appeared in his *Must We Mean What We Say?* His other books include *The Claim of Reason: Wittgenstein, Skepticism, Morality and Tragedy* and *The World Viewed: Reflections on the Ontology of Film.*

JEAN-PAUL SARTRE was the most influential of the contemporary philosophers of existentialism. Besides his philosophical works, the most important of which were *Being and Nothingness* and *The Critique of Dialectical Reason,* Sartre's works include novels (*La Nausée* and *Chemins de la liberté*), plays (*The Flies, No Exit*), and works on literature (*What Is Literature?, Baudelaire,* and *Saint Genet*). At the time of his death, Sartre was working on the latest volume of his monumental study of Flaubert, *L'Idiot de la famille.*

BERTEL PEDERSEN taught at Cornell University and completed the essay in this volume shortly before his untimely death.

SYLVIANE AGACINSKI is the author of *Aparté, conceptions et morts de Søren Kierkegaard* and of a long study of Wittgenstein that appeared in the collective volume *Mimesis des articulations.*

HENNING FENGER is a Swedish scholar who has published extensively on Kierkegaard.

MARK C. TAYLOR is Associate Professor in the Department of Religion at Williams College. He is the author of *Kierkegaard's Pseudonymous Authorship: A Study of Time and the Self, Journeys to Selfhood: Hegel and Kierkegaard,* and *Deconstructing Theology.*

LOUIS MACKEY is Professor of Philosophy at the University of Texas at Austin. His many works on Kierkegaard include *Kierkegaard: A Kind of Poet;* he has also published articles on literary theory and on medieval philosophy.

KEVIN NEWMARK is Assistant Professor of French at Yale University. He has published articles on Gide and Baudelaire and is now writing a book on French Symbolism and the problem of literary history.

Bibliography

Adorno, Theodor Wiesengrund. *Kierkegaards Konstruktion des Ästhetischen.* Tübingen. Mohr, 1933.

Agacinski, Sylviane. *Aparté, conceptions et morts de Søren Kierkegaard.* Paris: Aubier-Flammarion (La philosophie en effet), 1977.

Allemand, Beda. *Ironie und Dichtung: Fr. Schlegel, Novalis, Solger, Kierkegaard, Nietzsche, Thomas Mann.* Pfuhligen: Neske, 1956.

Arendt, Hannah. "Tradition and the Modern Age." *Partisan Review* 21 (1954): 53–75.

Auden, W. H. "A Preface to Kierkegaard." *New Republic,* 15 May 1944, 683–84.

———. "Knight of Doleful Countenance." *New Yorker,* 25 May 1968, 141–58.

———. "Søren Kierkegaard." In *Forewords and Afterwords,* 168–81. New York: Random House, 1973.

Beck, Samuel J. "Abraham, Kierkegaard: Either, Or." *Yale Review* 62 (1972): 59–72.

Becker, Ernest. *The Denial of Death.* New York: Free Press, 1973.

Bogen, James. "Kierkegaard and the 'Theological Suspension of the Ethical.' " *Inquiry* 5 (1962): 305–17.

Bové, Paul. "The Penitentiary of Reflection: Søren Kierkegaard and Critical Activity." *boundary 2* 9, no. 1 (Fall 1980): 233–58.

Bukdahl, Jørgen K. ed. *Kierkegaard and Dialectics: Lectures, Originally Delivered at a Symposium.* Aarhus: University of Aarhus, 1980.

Cole, J. Preston. *The Problematic Self in Kierkegaard and Freud.* New Haven: Yale University Press, 1971.

Daise, Benjamin. "Kierkegaard and the Absolute Paradox." *Journal of the History of Philosophy* 14 (1976): 63–68.

Dupré, Louis K. *Kierkegaard as Theologian: The Dialectic of Christian Existence.* New York: Sheed & Ward, 1963.

Elrod, John W. "Climacus, Anti-Climacus, and the Problem of Suffering." *Thought* 55 (1980): 306–19.

Evans, C. Stephens. "Kierkegaard on Subjective Truth: Is God an Ethical Fiction?" *International Journal for the Philosophy of Religion* 7 (1976): 288–99.

———. "Mis-using Religious Language: Something about Kierkegaard and 'the Myth of God Incarnate.' " *Religious Studies* 15 (1979): 139–58.

Fenger, Henning, and George C. Schoolfield, tr. *Kierkegaard, the Myths and Their Origins: Studies in the Kierkegaardian Papers and Letters.* New Haven: Yale University Press, 1980.

Gilson, Etienne. "Søren Kierkegaard." In *Being and Some Philosophers*. Toronto: Pontifical Institute of Medieval Studies, 1952.

Gilson, Etienne; T. Langan; and A. A. Maurer. "Søren Kierkegaard." In *Recent Philosophy: Hegel to the Present*, 69–78. New York: Random House, 1966.

Grene, Marjorie. "Søren Kierkegaard: The Self against the System." In *Dreadful Freedom*, 15–40. Chicago: University of Chicago Press, 1959.

Harper, Ralph. *The Seventh Solitude: Metaphysical Homelessness in Kierkegaard, Dostoevsky, and Nietzsche*. Baltimore: Johns Hopkins University Press, 1967.

Herbert, R. "God-man." *Religious Studies* 6 (1970: 157–74.

Hong, Howard V. "The Comic, Satire, Irony and Humor: Kierkegaardian Reflections." In *Midwest Studies in Philosophy 1: Studies in the History of Philosophy*, edited by Peter A. French, Theodore E. Uehling, Jr., and Howard K. Wellstein, 98–108. Morris: University of Minnesota Press, 1976.

Hook, Sidney. "Two Types of Existential Religion and Ethics." *Partisan Review* 26 (1959): 58–63.

Jaspers, Karl. "Origin of the Contemporary Philosophical Situation: The Historical Meaning of Kierkegaard and Nietzsche." In *Reason and Existenz: Five Lectures*, translated by William Earle, 19–50. New York: Noonday Press, 1955.

Johnson, Ralph Henry. *The Concept of Existence in the* Concluding Unscientific Postscript. The Hague: Martinus Nijhoff, 1972.

———. "Kierkegaard on Philosophy." *Dialogue* 17 (1978): 442–55.

Kaufmann, Walter. "Kierkegaard." In *From Shakespeare to Existentialism: Studies in Poetry, Religion and Philosophy*, 161–89. Boston: Beacon Press, 1959.

Kern, Edith G. *Existential Thought and Fictional Technique: Kierkegaard, Sartre, Beckett*. New Haven: Yale University Press, 1972.

Klemke, E. D. *Studies in the Philosophy of Kierkegaard*. The Hague: Martinus Nijhoff, 1976.

Krieger, Murray. "Tragedy and the Tragic Vision." In *The Tragic Vision: Variations on a Theme in Literary Interpretation*, 1–21. New York: Holt, 1960.

Lapointe, François, compiler. *Søren Kierkegaard and His Critics: An International Bibliography of Criticism*. Westport, Conn.: Greenwood, 1980.

Lawson, Lewis A., ed. *Kierkegaard's Presence in Contemporary American Life: Essays from Various Sources*. Metuchen, N.J.: Scarecrow Press, 1971.

Lowrie, Walter. *Kierkegaard*. London: Oxford University Press, 1938.

———. *A Short Life of Kierkegaard*. Princeton: Princeton University Press, 1942.

Lubac, Henri de. *The Drama of Atheist Humanism*. London: Sheed & Ward, 1949.

Lukács, Georg. "Kierkegaard." *Deutsche Zeitschrift für Philosophie* 1 (1953): 286–314.

Mackey, Louis H. "Søren Kierkegaard: The Poetry of Inwardness." In *Existential Philosophers: Kierkegaard to Merleau-Ponty*, edited by George A. Schrader, Jr., 45–108. New York: McGraw-Hill, 1967.

———. "Philosophy and Poetry in Kierkegaard." *Review of Metaphysics* 23 (1969): 316–32.

———. *Kierkegaard: A Kind of Poet*. Philadelphia: University of Pennsylvania Press, 1972.

Malantschuk, Gregor. *Kierkegaard's Thought*. Translated by Howard V. Hong and Edna M. Hong. Princeton: Princeton University Press, 1971.

Manheimer, Ronald J. *Kierkegaard as Educator*. Berkeley: University of California Press, 1977.

Marcuse, Herbert. *Reason and Revolution: Hegel and the Rise of Social Theory*, 262–67. New York: Oxford University Press, 1941.

Maritain, Jacques. "From Existential Existentialism to Academic Existentialism." *Sewanee Review* 56 (1948): 210–29.

Marsh, James L. "The Two Kierkegaards." *Philosophy Today* 16 (1972): 313–22.

McCarthy, Vincent A. *The Phenomenology of Moods in Kierkegaard*. The Hague: Martinus Nijhoff, 1978.

McKinnon, Alastair. *The Kierkegaard Indices*. Leiden, Neth.: E. J. Brill, 1970–75. 4 vols.

McLane, Earl. "Kierkegaard and Subjectivity." *International Journal for Philosophy of Religion* 8 (1977): 211–32.

Minear, Paul S., and Paul S. Morimot, editors. *Kierkegaard and the Bible: An Index*. Princeton: Book Agency Theological Seminar, 1953.

Muller, John D. "Between the Aesthetic and the Ethical: Kierkegaard's *Either/Or*." *Philosophy Today* 23 (1979): 84–94.

Nagley, Winfield E. "Kierkegaard's Irony in the *Diapsalmata*." *Kierkegaardiana* 6 (1966): 51–75.

_____. "The Concept of Irony." *Journal of the History of Ideas* 29 (1968): 458–64.

Norris, Christopher. "Fiction of Authority: Narrative and Viewpoint in Kierkegaard's Writing." *Criticism* 25 (1983): 87–107.

Pelikan, Jaroslav. *Human Culture and the Holy: Essays on the True, the Good, and the Beautiful: Kierkegaard, Paul, Dostoevsky, Luther, Nietzsche, Bach*. London: Student Christian Movement Press, 1959.

Percy, Walker. "The Message in the Bottle." *Thought* 34 (1959): 405–33.

Perkins, Robert L., editor. *Kierkegaard's* Fear and Trembling: Critical Appraisals. University: University of Alabama Press, 1981.

_____. *International Kierkegaard Commentary 14: Two Ages*. Macon, Georgia: Mercer University Press, 1984.

Pletsch, Carl. "The Self-Sufficient Text in Nietzsche and Kierkegaard." *Yale French Studies* 66 (1984): 160–88.

Pomerleau, Wayne P. "The Accession and Dismissal of an Upstart Handmaid." *Monist* 60 (1977): 213–27.

Poole, Roger. "The Travels of Kierkegaard," *Raritan* 4, no. 4 (1985): 78–90.

_____. "A Walk with Kierkegaard." *London Review of Books* 2, no. 3 (1980): 1–5.

Rohatyn, Dennis A. "Kierkegaard and his Critics." In *Two Dogmas of Philosophy and Other Essays in the Philosophy of Philosophy*, 103-36. Rutherford, N.J.: Fairleigh Dickinson University Press, 1977.

Rougemont, Denis de. "Kierkegaard." In *Dramatic Personages*, translated by Richard Howard, 27–74. New York: Holt, 1964.

Said, Edward W. "Molestation and Authority in Narrative Fiction." In *Aspects of Variation: Selected Papers from the English Institute*, edited by J. Hillis Miller, 47–68. New York: Columbia University Press, 1971.

Schacht, Robert. "Kierkegaard on 'Truth Is Subjectivity' and 'The Leap of Faith'" and "Kierkegaard's Phenomenology of Spiritual Development." In *Hegel and After: Studies in Contemporary Philosophy between Kant and Sartre*. Pittsburgh: University of Pittsburgh Press, 1975, 19–34 and 135–74.

Schleifer, Ronald. "Irony, Identity and Repetition: On Kierkegaard's 'The Concept of Irony.' " *Sub-Stance* 25 (1980): 44–54.

Schleifer, Ronald, and Robert Markley, editors. *Kierkegaard and Literature: Irony, Repetition and Criticism.* Norman: University of Oklahoma Press, 1984.

Schrader, George A. "Kant and Kierkegaard on Duty and Inclination." *Journal of Philosophy* 55 (1968): 688–701.

Shestov, Lev. *Kierkegaard and the Existential Philosophy.* Translated by Elinor Hewitt. Athens: Ohio University Press, 1970.

Smith, Joseph H., ed. *Kierkegaard's Truth: The Disclosure of the Self.* Psychiatry and Humanities 5. New Haven: Yale University Press, 1981.

Solomon, Robert C. "Søren Kierkegaard: Truth and the Subjective Individual." In *From Rationalism to Existentialism: The Existentialists and Their Nineteenth-Century Backgrounds,* 69–104. New York: Harper & Row, 1972.

Stack, George J. "Kierkegaard: The Self and Ethical Existence." *Ethics* 83 (1972–73): 108–25.

———. "Kierkegaard's Existential Categories." *The Personalist* 57 (1976): 18–33.

———. "The Inward Journey: Kierkegaard's Journals and Papers." *Philosophy Today* 23 (1979): 170–95.

Taylor, Mark C. *Kierkegaard's Pseudonymous Authorship: A Study of Time and the Self.* Princeton: Princeton University Press, 1975.

———. "Language, Truth and Indirect Communication." *Tijdschrift voor Filosofie* (1975): 74–88.

———. "Love and Forms of Spirit: Kierkegaard vs. Hegel." In *Kierkegaardiana* 10 (1977): 95–116.

Thomas, J. Heywood. "Logic and Existence in Kierkegaard." *Journal of the British Society of Phenomenology* 2 (1971): 3–11.

Thomas, Marilyn. "The Reader as Protagonist in Kierkegaard's Narrative Labyrinth." *Georgia Review* 36 (1982): 591–600.

Thompson, Josiah. *Kierkegaard.* New York: Alfred A. Knopf, 1973.

———, editor. *Kierkegaard. A Collection of Critical Essays.* Englewood Cliffs, N.J.: Prentice-Hall, 1978.

Thulstrup, Marie Mikulova, editor. *Concepts and Alternatives in Kierkegaard.* Bibliotheca Kierkegaardiana 4. Copenhagen: C.A. Reitzels Boghandel, 1980.

Thulstrup, Niels. "Introduction" to *Philosophical Fragments: Or, a Fragment of Philosophy,* by Johannes Climacus [pseud.]. Translated by Howard Hong. Princeton: Princeton University Press, 1967.

———, and Marie Mikulova Thulstrup, editors. *Kierkegaard's View of Christianity.* Bibliotheca Kierkegaardiana 1. Copenhagen: C.A. Reitzels Boghandel, 1978.

———. *The Sources and Depths of Faith in Kierkegaard.* Bibliotheca Kierkegaardiana 2. Copenhagen: C.A. Reitzels Boghandel, 1978.

Updike, John. "The Fork." *New Yorker* 26 February 1966, 115–18; 121–24; 128–30; 133–34.

Vick, George R. "A New 'Copernican Revolution.' " *The Personalist* 52 (1971): 630–42.

Wahl, Jean. *Etudes Kierkegaardiennes.* Paris: Fernand Aubier, 1938.

———. "Kierkegaard and Kafka." In *The Kafka Problem,* edited by Angel Flores. New York: New Directions, 1946.

_____. *Philosophies of Existence: An Introduction to the Basic Thought of Kierkegaard, Heidegger, Jaspers, Marcel, Sartre*. Translated by F. M. Lory. New York: Schocken Books, 1969.

Walker, Jeremy. *To Will One Thing: Reflections on Kierkegaard's* Purity of Heart. Montreal: McGill University Press, 1972.

Wyschogrod, Michael. *Kierkegaard and Heidegger: The Ontology of Existence*. New York: Humanities Press, 1954.

Zimmerman, R. L. "Kierkegaard's Immanent Critique of Hegel." *Philosophy Forum* 9 (1977–78): 459–74.

Acknowledgments

"The Foundering of Form against Life: Søren Kierkegaard and Regine Olson" by Georg Lukács from *Soul and Form*, translated by Anna Bostock, © 1971 by Hermann Luchterhand Verlag, English translation © 1971 by the Merlin Press Ltd. Reprinted by permission of The MIT Press and the Merlin Press Ltd.

"On Kierkegaard's Doctrine of Love" by Theodor W. Adorno from *Studies in Philosophy and Social Science* 8, no. 3 (1939), © 1940 by Social Studies Association, Inc. Reprinted by permission.

"The Importance of Kierkegaard" by Karl Jaspers and translated by Erwin W. Geissman from *Cross Currents* 2 (Spring 1952), © 1952 by *Cross Currents*. Reprinted by permission.

"Kierkegaard and Evil" (originally entitled "Two Encounters with Kierkegaard: Kierkegaard and Evil") by Paul Ricoeur from *Kierkegaard's Truth: The Disclosure of the Self* (Psychiatry and the Humanities, volume 5), © 1981 by the Forum on Psychiatry and the Humanities of the Washington School of Psychiatry. Reprinted by permission.

"Kierkegaard's *On Authority and Revelation*" by Stanley Cavell from *Must We Mean What We Say? A Book of Essays* by Stanley Cavell, © 1969 by Stanley Cavell, © 1976 by Cambridge University Press. Reprinted by permission of Cambridge University Press.

"Kierkegaard: The Singular Universal" by Jean-Paul Sartre from *Between Existentialism and Marxism* by Jean-Paul Sartre, © 1972 by Editions Gallimard, English translation © 1974 by New Left Books. Reprinted by permission of the Georges Borchardt Agency and Pantheon Books, a division of Random House, Inc.

"Fictionality and Authority: A Point of View for Kierkegaard's Work as an Author" by Bertel Pedersen from *MLN* 89, no. 6 (December 1974), © 1974 by The Johns Hopkins University Press, Baltimore/London. Reprinted by permission of The Johns Hopkins University Press.

"On a Thesis" by Sylviane Agacinski from *Aparté: Conceptions and Deaths of Søren Kierkegaard*, translated by Kevin Newmark, © 1987 by the Florida

State University Press. Reprinted by permission of University Presses of Florida.

"Kierkegaard as a Falsifier of History" by Henning Fenger from *Kierkegaard, The Myths and Their Origin: Studies in the Kierkegaard Pages and Letters*, translated by George C. Schoolfield, © 1980 by Yale University. Reprinted by permission of Yale University Press.

"Natural Selfhood and Ethical Selfhood in Kierkegaard" (originally entitled "Natural Selfhood" and "Ethical Selfhood") by Mark C. Taylor from *Journeys to Selfhood: Hegel and Kierkegaard* by Mark C. Taylor, © 1980 by the Regents of the University of California. Reprinted by permission of the University of California Press.

"Once More with Feeling: Kierkegaard's *Repetition*" by Louis Mackey from *Kierkegaard and Literature: Irony, Repetition, and Criticism*, edited by Ronald Schleifer and Robert Markley, © 1984 by the University of Oklahoma Press, Norman, Oklahoma. Reprinted by permission of the University of Oklahoma Press.

"Between Hegel and Kierkegaard: The Space of Translation" by Kevin Newmark from *Genre (Special Issue: The World as Text: Nonliterary Genres)* 16, no. 4 (Winter 1983), © 1983 by the University of Oklahoma. Reprinted by permission.

Index